CRUEL PARADISE

Moi de groetnes
fan

24-6 2017 -

CRUEL PARADISE

Life Stories of Dutch Emigrants

Hylke Speerstra

Translated and abridged by

Henry J. Baron

WILLIAM B. EERDMANS PUBLISHING COMPANY

GRAND RAPIDS, MICHIGAN / CAMBRIDGE, U.K.

This publication has been made possible with financial support from the Foundation for the Production and Translation of Dutch Literature and from the Sid & Margaret Baron Foundation.

This book is a translation and abridgment of
It wrede paradys: Libbensferhalen fan Fryske folksferhuzers,
published in 1999 by Friese Pers Boekerij of Leeuwarden, The Netherlands

Wm. B. Eerdmans Publishing Co.
255 Jefferson Ave. S.E., Grand Rapids, Michigan 49503 /
P.O. Box 163, Cambridge CB3 9PU U.K.

Printed in the United States of America

10 09 08 07 06 05   7 6 5 4 3 2 1

Library of Congress Cataloging-in-Publication Data

Speerstra, Hylke.
[Wrede paradys. Frisian]
Cruel paradise: life stories of Dutch emigrants / Hylke Speerstra;
translated and abridged by Henry J. Baron.
p.   cm.
ISBN 0-8028-2801-9 (pbk.: alk. paper)
1. Friesland (Netherlands) — Emigration and immigration. 2. Frisians — Foreign countries.
3. Frisians — United States.   I. Baron, Henry James.   II. Title.

JV8159.A2F757   2005
305.83'92 — dc22
                                        2005041733

www.eerdmans.com

Contents

CONTENTS

Contents

Translator's Preface

This was more than just a translation project for me. I was an immigrant child myself. I will never forget my parents' struggle with a new
language and culture, with hard work, little money, and homesickness.
Hence I felt a deep identification with many of the experiences recounted
in *Cruel Paradise*. The stories stirred memories and emotions that had been
submersed for a long time.

The author's enthusiasm for this project stimulated me throughout,
as did the ongoing encouragement of my beloved longtime mentor, Professor Bernard Fridsma. I felt fortunate to have the advice and help from
both readily available to me. Hylke Speerstra's suggestions for story selection (since we had to significantly reduce the number included in the original version) closely coincided with my own preferences. He was also very
helpful when place names, locations, intended meanings, and allusions
were not clear to me.

Cruel Paradise was originally written in Frisian and subsequently rather
freely translated by the author into Dutch. Thus I had both versions available to me, and I sometimes took advantage when I chose a more appetiz-
ing slice from one rather than from the other. A few stories appeared only
in the Dutch edition, and those gave me no choice. However, most of the
selections were translated from the Frisian only.

Throughout the book Frisian place-names are often cited in Frisian,
though a glossary has been provided that translates them into the more familiar Dutch. The map included should prove a helpful aid to readers in

placing the towns and villages from which the characters in these stories emigrated.

These tales — often poignant, sometimes amusing, always memorable — are now accessible to the descendants of these immigrants, as well as to a wide range of other readers. Immigrant experiences must not be forgotten; rendering them into a world language was a source of genuine satisfaction and has drawn me closer to my roots. For that I will always be grateful.

Author's Preface

A s writer-journalist, I traveled on vacation to all seven continents in the 1990s. My purpose was to enjoy the places and landscapes I would encounter, and I did. But I also became deeply impressed by all the life stories I heard from Dutch emigrants that I met. Their tales stuck with me. Emigrants, one might say, have a double life story to tell.

In 1997 I decided to travel the world anew, this time for serious interviews with a number of emigrants. I hope that I have observed the interviewer's art of not only listening to their words, but also to their heartbeat.

I didn't start out with a closely prescribed plan or rigid selection of interviewees. Rather, I simply traveled, and I became, so to speak, buried under the stories I heard. I traveled through America and Canada as my inspiring example John Steinbeck did in his motor home, for his *Travels with Charley*. His lesson: If you're a good, interested listener, each person will have a story, a book, an epic to tell.

I went to attend church services in Michigan and California, and of course also in Ontario. Already during the service, but especially afterward I drowned, as it were, in an ocean of life-lessons and stories. Those were not just about the pains of separating from the old country, but also about the challenges of connecting to a new society. Some were painful examples of displacement and sacrifice, but others told of hope and faith and trust, of persistence, acceptance, and, finally, of making it.

And thus became the writing of this book for the author a lesson for his own life: integration is a lifelong process. To emigrate in the fifties during the twentieth century was not more and not less than taking the first giant step in a search. For the wanderer there is no well-traveled path; that path emerges as one wanders.

The success of the emigrant, I learned, is not just defined in terms of the number of dollars earned. Though there are the unforgettable memories of an earlier life in the old country, in the final analysis success is more about finding peace of mind and soul, about living in harmony with one's family and with the new way of life and place — for self, yes, but especially for the succeeding generations.

I am myself a child of the Depression years of the thirties; I have personally experienced and have some feelings about World War II and the liberation of the Netherlands by the Americans, Canadians, and British. I know how the economy and the reconstruction of the old country stagnated behind the dikes. Therefore all the interviewing that led to *Cruel Paradise* awoke old memories. Repressed images became reality. I suddenly recalled that also in my village a busload of emigrants was waved a reluctant good-bye. That image really moved me for the first time during the writing of this book.

It turned out that there was a large reading public for *Cruel Paradise* in the Netherlands, and particularly in Friesland. Around the year 2000 and after, *Het wrede paradijs* generated a great many reactions. Fifteen radio programs and even national television took note of it. It's as if the Netherlands embraced anew those who left.

The Dutch reading public of *Het wrede paradijs* was not just comprised of people who had been around during the postwar era and its wave of emigration. It was especially the younger folk who read the book with increasing amazement. I hope and trust that this will also be the case in America, Canada, and the other English-speaking countries.

I conclude by noting that it was of course difficult to make a selection from that ocean of life-stories. For the truth is that each person, and certainly the searching wanderer, is worth a story.

A Glossary of Frisian Place-Names

Throughout this book many towns are referred to by their Frisian names.
Here their more familiar Dutch names are given.

Frisian	Dutch
Akmaryp	Akmarijp
Aldeboarn	Oldeboorn
Aldegea	Oudega
Aldeskoat	Oudeschoot
Aldeskou	Oudeschouw
Appelskea	Appelscha
Barhûs	Barrahuis
Berltsum	Berlikum
Blije	Blija
Boalsert	Bolsward
Burchwert	Burgwerd
Burdaard	Birdaard
Burgum	Bergum
Bûtenpost	Buitenpost
Damwâld	Damwoude
De Bjirmen	Bierumen
De Gaastmar	Gaastmeer
De Geast	Rinsumageest
De Jouwer	Joure
De Koaten	Kooten

De Lemmer	Lemmer
De Pein	Opende
De Sweach	Beetsterzwaag
Dearsum	Deersum
Droegeham	Drogeham
Dronryp	Dronrijp
Drylts	Ijlst
Earnewâld	Eernewoude
Eastermar	Oostermeer
Eastersea	Oosterzee
Easterbierrum	Oosterbierum
Easterwierrum	Oosterwierum
Follegea	Follega
Frjenstjer	Franeker
Fryslân	Friesland
Grekeskleaster	Gerkesklooster
Gordyk	Gorredijk
Greategast	Grootegast
Grinslân	Groningen
Grinzer Pein	Groninger Opende
Grou	Grouw
Grypskerk	Grijpskerk
Harns	Harlingen
Hartwert	Hartwerd
Heech	Heeg
Hilaard	Hijlaard
Huzum	Huizum
Ikkerwâld	Akkerwoude (Damwoude)
It Hearrenfean	Herrenveen
Jirnsum	Irnsum
Jobbegea	Jubbega
Koarnwettersân	Kornwedderzand
Langwar	Langweer
Ljouwert	Leeuwarden
Lúnbert	Luinjeberd

Lúkswâld	Luxwoude
Lytsegast	Lutjegast
Lytsepost	Lutjepost
Menaam	Menaldum
Menameradiel	Menaldemadeel
Mildaam	Mildam
Nijeskoat	Nieuweschoot
Nijhuzum	Nijhuizum
Nijlân	Nijland
Oentsjerk	Oenkerk
Oppenhûsen	Oppenhuizen
Ousterhaule	Ouwsterhaule
Ouwesyl	Oudezijl
Raerd	Raard
Rinsumageast	Rinsumageest
Seisbierrum	Sexbierum
Sibrandabuorren	Sijbrandaburen
Sibrandahûs	Sijbrandahuis
Sint Anne	Sint Annaparochie
Sint Jansgea	Sintjohannesga
Sint-Nyk	Nicolaasga
Skalsum	Schalsum
Skar	Schar
Skettens	Schettens
Stynsgea	Augustinusga
Surhústerfean	Shuhuisterveen
Sumar	Suameer
Terherne	Terhorne
Tsjalbert	Tjalleberd
Tsjerkgaast	Tjerkgaast
Tsjerkwert	Tjerkwerd
Tsjom	Tzum
Tsjûkemar	Tjeukermeer
Tsjummearum	Tzummarum
Twizelerheide	Twijzelerheide

A Glossary of Frisian Place-Names

Wâldsein	Woudsende
Warkum	Workum
Warten	Wartena
Wergea	Warga
Winaam	Wijnaldum
Wiuwert	Wiewerd
Wûns	Wons
Wûnseradiel	Wonseradeel
Wurdum	Wirdum
Wymbrits	Wijmbritseradeel
Ychten	Echten

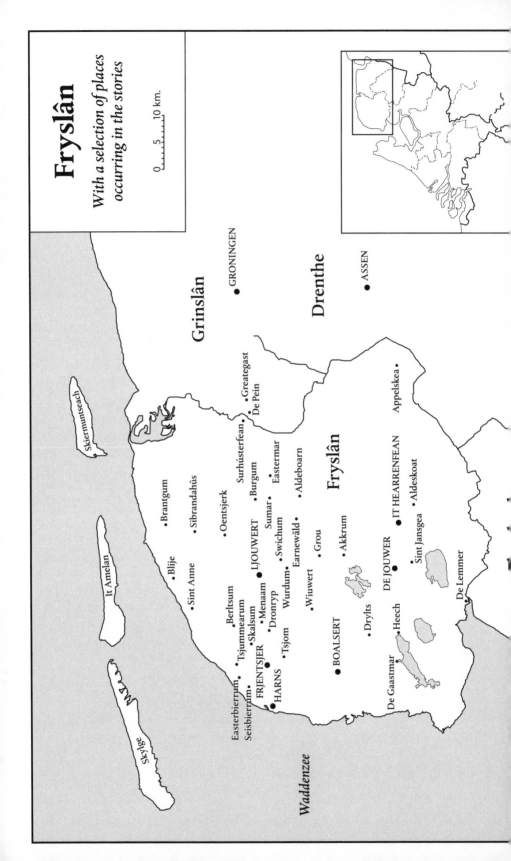

Fryslân

With a selection of places occurring in the stories

0   5   10 km.

Skiermuntseach

It Amelan

Skylge

Waddenzee

Brantgum

Sibrandahûs

Blije

Oentsjerk

Sint Anne

Berltsum

Tsjummearum

Skalsum

Menaam

LJOUWERT

Dronryp

Wurdum

Sumar

Swichum

Earnewâld

Grou

Akkrum

Wiuwert

Easterbierrum

Seisbierrum

FRJENTSJER

HARNS

Tsjom

Drylts

BOALSERT

Heech

De Gaastmar

DE JOUWER

Sint Jansgea

Aldeskoat

IT HEARRENFEAN

Appelskea

De Lemmer

Surhústerfean

Burgum

Eastermar

Aldeboarn

Greategast

De Pein

Grinslân

•GRONINGEN

Drenthe

•ASSEN

Fryslân

Crescendo

Hindrik Jeens Baron from Grand Rapids, Michigan, USA

Prologue: The Shattered Springtime

The day came that the suitcases were packed and ready to go. The luggage of Dad and Mom and their five children. The farm, the cows, the land, the tools and equipment — none of it was theirs anymore. As if they had become strangers in their own house, that's how the family felt as they looked out the window of the small farmhouse on the Skieding in Opende, Groningen (known to all the Frisian-speaking villagers in this border town as the Grinzer Pein). Even the clock, ticking away the last hours, didn't belong to them anymore.

An incident, in the second half of May 1948, through the memory of a boy of fourteen. It happened on an evening when the air was soft as silk, when the smell of spring hung over the fields, and the sun descended slowly, slowly to make the last day as long as possible.

People were coming up the path to the farm. Two men in the lead. One carried a trumpet under his arm, the other was the cornet player. More followed, men with shiny instruments hanging from their shoulder. Soon the whole membership of the Christian brass band "Crescendo" from Grinzer Pein had gathered on the yard of the small farm on the Skieding: the small and large bass horn were there, the small and large drum, the tubas, trombones, bugles, trumpets, and the cornet.

The men of the band tried to stand stiffly at attention, but it seemed as if they were waiting for a signal from on high. The man with the large bass rapped on the iron lid of the cistern with his wedding ring, and it became deafeningly quiet. And then the band played, exploding the last springtime on the Skieding in Grinzer Pein. Whether it was a chorale or a march, the boy from that time isn't sure anymore, but in any case it was music played so stately that it sounded like the death march from Beethoven's Third.

The family stood in the low side door and listened. Except one. The father, who had the tickets for the boat trip to America already in his pocket, did not appear. And the children, standing there without him in the low side door, did not understand why not.

The boy of fourteen eventually became an American. The images of their final hours were stored in his memory as a movie fragment that froze at their departure into a static picture. And now he looked back and began to tell the story. Everything was projected anew and the images became sharp again: the father with his secrets and sadness, the strong mother who saw her family through the tough times, and the good things that eventually came their way in the new land.

The boy would later return to the Skieding and discover that the camera had never stopped there on the old place. The country was not the same that he had left.

In one lifetime, the earth changed from a huge planet full of unknown places to a well-traveled world, and thus farewell serenades went out of style. But in the life stories of old emigrants the distances were beyond imagination. They ventured into endless space and had no idea where they landed. "To us New Zealand was even farther than the moon, because we could at least see the moon," said an old Frisian woman on the other side of the world. And to those who remained behind, the leaving of their dear ones felt like a live funeral.

The testimonies of the Frisian wanderers of the twentieth century teach us that emigration is in the final analysis the multiplication of life. One begins a new living in a new land with a new language, but at the same time hangs on to all one took along from the old country.

—❦—

The band "Crescendo" from Grinzer Pein was finished, and the springtime was shattered. Quietly, the musicians left the yard that evening
of the small farm on the Skieding. The family in the low side door that had
listened to the farewell serenade went back inside the house that wasn't
theirs anymore. And then the father, who had not wanted to listen to the
music, reappeared. He had stopped the clock. Now it wouldn't be long
anymore for the bus to come to take them away.

The boy from that time doesn't remember exactly what happened in
the hours immediately after. And for a long time he had no idea why the
music of "Crescendo" sounded so false in his father's ears, more false than
the rasping of the first scythe in his last Frisian spring.

The American Henry James Baron (b. 1934), a good fifty years later,
living comfortably in Grand Rapids, Michigan, doesn't often talk about
that leave-taking. But now as he tells the story, the dimmed and neglected
details begin to take on sharper contours, and he is again the boy from
that time: Hindrik of Jeen Sytses Baron and Afke Hoekstra.

Before he continues the story, we're going for a ride on his motorcycle
around his city of Grand Rapids in Michigan-USA. It's been hot for several
weeks already in North America. The wind is muggy, the fields are dry,
and the corn stands in withered rows. "That crop isn't going to amount to
much," observes Hindrik Baron. We pass a lot of farms, many still farmed
by descendants of families who bought their land from the Indians.

Kalamazoo. Now we've wandered far enough. Back to the city. It is
late afternoon when Grand Rapids comes back into view. The freeways
crisscross the suburbs like concrete ribbons. On the exit ramps swarms of
cars creep toward an ocean of homes, but that same ocean spews them
out again because just ahead the concrete curves are still strewn with
metal on wheels.

Before us lies a city of a good two hundred thousand residents. The
southeast side appears less crowded and greener. There the outskirts of
the city feature quiet avenues, the brick homes show off their Reformed
Church grandeur, and the way of life proceeds calmly and conservatively
along orthodox and Republican lines.

3

Hindrik Baron pushes the motorcycle inside the open garage, drops down in a chair on the deck, and tries again to begin with the beginning. When the band came to their place, it must've been one of the last, if not the last, evening in Grinzer Pein. In the middle of the night, the family walked from the Skieding to the Provincial Road. The bus stood waiting.

His first conclusion sounds like a variation on the first sentence, "The ashes of our mother," from the famous book, *Angela's Ashes*, by the son of Irish immigrants, Frank McCourt: ". . . Dad and Mom for their own sake could better have stayed in Grinzer Pein." But Jeen Sytses Baron and Afke Hindriks Hoekstra took the step, and then there was no going back. Their five children went along, of course. Hindrik was the middle child.

Events occurred in the village of Grinzer Pein that did not pass the Barons by. In the twenties, when Jeen and Afke threw in their lot together as husband and wife, there was hope for better times to come. They were happy. But then came the time of crisis, the Depression, and it knew no mercy. Just when things began to look somewhat rosier, the German trucks rattled over the brick-paved road of Grinzer Pein. A time of much betrayal followed. Men like the German collaborator Pier Nobach also knew no mercy. Jeen Baron, elder in the Christian Reformed Church, didn't slink away. He read Nobach the riot act. Not without serious risk. And that's how the family on the Skieding farm, including the people they kept in hiding, went through the eye of the needle.

But eventually, the Canadian vehicles came roaring through the neighborhoods, also in Grinzer Pein. Liberation. A new day; now let the good times roll! But in the liberated Netherlands nothing seemed to change. Where was progress? Where were the promised improvements?

Jeen Baron wasn't the average small farmer and feed dealer, that was true. He was a well-read community leader with a competent pen, and one with musical talent. As a former member of the military band in the time of mobilization of World War I, he helped found the Christian brass band "Crescendo" in Grinzer Pein. Baron was able to transpose whole pieces of music as well as compose new arrangements. He was able to inspire others. And so he became the band's conductor.

Then there was the *Gereformeerde Kerk* (Christian Reformed Church). As elder he was concerned not only for members in the congregation, but also for others. In the Grinzer Pein of today, old people who knew him still talk about Jeen Sytses with respect. But what often happens in a village? What happened in this community of mostly pioneer types from other places? What happened in this rather young community that stood with one leg in Fryslân and with the other in Grinslân? Were the people always agreeable? Oh, it didn't go too badly, but sometimes the bickering made it seem like they were still struggling for position or power.

In the Christian Reformed Church in De Pein a depressing conflict developed between those adhering to a synod ruling (the synodicals) and those rejecting synod's ruling (the liberated). A split followed. Elder Baron was a leader on the side of the liberated. That was in 1944. The whole world was practically aflame; why not add a church war too.

In time, the church conflict eased up a bit. Well, true, on the school yard the children of synodicals and liberated were of course not allowed to jump rope together. In less than a year, the separated liberated had built their own church. The split acted like a watershed: a river begets a side river and neither stream wants to have anything to do with the other anymore, even though they owe their existence to one and the same source. When four years later the household of Jeen and Afke left their village, the sharpest edges of the church conflict had worn off. No, that could not have been the main reason for their leaving.

There was more pain. Something happened that hurt the small farmer and feed dealer deeply and plagued him to his death. Not until years later would the children discover the how and what. The music. "Crescendo." Jeen would do anything for his community and for the band. For his role as conductor and all his efforts he didn't expect a penny. What counted for him was the unity of the village, the harmony, the musical development of the youth.

The band got better and better. Everyone was greatly impressed. Soon "Crescendo" moved from the third division to the second in the association of Christian bands. It was time to participate in another music competition, the board concluded.

It was a unified group that traveled to the competition in Grijpskerk. They practically knew their whole repertory by heart, that's how much they had practiced. They would show their stuff with *"Au Printemps"* ("In

5

the Springtime"). How does a farmer, a man of nature who spends much time in all kinds of weather, experience the springtime of his Frisian woodlands in the western district? The interpretation of Jeen Sytses Baron was this: first a restrained volume, then a gradual unfolding, followed by an almost majestic expression of the life force. All the members of "Crescendo" felt the springtime in this *"Au Printemps"* permeate their being. They played their hearts out.

The decision of the jury was bewildering. The men behind the jury table, those gentlemen who might never have watched a sunrise in the spring, did not share the interpretation of "Crescendo." The band fell from grace and was dismissed with a third instead of a first prize.

On the trip home, even before they reached Grootegast, some members of the board began to point the finger. The gentlemen of the jury must be right. They were experts, after all, and must know what they were doing. Their own prophet among them must've been dead wrong. And so it was secretly decided, in the delusion of the moment, that they needed a new conductor. One who was qualified and had papers to prove it, who knew exactly what the experts were looking for.

A few days later, the board sent a "representative" from "Crescendo" to the Skieding with the decision. On behalf of the board, Jeen Sytses Baron was dismissed. He felt humiliated and betrayed. What hurt him the most was the way it was done. After that encounter, Jeen Sytses never touched his conductor's baton or his trumpet again. Harmony was shattered. And each springtime after that, when in the woodlands and western district nature at first tried to restrain itself, but then in an almost majestic expression of the life force let itself be seen and felt, the small farmer and feed dealer from Grinzer Pein felt like weeping.

Hindrik Jeens Baron, on the deck behind his home off Burton Street in Grand Rapids, begins again. "It was still dark, very early in the morning, on the twentieth of May in 1948. We walked the path together to the Provincial Road, five of us as kids with Dad and Mom. Crates packed with furniture had already preceded us to Rotterdam. In one of those crates was a trumpet for me and a saxophone for my brother. Shortly before, we had gone to Ljouwert with Dad to buy them. In Grinzer Pein, playing had become taboo, but now it was going to be different. Dad had also packed his own trumpet. A new land, a new springtime, a new sound. To America, where everything, the whole way of life, would have a new chance."

Emigration. What objection could one make as a boy of fourteen? At that age one doesn't need a new beginning in a new world. One had barely begun to sink his roots. "For me the trip had something intimidating about it, but at the same time it held challenge. I think I smelled adventure. Though it's also true that I had just spent my first year at the Ulo in Surhústerfean, and I had enjoyed that because I liked to study. Now farewell to all that, to friends, to everything. I hoped that I'd be able to continue my education on the other side of the world.

"It was about half past two that morning when we left the place on the Skieding. I heard the mournful cry of a bird, a cry I would never forget. And then, all of a sudden, I heard myself say: '. . . Never again, never again. . . .' I thought I was speaking for all of us, but it turned out that I was speaking only for Dad: he would never return.

"Mom had heard what I'd said in my elementary, Ulo-school English, but for her they were foreign words. I felt her arm, her hand. I stopped as if waiting for and wanting a hug. 'Come on,' brother Sytse urged, who was carrying the heaviest suitcase, 'the bus is already waiting for us!'

"It was the bus of Uncle Marten Hoekstra from Feanwâlden. The door of the bus was wide open for us, but the engine had been turned off. 'Rotterdam, chauffeur!' Dad tried to break the tension with a joke. He put his suitcase on the running board, then turned. In the darkness appeared the faces of a few of my friends. Then all of a sudden I recognized relatives. Uncles and aunts, and cousins too. Dad was still standing right in front of me. He was not breathing quite so hard anymore. Then he went in. Uncle Marten dropped behind the big steering wheel and started the engine. The bus was almost full with people who were going to take us to the boat in Rotterdam.

"What I recall here may not be exactly the way it was. A half-century has a way of fading and shifting the images and conversations of so long ago. But I do know that in the very early morning hours we rode through the darkness toward a new day. A strange sort of tension hung over us in the bus, and I felt the old country glide under me mile after mile; I felt it glide away from me.

"What was that in my coat pocket? A mouth harmonica? Did Uncle Marten, who behind the wheel tried to lift the general mood, succeed in getting me to play and have the others sing along? I'm not sure anymore. I think it was my brother's friend who did the playing.

"The images of the harbor where the boat was docked, all the people, all the good-byes there — it's somewhat of a big blur to me now. We landed on the *Veendam* of the Holland-America Line. We discovered that Dad had booked first class because otherwise we would've had to wait another six months to get passage in tourist class. Now it became clear to me why we were all so dressed up. The dining room. The first dinner. All of us were overwhelmed, Dad and Mom included, by all the elegance. Satin table cloths, crystal glasses.

"I see Mom again sitting across the table from me. Timidly she pretended to read the French menu. Dad, next to her in his dark suit. Without a hint of diffidence he looked around. That's how Dad was; he was a man who knew who he was and where he was heading. But he had humbly hid his large milker's hands under the satin. And then the people who waited on us. They bowed. Some were brown-skinned, such as I had never seen in person. They bowed when they poured the drinks, ever so slightly. I couldn't shake the feeling that all the people in the dining room thought we were not only Baron by name but were really barons. Mom might've been regarded as a baroness, but especially for her it became a very miserable journey. Only once did she study the French menu; after that she got seasick. Almost all the way to New York, every bite she took came out again. For her, suffering had begun.

"Brother Sytse was eighteen. How did he experience the whole adventure? We've never talked about that much. His mind was full of electronics then already, and he'd planned to start his own business in Fryslân. In his heart he really didn't want to go, but he simply went. For Lys, the oldest at twenty, emigration must've been painful. Of all the children, her roots were deepest in Frisian soil. Then there were Grytsje and Marijke, but they were still young enough not to be bothered by much of anything. And that's how we left: the oldest of the five children was twenty, the youngest barely two, and the father already past fifty.

"They left home and hearth while they hardly knew what awaited them here. We never asked Dad and Mom about the whole array of motives before we left, and afterward it had little purpose, at least at first. It was a matter of survival. The questions come later. And then you have to speculate in part about the underlying background. It was never really discussed openly with us as the three oldest children. We didn't learn about the story of Dad and the band in detail until much later. From others. Isn't such a huge decision often the culmination of more than one consideration? The band, yes. And the strife in the churches likely caused some rancor too. But was it also maybe the madness of war that had hit Dad when he was in service during World War I? He hated the wars he'd been through himself. Did Dad and Mom leave, perhaps, to spare their sons another war? It was certain that they didn't want Sytse to go to Indonesia. And that they wanted to make a brand-new start. A new start on the other side of the world.

"Mom is still alive. She's ninety-six now and lives in a Christian care center in the Pacific Northwest, the state of Washington. Her memory isn't able to recall anymore the thoughts in her heart of long ago, but I remember hearing her sigh one time: 'We should never have left De Pein.' Why did they, then? Because she saw in the letters she received from her cousins in America the land of dreams and wishes? How much had the shakeup of "Crescendo" and the schism in the churches plagued her? Mom was there when late into the night Dad wrote his letters to the theologian Dr. Klaas Schilder, one of the brains behind the separation of the liberated. When the bombshell finally exploded, a judge was needed to decide which side would get the church building in De Pein and which the parsonage. It was a time when friends changed into enemies. Mom had to stand by when her husband was deeply humiliated through the action of the band's board. One of the consequences was that he could no longer exercise and share his musical gifts. Something else: Mom must've sensed fairly early that neither of her sons had a yen for farming. They wanted to go in other directions than their father had, namely business and academics.

"We landed in northwest Washington, near the town of Lynden. First, everybody had to go to work. Try to get on our feet. We didn't get the nicest boss to work for. A rough guy who swore and drank too much. In De Pein, Dad had always been his own boss; now he had to dance to another's tune. A boss who wasn't half the farmer he was himself, not half as intelligent, who excelled only in yelling and cursing. And then not to be able to understand a word of English; that time must've been torture for Dad. Fortunately, our kind of people had been well indoctrinated: look always to those worse off. Indeed, there were those who were worse off. The Oebele Boonstra family, for example, who had to live in a place that could hardly pass for a chicken coop.

"To master English as soon as possible, I attended the eighth grade of the local Christian elementary school. That stimulated my hunger for knowledge. I had my heart set on an education. But Dad's heart was set on getting his own farm, so of course Sytse and I had to help with the farmwork. 'First we have to make enough money, first we have to get back on our feet. Then we will look again.'

"That makes you want to fume a bit as a boy of fourteen, fifteen. 'I want to stay in school and study!' 'But first you have to help at home!' Dad said. That caused some misunderstanding between us. You're an adolescent in a new world full of uncertainty, and then you don't stop to think: Dad and I are partners in adversity, he needs me. Dad must've felt like a lost soul sometimes during those first years. He needed the support of his children. He must've felt a lot of anxiety that he wouldn't make it otherwise. And not making it was unthinkable.

"I came to realize much later that Dad had been extremely reluctant to keep me home from school. Only much later does one come to realize that a man of fifty-two is really too old to begin a new life as immigrant.

"So I stayed home, helping out, helping Dad, all the while taking high school correspondence courses, and cleaning countless eggs while thinking back to Grinzer Pein. Sometimes the fear and tension of wartime and church strife would all of a sudden hit me again. Sometimes in my thoughts I would be back in the time when the underground mistakenly killed Nazi-sympathizer Pier Nobach's son instead of Pier himself. Was it his fault that his dad was such a scoundrel? Had Pier become so frustrated when, after moving back from the States and stealing the show in his own town by riding around in a big Packard, he had not been crowned as king?

"Those times of reminiscing back then in Washington made me conscious of my history. What hadn't all happened in De Pein? Dad as elder had forbidden Nobach to participate in Holy Communion. Such a prohibition had to have consequences. Nobach was well known for reprisals; now Dad would certainly be shot too. While I was cleaning eggs, I experienced again our family's separation from the main church community and the gradual growth of a new identity. At first the church split seemed more like an excommunication. I was just ten, and on a Sunday morning I noticed how church people who had been close to us now passed us with hostility on their faces. With heads high they paraded to their own Christian Reformed Church while we shuffled to the village cafe. That's where we held church at first as a small group of about fourteen 'liberated' families. During the long prayer I heard kids outside make fun of us: 'From church to pub, from church to pub!' Some had changed from schoolmates one day to bitter enemies the next. How was that possible? Didn't we all have the same God?

"For the liberated Reformed members, their own kind of church stood waiting for them in the new country. But Dad decided that the whole family should join the Christian Reformed Church in the new land. Some of the immigrants who belonged to the liberated regarded that as an act of betrayal. But the choice had its logic: the Christian Reformed Church here had not had the theological conflict that had split the church in the Netherlands. Here Dad's ideal was still in place: 'one unified Reformed community.' It was an indication that the schism in Grinzer Pein had been an abomination to him.

"Sytse was in the meantime nineteen years old. 'I'm perfectly willing to help you now and again,' he told Dad one day, 'but I have to do my own thing, of course.' Dad was not interested anymore in fighting the will of his nineteen-year-old son. He had to let him go. Sytse not long thereafter married the daughter of a Frisian immigrant from the Lynden area and went on to become a very successful businessman.

"And then there was Lys. When she was eighteen in De Pein, Dad had hurt her deeply by personally terminating her relationship with a 'synodical' young man. One evening Dad had simply come into the house and said: 'Lys, your relationship is finished!' That's how it went in those days. Sometime after that, she became engaged to another who eventually followed her to America. The two youngest, Gryt and Marijke, hardly had problems with torn-up roots.

"I helped Dad on the farm, from my fifteenth to my eighteenth year. Each day I must've had the same feeling: farming would not be my future. In the meantime, Dad did get closer to the goal of owning his own place. He met a lawyer who had a farm and needed a partner on a fifty-fifty basis: each would get half of the profits. The partnership turned into a financial fiasco because of disease among the cattle. Instead of a profit, they had to split the losses.

"But Dad was not one to give up easily. Before long, he was able to rent his own place. Now he was able to practice his expertise to perfection; now he was able to get ahead. For Dad knew his cows! Before long he had developed a high-quality herd. That must've been a great relief to Dad and Mom. For me as well, for it gave me more time to hit the books. And I found a job in a store in the nearby city of Bellingham to earn a little money for myself.

"So things were looking up in the Baron home. Not that it ever came to a concert of two trumpets and a saxophone, but one mealtime I overheard Dad and Mom use the words 'a trip back home' and 'the Grinzer Pein.' It became clear that they were dreaming about a visit to the old country.

"It had been six years in America. Tough years for all of us. But we no longer ran to meet the mailman when he would deliver the illustrated weekly *De Spiegel*. A sign that we had integrated at least to some extent. And I had my hands full continuing an education by correspondence as well as participating in youth work in the church.

"I relied on the possibility that the American military would be my springboard to the future. If I served in the military, the GI Bill would cover my future educational expenses. So, facing an imminent draft anyway, I volunteered. There was an additional incentive: suppose that they would send me to serve my military duty in Germany; then an excursion to Grinzer Pein would certainly follow. Had my letter writing to the Frisian girls resulted into a tinge of homesickness? I don't know, maybe it was a bit like the little tree that couldn't get used to the strange soil in which it had been transplanted.

"However much I had been toughened by the heavy manual labor on the farm, I managed to catch a cold during basic training in Fort Ord, California. It eventually became TB. After a stay in the military hospital in Denver, I was sent to the Veterans Hospital in Portland. When I got well enough to be released but not ready to go back to work, I eagerly grabbed the opportunity to pursue the education I had been longing for in all these years. Western Washington University of Bellingham was my goal. They accepted me on probation. I gave it all I had, and soon the probation was lifted.

"The parents had now bought their own farm and were doing well. Too well? One morning, Dad was finishing the morning chores when he suddenly became ill. It looked grim. The doctor, who, it turned out later, was not a real doctor but a quack of Dutch origin, misdiagnosed the situation completely. Sixteen hours later, Dad, fifty-nine years old, passed away from a bowel obstruction.

"The enormous task to which Dad and his family had set themselves had not been finished. His journey back home was not to be. But in those last hours, Dad and I came to feel very close to each other. And Dad knew that he was going on his Home Journey after all.

"That left Mom, who had always stood by his side, who as mother had pulled the family through the storms of adjustments and uncertainties and lean times. I had to face the question, the dilemma really, whether I should turn to farming after all as Dad's successor. But everyone realized that that in all fairness could not be a legitimate option. So the farm was sold. Prices were not high at the time, but the sale enabled Mom to buy a decent house in Lynden. Marijke, the youngest, was only nine, so Mom faced the need to make a living for many years to come. She got a job in the Christian care center, where she herself is receiving care now.

"At the university in Bellingham I encountered Shakespeare and American literature. And genetics too, a subject that fascinated me a great deal. I graduated, married Ruth Bosman whose grandfather was an immigrant from Zeeland, became the father of a wonderful family, earned the Ph.D. in English at the University of Illinois, and have been a professor of English at Calvin College in Grand Rapids for many years.

"How could I resist? My 'never again' from long ago needed to turn into a comeback. I walked the path to the Skieding again, the path now shorter and narrower than on that night when a heavy blanket of dew lay over the land. Halfway to the old place, I stopped. I smelled hay as I hadn't smelled it for years. The bird that had given me such a sad send-off was now silent. Now only some fragments of a solemnly played chorale echoed in my head. I turned, and I saw Dad. He stood in the front room and stared out the window. Not far away, by the side door, the band was playing. Dad stood there, his hands over his ears, and for the last time he looked at his parcel of land and the cattle that no longer were his. It was in a terrible crescendo that the clock ticked away the last hour."

The Flight from Sibrandahûs

Hetty Seif-Lettinga from Grand Rapids, Michigan, USA

The shimmering avenues of Grand Rapids lie silently under a burning sun that seems to have paralyzed the city. It's close to three o'clock in the afternoon; the thermometer indicates that it's ninety-five degrees in the shade. Even the rose gardens behind Luther Home, where a few days ago the aged shuffled, some in short pants and white shoes, are now forsaken. Grand Rapids is slain by a Michigan heat wave.

In the hallways and rooms of the rest home, the air conditioners are busily playing catch-up. On the third floor, Hindrikje Seif-Lettinga has turned on the fan as well. There's a veritable gale blowing in the confined living quarters of the little old lady.

There's nothing in the room that harks back to the past; no pictures from long ago are on display. There's supposed to be a family picture somewhere from 1907 or 1908, but here the distant past seems forgotten.

"Later," she says, "later, after the last great war we began to do a little better. And now the children and grandchildren have everything they want. The Lettingas here have at least ten big farms, some are millionaires, one has an embryo-factory where they, so to speak, make cows. There's one farmer who has more than a thousand cows. And in Kalamazoo, if I got that right, there's another 320 head of cattle.

"But what I wanted to ask you: what do you think, will there be factories in the near future where they can make both cows and people? I don't think they should do that. They should leave that to the Creator. Though it's true that there are some strange creatures running around.

"My sister Sally, I mean our Sytske, went south, to Florida. Later she married a circus manager. So our Sally is more worldly than I am. The other day she told me on the telephone: 'I don't risk myself on the trapeze anymore, but to make your grand entrance into the huge circus tent on top of an elephant — to the accompaniment of an orchestra — that I could still do.' I said, child, you will soon be ninety-nine years old! She said: 'But I can hang on to my dreams, can't I?'"

A little old storyteller, as sharp as a tack. The widow is according to appearance and reports in her nineties. As turbulent and miserable as her childhood was, she begins her story with a cheerful face. For when life hits bottom, it can only get better.

"I can still hear the wind in the trees by Sibrandahûs: it was on a stormy night. We were children and were hauled out of bed. A single candle was burning in the front room. And there, oh, I couldn't believe my eyes: Dad came walking in his barn clogs to the table. Isn't that shocking; the farmer himself striding to the table of his obsessively clean wife's front room in his manure-covered wooden shoes!

"Dad was furious, ran in and out. A little while later he hit the open front room door with both fists. 'Woman, you got to quit whining!' He couldn't stand Mom's crying. 'I'm not going to back out anymore, the cow stalls are empty, and it's time to get the kids ready!'

"All of us had to go to the barn: Mom with our Sytske who was eight, I and our little Heabele who was just past two. I'd become six in August of that year. We were wearing new white wooden shoes. A new pair of shoes had come for each of us from Dokkum, but those were for later, Mom said, they had already been packed for the big trip in the afternoon.

"On the yard behind the house, a horse, harnessed, stood waiting, a black horse wet from the earlier rain, now shining under the light of the moon. Dad and the old hired man pushed a hay wagon out of the barn. A crate was on top of the wagon, a large crate, and there was also a bale of straw and some hay. We had to settle down on the wagon, Dad said. We landed behind the backs of our parents. I lay listening to the squeaking of the wagon wheel. When I pushed myself down tightly against the wagon-bed, I felt the vibration through my whole body.

"That evening two cattle dealers from Rinsumageast had hauled the last of the young stock off the place and taken to Dokkum's Ie. Now the animals were already headed to the Friday market in Ljouwert on the Dokkum cattle boat.

"That's how we left the farm in Sybrandahûs below the Geast. On a stormy Thursday night in October 1909. 'NOT go through the Geast to the Woodlands!' Mom heard Dad sneer. 'We're going through Dokkum to Groningen. There we will take the ferry and land up in Germany.'"

It is the reconstruction of a drama. Through a person ninety-five years old, the widow Hetty Seif-Lettinga. The images from her own observation and memory of that dramatic departure have become merged in those ninety years with the images her mother sketched of the incident. However, her mother seldom spoke of that time, and when she did, mostly in very sober language. For the departure from the farm in Sibrandahûs was nothing but a flight. And the beginning of a time of poverty and destitution. Later on even the father would now and then comment on that time. Even in Friesland, in De Geast and Bartlehiem, some still know about the circumstances. But only from what was passed on.

It was really poverty from the beginning, there on the farm of Wybren Lettinga at Sibrandahûs by Rinsumageast. The details of the situation remain somewhat sketchy, but the young farmer and his family had a tough go of it.

"One morning around four o'clock, the farmer came into his cowbarn and found two cows down. They couldn't get up. It might have been splenic fever, or maybe foot-and-mouth disease, but it was certain that some contagious disease had taken hold.

"Dad had figured on help from his mother-in-law, Grandma Sytske. They had money, those Postmas. But Grandma Sytske, who had become a widow when she was only twenty-nine, got married for the second time to a smart, decent farmer, a Tamsma. And he talked Grandma out of giving Dad a helping hand. Klaas Tamsma saw what was going to happen. Tamsma didn't think that Wybren Lettinga was careful enough and would probably fail to make a go of his place. In fact, Wybren Lettinga had also failed to repay the milkman from Bartlehiem the hundred guilders he owed.

"When the farmer fled that night with his family, he had nothing but hate in his heart for the second husband of what had otherwise always been a gentle mother-in-law. But there was also a handful of people in De Geast who'd rather see Wybren Lettinga go than come.

"It was the duped milkman from Bartlehiem who was the first to alight on the Lettinga farm the next morning. What he found there was an empty cow-barn, according to the stories he would tell later. He cautiously investigated the front part of the house. In the front room he saw the traces of an unbalanced farmer. Here and there stood a forsaken piece of furniture; even the tablecloth was still in place. There was a marble clock and two candleholders on the mantel. The clock had stopped at a quarter to twelve.

"That same Friday it was the talk of the town in the taverns along the Market Street in Ljouwert: Wybren Lettinga, the blustery farmer from Sibrandahûs, fled in the middle of the night with wife and kids. And as sly as he was, he had sold his last cows in the afternoon for cash. That's how he was able to afford a second-class ticket to America, which meant that he didn't have to head for the new world in third class, in the company of those dirty Poles and all their lice.

"'He must've taken off to visit distant relatives in Germany,' the feed dealer from De Geast thought. 'Wybren was talking the other day about how the German emigrants became filthy rich in America.'

"'Yeah,' opined another one, 'I bet he's on the way to Germany. In Bremerhaven or Hamburg he'll be able to find a boat that takes him to America, for in Amsterdam they might grab him at the Holland-America Line. There are too many people he owes money.'

"'Ja, there are quite a few merchants who have money coming from Wybren,' commented another. And a cousin said: 'I'm not surprised he's gone, because he stopped by the other day and said: 'I thought I'd come by because something could happen that we wouldn't see each other again!'

"Somebody by the name of Prins farmed on our place later," Hetty Lettinga remembers. "I went back there once, years and years later. That brought memories back to the surface. Yes, it was a terrible October night.

I lost one of my nice white, little wooden shoes on that wagon ride. When Dad noticed it, he said, 'Here honey!' and he took the remaining clog from my foot and threw it in the canal. I cried my eyes out because I was so upset. Then Mom said: 'Dear child, Dad's right, you can't do anything with one clog.'

"That flight from Sibrandahûs really went on for years. I remember the first days and nights as an endless, gloomy time with lots of delays and discomforts. I remember that Sytske kept asking if Grandma knew that we had left just like that. Those questions made Mom terribly upset. Dad was angry. One early morning a couple of strong men lifted the crate from the wagon, the horse and wagon were sold for cash, and we boarded a ferry with a couple of horses pulling. We spent long, long days en route, slept in strange places, heard people speak in foreign languages. But I know that Dad gradually became milder. The time came that I wasn't scared of him anymore; he even hugged me. He preferred Sytske otherwise, Sytske was cuter. I looked like a scruffy alley cat, he'd always say.

"Dad got a stranger involved, got papers from him, took money out of the billfold, we landed in a train, and later came to a huge steamship. It rained.

"At sea we threw up; it was like vomiting our whole insides. It must've been the beginning of November by now, with stormy weather and high seas. I learned from Mom later on that at one point the ship couldn't make any progress against that northwest gale, it could only bob up and down, its bow pitched sideways into the wind. Everything around us creaked and groaned. It must've been a hurricane, a hurricane that seemed to last forever. We spent almost three weeks on the high seas. At one point, I heard later, Mom said: 'We have to put it in the hands of the Lord Jesus.' And Dad said: 'In Sibrandahûs the barn is empty.'

"When we arrived in New York, I was badly dehydrated. Later Mother used to tell others that there wasn't much life left in me. Dad, she said, was beside himself when he saw the Statue of Liberty rise before him in New York. He got all choked up about that. 'In this land I will become a farmer, on a farm which Klaas Tamsma from the Iewâl below Sybrandahûs can't stand in the shade of!' When he spoke those words, one of my nice white wooden shoes must've been hanging out somewhere around Damwâld.

And the other one was probably still in a ditch close to Boerum. In any case, I arrived in America in my socks.

"I can hardly remember waiting in those huge immigrant reception halls in New York. I must've done nothing but sleep. At the exit, the Jews warned Dad seriously about a severe winter. So we bought a bunch of heavy, woolen underwear. The train ride to the Midwest is hazy in my memory, except that it seemed endless. It took us right across Pennsylvania, through Ohio, Indiana, Illinois, and Missouri.

"If I'm not mistaken, one early morning we stepped from the train in Dodge City. That's a good ways into Kansas, not even so far from Colorado, because we had left the prairies behind us long ago. Past Dodge City the land becomes elevated. What I still remember is that at times Dad became irritable again. Mom wore a round, black little hat. Now that I think about it, I believe it was a hat with a mourning veil, though I'm not sure why. Dad wore the striped trousers he had bought in New York. And he wore a straw hat he had bought in the train station in Missouri and paid for through the window of our compartment. Later on, when I went to school already, I read the name where the hat was made: St. Louis.

"So we landed on the other side of Kansas. When the train went on, three men approached us on horseback. They had another five horses on a line with them. Fine-boned brown horses. The leader, while spitting on the ground every few words, talked to Dad with a strange, harsh sound, but Dad didn't understand the man. The intention was that we would ride in a buggy, a kind of gig but a bit more primitive. One of the horses was hitched to the buggy. The five of us just fit. The crate with our goods would follow later, they said.

"That evening some five buggies came behind us, so there were more newcomers. That put Dad in a better mood.

"'We're almost there,' he said.

"'The land looks dry here,' Mom observed critically.

"'The men look trustworthy to me,' Dad said.

"Dad was wrong, he hadn't understood the men rightly. Late that evening we discovered that we couldn't get across a river. The horses drank from the river; the men explained to Dad that the river stood much higher than two days ago. It must've been a tributary of the Arkansas River, or a creek coming from Smoky Hill running south. In any case, it wasn't safe for the buggies to cross. They made a fire, something to eat, and then we slept in the outdoors. We actually were lucky that it wasn't a very cold November night.

"The next morning, we went further south, as I was told later, to cross the river, and finally arrived at our destination on horseback. I believe that we ended up in Big Bow, but it could've been in the area of Lakin. There they had a sod hut waiting for us. Maybe I could better call it a hollow, because the accommodation was dug out of the side of a hill. Dad was lucky, there were settlers who talked German; he was better at understanding that than English.

"Dad took off very early in the morning on horseback to meet the farmer he was apparently assigned to as hired hand: Gerald Hitchman. Hitchman owned a world of land behind the hills. When Dad came back home after a few days, he had blisters on his seat from all the horseback riding.

"Then the winter began, a short but severe winter.

"'Dad let them paint too pretty a picture,' I heard Mom sigh once. But for the most part, though a farmer's daughter from a well-to-do background, she didn't complain much. It was as if she resigned herself to her plight after the flight from Sibrandahûs: to the plight of having to go through life with a man like Wybren Lettinga. In reality, she loved Dad a lot; at least she always tried to smooth over and defend his actions. To her the man must've had something irresistible about him. After all these years I can see that a little; there was something attractive about him. He could also be very persuasive.

"Dad claimed that he could earn more by milking cows than working for Hitchman with his huge herd of beef cattle. So that same winter he traveled to another farmer even farther away. He'd come home only once a week. Still always on horseback. When the first snowstorm out of Nebraska blew over our sod hut, the three of us shivered all by ourselves. The next morning we couldn't even get out. That's when Mom for the first time faced up to the reality. Somehow a narrow path was dug through the snowdrifts to the neighbors' hut. About four days later Dad came home.

Without a horse; he'd sold it. It had taken him four days to get home and he had been worried sick about us. Mom cried.

"'When spring comes, we'll go to Iowa, that's on the other side of Nebraska,' Dad said. 'They have great clay there. On the other side of Omaha, in Iowa, I'm going to try farming.'

"We had winter weather with lots of sunshine. A farmer from Burlington came on a sleigh to pick up Dad and a couple of men. Dad had a chance to earn five dollars a week somewhere. 'That's better than nothing,' he said. So we were alone with Mom again.

"'Who's crying so hard, Mom,' Sytske wanted to know one evening. 'They're small dogs, honey, not bad dogs. They're just hungry, that's all.' That's what Mom said, but they weren't cute little dogs, they were howling wolves that each night came a little closer to the sod huts of Big Bow.

"When Dad came back home by the end of January, he gave his gun to Mom and explained how to use it.

"Spring came and Dad had bought a milk cow. The weather had turned mild, the field was drying out fast, and it wasn't long before you could hear the grass grow. 'I don't think we should leave here,' he said. 'Winter is going to be back,' Mom objected. 'Gerald said that we'll never have a winter as cold and severe as this last one.' That was Dad's way of reasoning.

"One morning, when he was back to work, the mailman came with the first letter from Fryslân. From Grandma Tryntsje in De Geast. Much later I got a chance to read that letter, and one sentence from it I have never forgotten: 'I have, my beloved daughter, pain in my heart because I miss you so much.' We were too young to realize how much Mom suffered too. Later, when we were older, she confided that she had cried every day. Because she knew that she would never see De Geast and her parents again.

"She milked the cow three times a day and tried to make butter and cheese from the milk. But way before the longest day, it got so terribly warm that the milk turned sour in no time. Then she dug a hole in the ground to keep the milk cool in and possibly manage to save the cream. When one morning she was going to haul the pan of milk to the surface, she saw a large snake slobber up the cream. Mom took the gun and shot the snake.

22

"'We have to get out of here, Wybren,' she said when Dad jumped off the horse that Saturday night. I can still see the man with the salt rings in his sweaty woolen undershirt. It was as if he didn't even hear what Mom said. 'In a couple of weeks I can afford two animals,' he said. 'And a ways from here I bought a tin shed. If I can get that snow-tight before winter, we'll be in good shape.'

"But then something happened that would drive us out of Kansas. It happened the next day already: a tornado from the direction of Ulysses came our way. With a whirlwind preceding it like a doomsayer. It was about two o'clock on that Sunday afternoon. 'There are funnels in the sky,' Dad had said several times already. Like a long-necked, all-devouring dinosaur, the tornado devastated the land. At first it seemed like it was going to go in another direction and dissipate, but then it loaded up all over again with dust and water and the hay that lay in piles here and there on the land. Then it was up to our little settlement. We flew into the hut with Mom and Dad and felt how the sods above us were torn away. Suddenly we lived outdoors.

"'It's getting lighter already, soon we'll have the sun out again,' Dad said.

"'We have to get out of here, Wybren, we must go to Iowa as soon as possible.'

"'Ja,' he said, 'there in the area of Marshalltown and Waterloo the soil is supposed to be much better too. That's what Jerry Griffith said. And the weather is more reliable.'

"'Jerry Griffith drinks too much,' Mom warned, 'we better not get mixed up with him.'

"'Jerry Griffith is going to Iowa because the land hasn't been drained there yet,' he grumped, 'but he's going in the first place because it has a better growing climate.'

"I don't remember much of the trip to Iowa, but I do remember that it was a depressing time for us. Our life was so insecure, we felt so forsaken. Because that's how Mom experienced it, we felt it as children that way too. All the happenings on the way to Iowa were erased from my memory.

"I believe that we traveled via Kansas City and Omaha. It was at the time that the automobile factories of Henry Ford began mass production and the first Model A's appeared in Omaha. I can still see that first car driving the streets. Along the way Dad heard that a certain Jackson drove one and the same car all the way from New York to the Far West. In sixty-five days. It was hard to believe all the things that were possible in this new land. And we, we wandered from one place to the other. Now in an overheated train, then in a rickety buggy again, or on horseback. And always we had to keep searching for lodging somewhere else.

"Past Des Moines in Iowa, the winters appeared to be much more severe even than in Kansas. Around Christmastime, Dad had to tie a rope between the old cow barn and our little wooden shack fifty meters away. If he hadn't done that, he would've lost his way in the snowstorms and died.

"At last we landed where the Almighty God wanted us: here in the area of Grand Rapids in Michigan. Two healthy little ones were added to the family — August and Tina — but Dad's farming floundered. He worked for a while for a farmer named Folkertsma. During that time we often had to listen to Dad's tirades about the rotten folk of Sibrandahûs and area. According to him, the family there had plenty of money, but they begrudged him any of it. At one time he milked seven or eight cows. We could just squeak by on that. We gave the money we earned later on as kids to Mom.

"One Saturday morning the mailman came with a telegram: Grandma Tryntsje had been buried in Rinsumageast. They claimed that her heart had failed from grief over the loss of her daughter. Dad came immediately to his own conclusions: some inheritance money should be coming to America. What's right is right. 'Even if I have to go and get it myself.'

"But that wasn't necessary. Mom's part of the estate soon arrived in America. During that same period of time, Grandpa Heabele — Dad's Dad — passed away. 'And now I'm going to pick up my share myself, otherwise I won't get it at all!' Dad exclaimed when he had read the telegram and put it down on the table in front of him. That same week he got on the train to New York and stepped onboard the boat to Amsterdam. Wybren Lettinga liked to have money in hand. That must've been in the twenties.

"It wasn't until a half year later that he returned to Grand Rapids. With a cousin, a Gysbert Lettinga from Hilaard, whom he had persuaded that America was a land of milk and honey. True, he brought a string of jet pearls along for Mom, but he had a smaller inheritance than he had expected. Grandpa Heabele in De Geast had assumed Dad's debts, and those had been deducted from his share of the estate. And then there was the milkhauler of Bartlehiem who had never gotten his hundred guilders back from Wybren Lettinga. The milkhauler biked from Bartlehiem to Hilaard, where Dad was staying, and demanded his rights.

"Still, Dad had just enough left to buy a farm in Michigan. But then came the crash and the Depression of the thirties. Those tough years took their toll; it was terrible. A couple of summers of drought came on top of that. The farm had to be sold again, because the debt load was too much. Dad's dream to show up Klaas Tamsma from Rinsumageast on his mother-in-law's place would never be realized.

"Mother died when she was eighty-one. And then it became clear that Dad could not do without Mom. He was completely lost. One year later he joined Mom in the grave."

Initials on the Stairs

Anna Postma-Wielinga of Oakdale, California, USA

I t is springtime in the Sacramento Valley. Though the winters are mild
here, everything looks full of new life. The fields are bursting out all
over. Now and again I cruise through oceans of flowers in my Chevrolet.

An hour later, on the other side of Sacramento, it's warming up rap-
idly. Endless lines of cars come streaming out of San Francisco and rush
down the freeway toward Los Angeles. I listen to the radio as I eat up the
miles through the almost flat landscape. I catch a glimpse of cows staying
close to their shed, looking for some shade. Then I see a huge herd of grazing black and white cows. In another month or two, most of the fields here
will probably look dry and yellow.

After another hour, I'm in the San Joaquin Valley. Close to Modesto I
have to turn left and drive east. On a clear spring day one can make out the
contours of the Sierra Nevada Mountain range, but I don't have to go that
far. In the town of Oakdale I reach my destination: the sunny home of Anna
Postma-Wielinga, who has just been watering the flowers. Since 1993, the
sad year in which her husband Nies passed away, she's been alone. Most of
her children and grandchildren live in the area, so this is home for her.

But there is still another place she feels close to, though that place has
become almost unreachable.

Her story begins in Seisbierrum, right after the war.

"For a moment I had the hope that Nies wouldn't pass the physical,
that's how much I dreaded to leave Seisbierrum. But Nies wanted to move;
he dreamed about having his own farm in America.

"One day he was talking about Canada; 'Canada is the heart of America,' you said. That's how much we knew about the world.

"I thought for a minute about pretending to be simple for the emigrant examination. There was a chance that they would ask the women questions like: 'How many kilometers is America from the Netherlands?' Afke Wiersma from Dokkum had answered that question: 'At least a hundred, sir.' She was rejected. But there was something wrong with her physically too.

"They didn't ask me anything. I didn't even have to take off my underwear there in The Hague. Nies did, and he didn't come from such a strong family; he became an orphan early. We were in the same examination room, and the pressure was killing Nies. When he had taken off his clothes, when everything hung on the chair, the doctor came in and said right away: 'That doesn't leave much of you, Postma.'

"'No,' Nies said nervously, 'I don't have too much fat around my ribs, doctor, but I'm as tough as nails.' Nies was so eager, he raced through the exam, and I did too, and well, we were really happy about that. Something serious could have been wrong with him and with me too, as far as that goes, because I came from a family with TB.

"It was in late spring of 1947, and we were heading for a dry summer — though we didn't know that then — and if you'd listened to the people from De Bjirmen, it seemed like the whole world was bent on emigration. Nies had made one more stab at trying to get work: he had applied to the civil service. But that didn't go anywhere; he didn't have the education.

"Then all of a sudden the day came when the mail brought a letter with the results of the emigration physicals. Passed. We had ten days to get our stuff packed. Canada. Oh, how I dreaded it. And how I tried to talk Nies out of it. But the minister of our Christian Reformed Church was all in favor of emigration too, and he encouraged me. We were an ideal family for such a move, he said. 'The Lord God will be there for you on the other side of the ocean too.'

"We had married during the war, in 1941, and now we had three children: Sjoerdsje Johanna who was four, Willem Siek was three, and Jan Bieuwe was one and a half.

"The crate was soon filled: the tea table, the coatrack, the clock, the chamber pot, and some other pots and pans. And Nies's ice-skates which he had used in the Eleven-City Race of 1942. He also put his race medallion in there, but that somehow got lost in transit, and that bothered Nies for a long time. Even though he finished the race more dead than alive, that medallion symbolized his rehabilitation from TB.

"The good-byes in Seisbierrum, on a Sunday in the middle of June in 1947. Beautiful weather. A lot of people over at the house, for I came out of a family of nine children. At one point, Nies and I wanted to go outside, walk through the neighborhood, sit on the lawn for a while, but Dad insisted we stay inside. Mom had closed the curtains halfway. Dad apparently wanted to say some words to us while everybody was still there. He rose, held on to the table with both hands, was going to open his mouth, and got stuck. Then, for the first time in my life, I saw him cry. Mom did not cry but proved to be tougher than Dad in the present circumstances. Of course, she believed that the tragedy of emigration was God's will, and that meant that you had to accept. Still, it was a disaster for her too. 'All at once I lose a daughter with her husband and three children.'

"The next morning we bounced to Ljouwert in a truck, and from there on the train to Rotterdam. 'Let us pray for a peaceful journey,' the minister had said in his last sermon.

"But it wasn't peaceful. It was already terrible on the first day of travel. Nies lost his passport: a stranger took it and then took off with it. Nies and I and the children were still on shore when they were already casting the ropes loose. It was like a nightmare. They thought that Nies had maybe stuck the passport in some secret pocket, so they made us go through all the clothes. We were shunted from one window to the other, there on the Lloyd Harbor pier of Rotterdam.

"I could've been happy to still be on shore; at least there was a chance now that we wouldn't be going away. But toward evening, the news came that the passport had surfaced on board. A small boat came to take us to the big *Waterman*. We had to crawl up on the rope ladder, and that was no small task. First a dockworker climbed up with our little Sjoerdsje; the poor child screamed like bloody murder. Then our Willem was hauled up. After that Nies went with the baby in his arms. And then it was my turn, as the very last emigrant on the very first postwar emigrant ship to Canada. I didn't dare, I couldn't do it, but I had to. And I did it.

"When we were out on deck that evening, Nies admitted that he hadn't had anything to eat or drink for a day and a half. But that was his own fault, because he kept saying he didn't need anything. The kids were eager to get to bed, they were all tuckered out. And there was a new neighbor lady — from the area of St. Nicholas — who was keeping an eye on her and our kids.

"It was around nine in the evening as the ship, high above land and sea, pushed steadily on the New Waterway toward sea. The dew passed over the fields. On the other side of the small houses, we could see the gardens, and herds grazing.

"Then we reached the sea. The weather was calm; there was still a sliver of the sun above the horizon, coloring the waves a bright red. That special moment I will never forget. Nies said: 'So that's that.'

"We just lingered there by the railing on the back of the ship, and suddenly he got all choked up. I quickly handed him a piece of bread, for the umpteenth time urged him to take it, said, 'You got to have something in your stomach!' A little later he ate the bread. He wasn't thinking about sleeping, tried to explain why he had moved from Tsjom to Seisbierrum. Because of work, to make some more money, because in Tsjom he would always have the feeling that he was a little orphan boy. It was as if only now, here on the *Waterman*, he had found the excuse for the huge step he had taken with me.

"'I was making cheese for seven guilders a week, I didn't have a home as an orphan, in Seisbierrum I also had to pay seven guilders for room and board, I became skinny.'

"I had often asked myself why he couldn't get back into the factory after the war, because he was a first-class cheese-maker. Later he looked for other motivations: 'I didn't leave because in the war the Germans were after me all the time, Anna, and neither did I leave, as so many others did, out of fear for the communists, I didn't let others talk me into it, I just wanted to get away, and I will probably never know for sure why.'

"The two of us stood by the ship's railing. 'Look,' he said suddenly, 'look at these names.' In the heavy wooden railing, the boys who had sailed to Indonesia, had carved their names or initials. Nies tried to read all the names, to decipher all the initials, he looked for the names of men he knew. Boys from Tsjom and area, and from our neighborhood in De Bjirmen. There were a lot of names he knew, guys he had gone to catechism with and others he had gone into hiding with. He thought he discovered names and initials of some who had been killed in action: Andele Lautenbach from Berltsum, Lieuwe Greidanus from Tsjom, Wiebe Bruinsma also from Tsjom; Lieuwe who was so good on the trombone in the band 'Praise the Lord.' He too had taken his knife and carved his initials in the railing.

"Let me be honest, we had no idea where we were going. Montreal, yes, but where then? And was Montreal in Canada? Three days after arrival as a troop transport from Indonesia, the *Waterman* turned right back out to sea with its first load of emigrants. The ship was designed as a troop carrier in wartime. Now it had stuffed almost two thousand adults with an army of kids together for nine long days and nights. There were no cabins, only halls and hammocks. Nies had to sleep with the men. There was so little privacy. Fortunately I had grabbed the chamber pot from the crate at the last moment and kept it with me. We threw up in that pot, relieved ourselves in it, and washed ourselves in it. Halfway on the voyage, the toilets plugged up. It began to stink like the human waste wagon from Berltsum. And the children? There was no entertainment at all for them.

"When we finally moored in Montreal, the rats raced on shore across the ropes. But our first card to Seisbierrum said: 'The food was wonderful, we had white bread all the time on the *Waterman*.' And that was true, we hadn't had white bread for seven years, and it tasted like cake to us.

"At seven o'clock in the morning, after a sleepless night, we landed in a large immigrant hall. Red Cross personnel were everywhere. They were better organized here than in Rotterdam, Nies observed. He was almost cheerful. But then we had to go back to administration officials. 'Where are we going?' Nies wanted to know, but the man didn't understand his Dutch. Nies had taken some English lessons, though, from a young farmer below Winaam who later became an attorney. 'They talk different here than the farmer,' he said. We stopped at a high gate, and there a man from the Christian Reformed Church met us. The 'Field Man.' He could speak

Dutch, and then we felt at ease. We found out later that the Field Man also decided where we would go.

"It was almost dark already by the time we were on the train. A lady came around with ice cream. That was a mistake, for we got upset stomachs. A shame, for one car ahead tables with delicious food were waiting for us.

"'Yes, they're much better organized here than in Rotterdam,' bragged Nies.

"But in the meantime he felt as sick as a cat and couldn't eat a thing. And the kids didn't want anything either, they just hung around. When we had been on the train for five hours, Nies and I got into an argument. We had never had a fight like that in our marriage. I almost exploded, all the tension got released. When we stepped out onto the platform in Trenton, Ontario, Nies and I took a good look at each other, and then it was done. We still had a long car ride ahead of us, and then we arrived at a farmer with a herd of cows, some pigs, and a large apple orchard. 'Such farm-workers homes they don't have in Bjirmen,' bragged Nies. Well, it was a house with a lot of space, that's true, but we had to share that space with another family, the Streekstras, who came from the area of Birdaard. There were now altogether eight children. After a few days you could cut the tension. The men were gone during the day, but the women were stuck. Inside of me, I was furious. For years Nies and I both had had our feet under someone else's table. He as a boarder, I as a maid working for somebody else. As nine children in my own family in Seisbierrum, we had to get by in the quarter part of an old farmhouse. There was so little space, Dad and Mom had to sleep by an open door, and that's how he got TB.

"Nies and I wanted to get married in the early years of the war because we so much needed to finally have a life to ourselves. I literally got on my knees by my parents' bed to beg their approval. And when I got it and told the woman I worked for, she became furious. 'You're gonna leave me? Is that why I provided work for you? Is that why I was always so good to you?'

"Whenever I reflected on life in Seisbierrum there by that Canadian farmer Nies was working for, I always thought about those kinds of incidents. Nies was working in the daytime, put in long days, and had his good appetite back, but now it was me that couldn't swallow a bite. I watched our little children get teased by the other people's big ones in our shared quarters. And evenings, nearly every evening, I could hear the noise of stormy weather in the hills. It was as if a war was heading my way all over again, reminding me of the time when Nies was chased like an animal by the Germans and had to keep moving from one hiding place to another.

"I became a nervous wreck, with a strange feeling coming over me that I couldn't identify. 'We have no trouble with homesickness,' the Streekstras cried in chorus, 'because we can never have it worse than we had it in Birdaard.' And I took Seisbierrum to bed with me every night and woke up with it every morning.

"Nies earned fifteen dollars per week by his new farmer, Kenneth Crews, and we had fuel and electricity free. We had never made that much before. Why in the world wasn't I happy now? That Crews was not one of the best, I need to add, because it turned out that he deducted a scandalously high amount from the pay for the milk Nies took home at night and for the rent of the place. That farmer figured of course that we weren't well informed or advised about such things, and we didn't have a car to go somewhere else.

"Nies was out the door every morning by four, and I would see him again around bedtime. And how much did we have left each week? One dollar. The house was far from other homes, even far from the farm itself, right in the middle of nowhere. Not till fall were we finally able to get a place of our own, closer to the farm. But this time I could hardly call it a house; it was nothing but a dilapidated shed. From our sleeping corner we could see the stars shine. Fortunately we had a dry, mild summer and fall.

"But the good fall weather didn't last long. It turned stormy, with wet snow. And after that, dry snow. One morning I had to shovel three buckets-full of snow from the blankets.

"One late afternoon in November, the farmer's wife came to the door. She wanted to check how things were going with me and the rest of the household. I said: 'I am too busy to be crazy.' She didn't understand what I was talking about, chuckled, and only later realized that I was in the process of going crazy. Homesickness, as I would still find out, is like a terrible venereal disease: at first you hardly feel it. But then suddenly you don't have an appetite anymore, and then you can't sleep anymore. Still later you suffer the consequences of that, and at last it seeps through your whole system and settles in your marrow. Finally, in the last phase, it attacks you mentally, and you go crazy. You die from it.

"I didn't want to complain when Nies got home late at night, because he had his needs too. He noticed of course that I was down. One night I admitted: 'I haven't had my period for a long time.' I had lost weight, but it turned out that I was pregnant again.

"It got harder all the time, I felt forsaken, and eventually didn't dare to leave the house anymore. The farmer's wife now picked up groceries for me in Trenton, because they wanted Nies to stick to his farm work, of course. For a long time I didn't want to complain. Something like 'maybe it'll go away by itself.' I knew that Nies was learning some English from an old Englishman: five new words each day. And he did very well. At night he'd study the new vocabulary, wanted to teach me some too, but I couldn't concentrate. I cried all the time. 'Something seems to be wrong with you,' he said. But who could understand what was happening to me; I had always been such a steady and strong woman.

"It became a cold winter, I didn't dare get out of bed anymore, was scared that I couldn't stand anymore. The temperature went down more than thirty degrees below zero, and we could hardly keep the place warm. But that wasn't the worst. The snow, the holes in the roof, which Nies never succeeded in plugging up completely, that was the worst.

"My mind was falling apart, and I had to be hospitalized. Does misery love company? I found out in the hospital that there were many more immigrant wives who had lost the battle. In the meantime, two new shiploads of immigrants had come to Ontario; so Nies had no trouble finding a good place for the three kids. One went here, the other there. And Nies had to take care of himself. After a year, the whole household was in disarray.

"After a few months, I began to get my act together; I was no longer preoccupied with life in Seisbierrum. I just wanted to get back to my own home, to the kids, to Nies. 'All right, now we're really moving in the right direction,' said the Christian Reformed minister in the hospital.

"One of Nies's sisters had married Jabik Hoekstra from Ikkerwâld, and they were now coming our way with the whole family. They had five children already. That's how I got more and more support and could even offer advice to others and help newcomers get on their feet. Yes, I do believe that that did me a world of good. And then Ed was born, and everything looked good. Our first little Canadian. The oldest kids were excellent students, took schoolbooks home with them, and played the teacher to help me learn the language.

"It was kind of strange, but Nies in his heart had never liked farmers, and now he had one goal: to become a farmer himself. We hadn't been allowed to take a dime with us when we crossed the ocean, so now we borrowed some money from Tsjerk Bylsma, from St. Anna. Six hundred guilders. With that we could start a small farm. Pigs. Nies in the meantime began to work for another farmer, one who was easier to work for than Kenneth Crew, and he brought home twenty dollars a week. And then in the evenings he'd be working for himself. But we ran into such a terribly cold winter that we brought some bales of straw into our basement. You might say that our life in Canada was marked by anecdotes: that winter we brought our three sows with piglets into our basement. It froze thirty-two degrees below at night, and sometimes a hard wind on top of that. Eventually we even had to turn on the heat lamps in the basement. Let me tell you, farming in Ontario was no picnic. But after a few years, we did manage to have some cows of our own, some pigs, a coop-full of chickens, and a couple acres of tomatoes. And, I almost forgot to mention it, we now had six kids. The oldest worked hard alongside of us; as kids of eight, nine, they were already driving tractor. That got us in trouble once when a jealous neighbor accused us of 'child labor.' But the kids loved to help out.

"Nies was aging fast, the cold weather bothered him, got back trouble, always had to wear wool in the wintertime. But that makes your skin break out in the spring, so one evening he got all excited when he got a call from Neal Visser from California. Neal, a son of Jetse Visser from Tsjom, had already come to California around 1930 when he was just a boy of six.

"'Why for goodness' sake don't you come this way, Nies.' According to Neal, there were enough farms in California, and the land at that time was still reasonable. That's how Nies's American Dream resurfaced, the dream that had begun in 1938 in Tsjom. Just the word California sounded like music in his ears. Neal hadn't been his first schoolmate for nothing; he could sponsor us. And he did: he signed for our whole household and vouched for us for a period of five years.

"In November of 1954, we had an auction. The price of cattle that year was terrible. We lost money not only on the land and cows, but also on the new tractor and other equipment. So when all was said and done, we had practically nothing left. Without money we landed in the neighborhood of the Vissers in Artesia, California. Nies had no more trouble with cold weather. And two more kids joined the family in the States. As far as farming goes, it seemed that Nies was more relaxed, because he no longer slaved from early in the morning to late at night. That's why things went better, he had more confidence, and became physically tougher. Because if you want to succeed in the States, you simply have to be physically tough. Because of the appreciation through inflation, we really saved more money in California with buying and selling land and cattle than from all the toil and shivering we did in Ontario. By 1961 we had our own nice house in America, and around 1972 we moved here to Oakdale, and then we had it even better. Land that he bought for fifty thousand dollars, he sold in 1982 for three times that.

"Before long, Nies saw his ideal become reality: his own farm with a hundred cows. When he got that far, he was content.

"But tragedy would still strike: in 1989 our youngest son died in an accident. Nies could not get over it; it did him damage. No doubt that caused him heart trouble. It turned out that he twice needed bypass surgery. He picked up again, but then added another problem: homesickness. 'I know now what you had in the beginning of the fifties,' he said. As therapy I went back eight times with him to Tsjom. When he would walk through the neighborhood there and stand by the church, he would be kind of excited. Emotional. And then I thought: how is it possible to love a village so much in which as an orphan you were so lonesome?"

Return to De Gaastmar

James Jelle Wildschut, Tampa, Florida, USA

The waves wash lazily over the West Coast beach of Florida. The Gulf of Mexico gasps in the bright morning light. Then the silence is disrupted. Rumbling machines level and rake the powdery white sand, and gratefully a flock of stilt birds descend, in search of food. Among them are oystercatchers that stand a little higher on their legs than their relatives that forage at the flood line of the Dutch Wadden region. Clearwater Beach has its own flora and fauna.

It's close to ten o'clock when the first "snowbirds" begin to arrive, the Americans and Canadians from the cold north who spend their winters in Florida. They emerge from their second homes: a condo, apartment, or mobile home. They first tiptoe across the beach that has just been evened especially for them. Old, gray, and yet vital. She's decked out in soft pastel colors, he in multi-colored Bermuda shorts several sizes too big. On top of the beach bag with a small cooler is a copy fresh from the press of the *St. Petersburg Times*, the respectable daily in this area. Practically every page features small ads for the hope-giving Viagra pill. No matter what need is uncovered on the American market, it is sure to be filled.

The license plates of the four-, six-, and eight-cylinder automobiles on the huge parking lot reveal which winter each snowbird is escaping: the one in New Jersey, or Ohio, or Michigan, or Wisconsin, or Minnesota, or Illinois, or the Dakotas, or Maine. There are even birds from the distant

Canadian province of Nova Scotia. In the autumn of their life, they search again for springtime.

Tonight they will meet each other again, a bit more of their bodies covered this time. They will meet in the small gardens behind their second homes, or in the trailer parks, or at the buffets in the cafeterias of Spring Hill, Holiday, Port Charlotte, West Palm Beach, or Miami. In many eating-places the gray invaders enjoy a discount. Why? "Because we made the States strong, you know!"

The words tumble out of the American James Wildschut Wilson. He adopted his second last name because he wanted to be both a hundred per-cent American and a hundred percent Frisian. As a boy of six, he came across the ocean to the States in September 1924 with his parents, four brothers, and a sister. First they took the milk boat from the village of De Gaastmar to Warkum. That wasn't so far: in clear weather one could easily see Warkum in the distance. But from Warkum all the way to Amsterdam! And from there across the ocean in the *Nieuw Amsterdam*. And then from New York across large lakes and endless hill country to the town of Zeeland in Michigan.

The journey was the continuation of a family tragedy. That really al-ready got started in the family of the grandparents of Jelle-alias-James: the shipbuilder Lourens Roelofs Wildschut from the close-by village of Heech, and his wife Aukje Tjipkes van Netten from De Gaastmar. Most of the ten children of Lourens and Aukje did not manage to escape disaster: a number of them died young, and a number of others became widow or widower at a young age. Nevertheless, a couple of successors to the Wildschut slipway survived.

The times turned bad, and the demand for the skilled craftsmanship in the making of wooden barges, vessels, and Zuiderzee yawls dropped dramatically. In the eyes of the old Lourens, the skippers of iron and steel on wooden boats were being replaced by wooden skippers on boats of iron and steel. This called for a lot of adjustments, and tensions developed within the family. Some beautiful iron boats were manufactured now all right, but Age, the son of Lourens and the father of Jelle, began to dream of America. There were Wildschuts in America already, and they had pre-sumably become rich. It wasn't long before Age's wife, Ytje Luitzens Ypkema from Nijhuzum, shared his dream.

Now it's three quarters of a century later, and James Wildschut, one of the more permanent snowbirds in Florida, tells the story. In his old age he has begun to reconstruct the dark journey of Age and Ytje's life. He hauls out an old picture, a farewell portrait, made a good seventy-five years ago in front of the house on the Hellingpath in De Gaastmar: Age and Ytje with six children at that time. In the middle is the brave mother, pregnant again as it turned out. Next to her an absentminded father, not young anymore. Thick mustache, vacantly staring into the merciless eye of the times and the camera.

Around the parents stand the five sons, dressed in the sailor suits sewn by their mother. A somber-eyed daughter, the oldest. Not a trace of a smile on the round faces, but that was the mode in those days. Only after the Second World War would children laugh or smile on pictures.

"I can't remember much of the long trip from De Gaastmar to Michigan," says Jelle, who now lives in Tampa, Florida. "But I must've had a vague feeling that something was not right. Dad was so quiet, so distant, so dejected. And that got gradually worse.

"The move from the old slipway that no longer had enough work to a lumber factory in the new world was a big change. In the evening, exhausted from the factory work, father Age would sit and stare with moist eyes at nothing. Could his sadness possibly be the consequence of the Spanish flu he had suffered as a young man? Or was this man, who had always been so strong, homesick but didn't dare talk about it? In time, the whole family felt smothered by depression. When the day came that Dad could no longer hack the work or the world, Mom had to do the washing for even more homes in the neighborhood. In the meantime a seventh child, a daughter, was born. And it was Mom who had to take responsibility for putting bread on the table.

"'What in the world is wrong with you, Dad!'

"'My head feels so funny.' That was all he could say. When the doctor didn't know what to do anymore, the minister was consulted. And when he too could not think of a remedy, the idea was advanced to scrape together all the hard-earned money so that Dad could travel back to Fryslân. Surely, a doctor and a minister there should be able to understand him better and put some life back into him."

Age Wildschut traveled back to Europe, less than two years after his arrival in Zeeland. Alone, because it took more than a year's wages for just one ticket.

Thanks to the help of fellow passengers along the way, Age arrived one late afternoon back at the slipway in De Gaastmar, a vacant look in his eyes. He had become a stranger.

"Where in the world are your wife and children!" But Ytje on the other side of the world tried to keep her family alive. Which was the good side of the world? Ytje, the washwoman, was now a grass widow. Because Age wasn't coming back.

At the old wharf they didn't know what to do with him. He wasn't able to work; he just sat there, staring blankly ahead. Sometimes he would stare at his trembling hands, and then he started to cry. "Are you homesick for your wife and kids, Age?" "No, no, it's just that my head feels so funny."

A yellowed picture from the years that followed, dug up in a drawer by Jelle James Wildschut Wilson in Lutz. Age sits in the door opening of the poorhouse in Heech, an expressionless look on his face. Another picture: a bus outing with the residents of the poorhouse to hotel Tjaarda in Oranjewâld. A small revival?

The presumed facts are hidden in old stories told in Heech: "His steps kept getting shorter on his daily walks through the village."

He must've had Parkinson's. It's certain that Age Wildschut at that point hardly knew anymore where he was.

In America the Depression began to ruthlessly fell its victims. And there was dire poverty in De Gaastmar as well, which was so dependent on fishing and agriculture. Under these economic circumstances, Age could not return to America, for there was no place for the disabled in that land. Mother Ytje had her hands full in Zeeland, Michigan, with her seven growing children. And she wanted an education for them too.

Age Wildschut, son of Lourens, wasn't able to eat anymore and died at the age of sixty-five in the middle of the wartime, on June 21, 1942, in the Dr. Wumkes Home in Snits. Because of the war, Ytje and the children did not learn till February 1943 that their husband and father had been buried for more than a half year already. The strong young man who had carried his bride Ytje on the 11th of May, 1907, into his milk scow was no more.

Ytje Ypkema would never return to Friesland. She was interred at age ninety in the red-brown earth of Zeeland.

"As seven children of Age and Ytje we turned out very well," observes James. "To a great extent we have to thank our plucky mother for that. Our dad was a mysterious gap in our existence for a long time, but in the eighties we were able to talk about it more. That's when we decided to go back together as brothers and sisters to De Gaastmar. We enjoyed beautiful summer weather, and Fryslân looked like a prosperous paradise with luxurious pleasure yachts floating on water everywhere. In the café of Mama Ozinga we gathered around the table and together tried to get a handle on what had happened. How was it exactly? What did that invisible Dad have to go through? We decided to have a stone placed on father's grave. Under the name of both parents it now says: 'Apart in life, together in death.'

"We took a boat ride through the Frisian Southwest corner. In Langwar we couldn't go any farther, for they had barge races on their lake. That afternoon, skipper Lammert Zwager won the race with his Langwar barge, the barge that Dad had helped to build in 1914. He was thirty-seven at the time and did not yet dream of a happier life on the other side of the ocean.

"We sat on that sightseeing boat and saw how that beautiful barge sliced through the water of that lake. A ship with huge sails billowing and a white mustache in front of the bow — oh my, oh my, it was such an emotional moment! A dead father came to life in a living ship, in a monument. A white swan had been painted high on the great sail, a bird poised to fly away.

"Dad's barge gained the lead, the wind kept getting stronger, the ship began to lean dangerously, everyone held his breath, but it stayed up, and won. With the ship, Dad won first prize."

Breakfast of Champions

John Reitsma from Jerome, Idaho, USA

"**I**t's a weird situation here right now," the farmer says. His beautiful home in a spacious setting near Jerome, Idaho, USA, is being used this week as a film location for the movie *Breakfast of Champions*. "The whole place has been rented to the movie people for four days. That brings in a lot of money, but that's not what it's all about for me. Movie-making is educational, it's a creative activity, it's by a top organization, it's big business."

So for four days film stars and a whole armada of support crew are rushing around the place: an editor with assistants, camera-, light-, and sound technicians, costume people, nonentities, floor-managers. And why did they pick this spot exactly? Because in all of the country you're not likely to find a place with a more beautiful view.

A look through the front room window of John and Susan Reitsma: the décor of a surrealistic painting by Salvador Dalí. Beneath a cloudless late afternoon sky, the Snake River twists itself through walls of rock nearly five hundred feet high, a silvery snake which farther on slithers inside the brown-red mountains of the Canyons. The sun sinks; soon distant rock formations will drain the red globe. "What a shot!" groans the cameraman.

In the large kitchen of the villa, breakfast is waiting to be filmed. There's caviar for the champions, and the cameraman is preparing with a few technicians for the awesome moment when the sun finally disappears behind the uneven horizon. A purple-like curtain is drawn across the glaring colors of the day. A few more moments, and the day has ended.

The farmer takes a walk in the purple-tinted evening. The contours of a paved path emerge in the twilight, then an open-air milking parlor with endless rows of cud-chewing black-and-white cows, and in the distance the headlights of a feed wagon. Breakfast for champions. "They're not all champions," says Johannes, son of Durk Reitsma, from the town of Wurdum. "We milk a good six thousand cows on this place. Three times a day. That means we touch a cow's udder 18,000 times a day." His laugh echoes through the quiet evening. And then: "Those are the kinds of figures that would probably blow the minds of the old Frisian farmers, but this dairy farm is not even one of the biggest. The numbers keep going up. Before long they will say, 'John Reitsma in Idaho thought he was one of the biggest farmers in America, but take a look at this.' There are farmers already that milk more than 10,000 cows."

Open-air cow barn — how does that work out in the wintertime? "Sometimes we have a bunch of days when it freezes fifteen degrees or so. That's not much of a problem when there's no wind, but when a blizzard comes whipping across the prairie or a storm blows the snow in huge drifts, then you won't get the same production from the cows for a while. But even then farming is better in Idaho than it is in Texas. When it's not too muggy there, it's too wet or too dry. And then you get the grasshoppers, worms, and all kinds of weeds on top of that yet. I understand why in recent years so many Frisian farmers went to Texas," he laughs. "A few shrewd Frisian wheelers and dealers came ahead and bought huge tracts of land for a scratch, and then turned around and parceled it out to Frisian farmers who had no idea what to do with all their milk-quota money. And so like a fad, one after the other immigrated to Texas."

Jerome, and an open-air cow barn that would stretch from the town of Wurdum to Swichum. John Reitsma: "That mass kind of emigration isn't a new thing, of course. How did the immigrants fare here in Idaho in the nineteenth century? I'm thinking of all those boatloads of immigrants that arrived in the fifties and eighties during the 1800s! Those poor women. And kids! First they hung over the railing for weeks, sick most of the time, then they bounced for days, maybe weeks in the direction of the Midwest, where a relative or so might have settled earlier.

"A group of immigrants like that arrived here too, a bit farther on, in Sun Valley. In the springtime. They named their settlement New Amsterdam, but they might better have called it Dry-dwellings, because it was as dry as dust there. Now and then I see in the Obits an old Dutch and Frisian name. Their great grandfather and grandmother one day accepted Sun Valley as their paradise and after that as their final fate. But, you know, our kind of people in this day and age don't believe in that kind of acceptance anymore. When I emigrated, I refused to adjust to the way things were, wandered from the far north of Canada to the deep south of California, rummaged around in Texas, made tons of money, in between business deals did some gambling in Las Vegas, gradually calmed down a bit, met Susan, an Irish woman with a strong will, landed here in Idaho, and gradually caught on that nothing, absolutely nothing, is constant. Nothing is forever."

Johannes Reitsma, from the looks of things, is likely going to be all right for a while in Jerome, Idaho. "A wife from Irish descent. Her great grandfather and grandmother came here because of the potato disaster in Ireland. It's the same with the Irish as it is with the Frisians, they feel different from the rest, and what they get in their head, that's the way it's going to be. That's why I don't insist that our kids succeed me as farmer. They must and will go their own way. I bought them nice Frisian horses, but they probably see those beautiful animals as nothing more than as something Frisian and therefore as something unique."

He was nineteen and wanted to get out of Wurdum. "What? I was a boy of hardly seven, I could read, and I saw the word 'America' somewhere. And 'California.' 'That's where I want to go someday, Mom!' I said. I dreamed about going far away. When parents begin to show their opposition later, you're going to get into tensions and disappointments. That 'drive' to seek adventure was in my case irrepressible. If I had been born thirty years later in Fryslân, I would emigrate all over again because I heard that the Frisian farmer has to have a permit to go egg hunting in his own fields. They make regulations like that for just one purpose: to get farmers to leave the country."

John Reitsma is thinking about buying a couple thousand more milk cows. To milk ten thousand cows, that looks good to him. Seventeen dollars for one hundred pounds of milk — the price of milk has never been that high. And the price of feed is good too. "But how am I going to get a good cow for a reasonable price, that is the question. I'm crazy about wheeling and dealing. Let others do the raising part; I'd rather do the dealing and travel all over to find quality young stock at a good price. To Minnesota, Sioux City in Iowa, Wisconsin. Then I hit the cattle auction there around eleven o'clock. No sleepwalking, clear minded, not too slow, don't look for the very best cow, just make a good deal on a first-rate cow. Sometimes I'm satisfied with just a trailer full of some forty animals, but at other times I can use five of those loads on one and the same day.

"There are farmers here of Frisian background who can see right through a cow. They're so full of cows, that they have the register of the great grandmother of their first purebred cow hang by the headboard of their bed. But that doesn't make them do any better at the cattle auction. You have to be able to make up your mind in less than two seconds.

"I have a Mexican on my other place. That boy is such a good milker and is so sharp and able, that I made him my partner on the place. 'I believe, Mr. Reitsma, that I can do it.' OK! He's capable of milking four thousand cows in seven hours with his men. The Devries boys — they come from the Hearrenfean area — discovered that they were farming in the wrong place. That takes the fun out of it after a while. They were hard workers, so I said, 'Why don't you join me with your six hundred cows, then you can just keep on milking, and I will take care of the management end of it.' Now they're flying high again. Not that I'm such a hero. It can go the other way too in the States. I mean it's possible that in the future those men are going to take the whole business over from me, because I'm not able to make it anymore and they are.

Last week John Reitsma was back "on the other side" in Fryslân for a little while. Below Sint-Nyk he discovered a decent golf course. "And there I met a boy from Skettens, one my age. I asked him what business he was in. He had been a milk inspector, he said, but now he had become an assistant minister for Economic Affairs. Gerrit Ybema; I said, 'How's it going to go with the interest rates, Gerrit?' 'If I knew that,' he said, 'I'd be joining you in business, John.' As we walked to the eighth hole, somebody in Idaho called on my cell phone. 'Well, I'm going to get a fax pretty soon,' I said. That same day I got a big loan at very low interest. Low interest, a high milk price, low feed costs, what are you waiting for. I know of course that things can change a lot in six months.

"Sometimes everything goes your way, and other times you lose your shirt. A few weeks ago I took my race horse, Just Take It Easy, to Texas. A big race in Dallas. Frisian farmers from everywhere were swarming the place. All men who, from the sound of it, were in the middle of a big adventure. That's just the way the life of an immigrant is. The atmosphere, you know; as if there was going to be an American version of the *Golden Whip* by Abe Brouwer.

"'If that odd goat of yours is going to win a prize, we'll never make it back home!' one of the men hollered. He meant that they expected me to buy them drinks. Well, Just Take It Easy hauled in twenty-four thousand dollars. We had quite a party afterward.

How did a boy of seven get so excited by just hearing the word "America"? "That has to do with something deep inside you. Dad was often sickly, so the man had really no chance of going anywhere. He liked a good cow, and we won the Exchange Prize with our livestock at the Wytgaard-Redezum breeding stock inspection. A silver wheelbarrow from Frico [a major dairy products manufacturer]. It happened to be the last inspection in that category held there, so we could keep the prize. My brother thought it was great, but to me it was like taking a challenge away from me. It was 1967, I was nineteen, and I took off for Canada."

After a year he returned to Friesland for a little while. "Our farmhouse had burned down. There was a hang-up with the insurance in Wâldsein, because they insisted that it should be replaced with an authentic duplicate. That right there made me look cross-eyed. I had been spoiled by the 'Great Open Spaces.' Back in Canada, I took off in my old 1961 Plymouth for Chino, California. Clipping and washing cows. A rotten job. $1.25 per cow, hundred cows in a day. And then a quick jaunt to Las Vegas for some first-rate gambling. Bachelor. Always messing around with cow hair and women's hair. And that's how I met Jack Vanbeek and all the other guys, and landed in the calf-dealing business. Till that time I had assumed that people are honest, with a rare exception maybe. But after eight years as a calf dealer, I knew that the truth was just the opposite."

It's late when we walk back from the paved milking areas of Idaho to the villa of John and his Irish wife, Susan. The dishes with caviar are still set up in the kitchen. They will do the last takes early tomorrow morning for *Breakfast of Champions*.

The Horse-Sleigh of Ithaca

Klaas and Mares van der Ploeg from Ithaca, Michigan, USA

K laas van der Ploeg doesn't easily get excited, but this morning the anxiety level is rising. Here, on his farm in Michigan, his Frisian mare Nynke is in heat, and two thousand miles away is the stallion Pyt. How far a reach does modern technology have? Last night in California, an artificial inseminator collected the seed from Pyt, which is is now, in frozen state, on the way to Nynke. By air. Will Nynke still be in heat when the airplane arrives?

Klaas is scanning the skies like his dad, Joris, as a crop farmer in Skalsum would do after a prolonged dry period. If the airplane with Pyt's seed should come too late, Klaas will have a problem.

"A problem of affluence," Klaas concedes. Work can rule a farmer's life, but so can details. The American livestock farmer from Skalsum has as purebred breeder all the marks of a champion sportsman. When still a farmer and breeder behind the sea-dikes, he climbed the winner's podium with the highest average milk production of all farmers milking more than a hundred cows. And then he crossed the wide channel, looking for new challenges. His herd of more than nine hundred cows now produces more than twenty-five million pounds of milk annually. Whatever he undertakes, Klaas of Joris van der Ploeg from Skalsum wants to be the best.

The stallion Pyt performed, the airplane arrived in time with the sperm, the mare was still in heat, Nynke would have its foal, and the farmer calmed down. And high above the Atlantic Ocean, an Air France Boeing 747 was on its way again with a couple of containers loaded with Frisian star-mares (a *stermerrie* or star-mare has received a distinction awarded by the purebred breeders association for outstanding physical features as well as for the quality of its offspring). *Chevaux par avion.* Horses by plane.

The reputation in the States of the four-legged Frisian immigrant — the horse — is not less than that of the farmer himself. In Kentucky there's another bunch of purebred Frisian horses in temporary quarantine every week. At first a bit listless from jet lag, then another week or so as home-sick as cats. But when Black Trude and Black Fedde have become used to their new boss in the new land, the knees are lifted high off the ground again. And thus has the Frisian horse, from San Francisco to Boston, be-come the status symbol of the Frisian-American farmer's success story. In the meantime the Americans, too, have developed admiration for the Frisian horse. It won't be long before there will be as many Frisian gigs rid-ing on the other side of the pond as in Fryslân itself.

Klaas and Mares van der Ploeg live close to the town of Ithaca, an hour and a half north of Lansing, Michigan. Their brand-new ranch-style house features windows on all sides that look out on gently sloping pastures, al-ternated by level stretches of dark-green cornfields. The basement is large enough to qualify as a town hall, or, with some remodeling into a milking parlor, large enough to accommodate thirty cows. Upstairs, in the living room, there isn't a picture or painting or relic from the old country any-where. Instead there's a picture of the whole farm spread taken from the air that shows off the large stables and barns, with next to them the verti-cal and the flat silos. Clearly, the farmer and his wife don't stand here with one leg in the old and the other in the new country. It's always been a mat-ter of all or nothing with Klaas and Mares.

"Just this yet about the horse business: I'm thinking about getting a gig from Fryslân over here," he says. "I've already had a nice-looking carriage flown here from Jannes van der Wal from the Stellingwerven [a Frisian area close to the province of Drente, where a non-Frisian dialect is spoken], but of everything that rides, nothing is more beautiful than a real gig."

Later in the evening, the conversation around the kitchen table focuses on cultural criticism. "What was left of the old farm culture when we left the Netherlands? Did the farmers have any respect left by the end of the eighties? No way! They were viewed as the great polluters!"

The old parents of Klaas, both in their nineties, still had some left. In their long life they had their fat and lean years, but there was always a sense of their uniqueness and respectability as farmers. You could find it in the architecture of their particular farmhouse. You could see it in the cut of their clothes, in the decoration of their carriage. Then the age of the automobile arrived; the farmer got off the yard. And he got strange visitors. In the fifties, dairy farmers and cattle importers came from more than thirty different countries to the breeding-cattle inspection days of the Frisian Purebred Association in Ljouwert. The Shah of Persia, who was interested in the dairy industry, rode together with Queen Juliana through the Nieuwstad of Ljouwert and was able to pronounce flawlessly the names of the pedigreed bulls Súdhoekster Piet Eduard and Amarilla Keizer Annes Adema.

After those heyday years, the Dutch farmer found it increasingly more difficult to maintain his status as steward of the land. Through the environmental movement, and thereby also through politics, he was tagged as one of the chief if not the chief environmental polluter. Besides, agriculture was no longer a kind of war industry; now there was overproduction and scarcity of land. The fact that in the eighties and nineties more and more Dutch farmers emigrated was not in the first place for the reason of economically improving their life. It was more a reaction to their loss of status.

The Americans presumably still have something of the old drive to perform and accomplish. There, the appreciation among the immigrants for their own Frisian lifestyle and the admiration for their own cooperatives and accomplishments are still in evidence in the country cafés and taverns where farmers hang out in Stephensville, Silver Springs, Chino, and Sioux City. There the myth of the farmer's way of life, yes, even the Frisian farm-class, is still alive and well, even if the brandy has become blended whiskey. As in the last years of the forties, when the top breeders paraded — some even in striped slacks — around the establishments on the Sophialaan in Ljouwert, so the Frisian Yankees now descend in "country style" on such watering holes as the Horse Cutter Bar in Grand Prairie, Texas. And they come with a good story. Whoever checks out the market days and cattle auctions of the nineties on the North American continent can only come to the conclusion that Fryslân's agrarian elite is no longer to be found in Fryslân itself but on the other side of the ocean.

The elite of course come in various stripes. Not a few Frisian farmers emigrated in the eighties and nineties, especially to Canada, under somewhat of a cloud. They had sold their land and their milk quota for a huge sum and forgot afterwards to pay the treasury what they owed. They essentially made their getaway with a stained conscience. Quite a few farmers this way saved themselves between two hundred thousand and a million and a half guilders. It turned out to be a matter of who had the most nerve.

But then a letter of the Dutch internal revenue service was delivered at their new address. Now there was no time to waste in taking care of unfinished business, for there was the danger of attaching property. What a mess! Mom, who already had trouble sleeping because of homesickness, now was close to a nervous breakdown. Some, with the hot breath of the treasury breathing down their neck, decided to meet their obligations after all; others became so frightened that when they went back for family visits, they didn't dare to land at Schiphol but instead flew to Brussels, Düsseldorf, or Hamburg, afraid as they were that they were going to be collared.

The Dutch treasury went on alert. By the end of the nineties they were lurking on the farmyard, so to speak, at the sale of each farm, quota, and cattle, and demanded, with the threat of attachment, a prepayment of the tax bill.

But just as there have always been, now too there were the cold-blooded reckless ones who wanted half the world for themselves. A small percentage of the "quota escapees" never paid up, even though their necks felt damp from all that hot breath.

In the meantime the last November storms of the twentieth century launched their ultimate attack on the last *ûleboerd* (owl-board, an ornamental triangular wooden board, flanked on both sides by carved swans and traditionally marking both ends of a Frisian barn's roof) of the Frisian farmhouses. New ones were made all right, but now in plastic and used as decorations for the recreational cottages that dotted the water-lands of Fryslân. Thus the farmer suffered the theft of his symbols.

We're back in Ithaca, Michigan, where, by long distance, the mare was bred by Pyt. How can a Klaas van der Ploeg, a dairyman through and through, become so obsessed in America with the Frisian horse? "Maybe," he muses, "maybe the show-horse is much more than a status symbol. The dirt-poor farmer from the past had to try to hang on to his ties to the fatherland and to symbolize it by putting Grandma's thin silver cap brooch (the headdress of the traditional Frisian women's costume) on display, or a picture of the old homestead. The neo-immigrant there has a twenty thousand-dollar Frisian mare come over. Times change; we now have eight Frisian mares on the place, all with foal. In comparison with the old immigrants who came before us, we shouldn't even call ourselves immigrants. In Fryslân we sold a four-million milk quota, cattle, and land; we came here with a bagful of money. Our kind are not immigrants but movers of capital."

But now "on the other side," in three days, at the Frjentsjer Sjûkelân (the playing field by Frjentsjer which each year on the first Wednesday in August hosts the tradition-old, climactic match of the Frisian sport, *keatsen,* an event that to the Frisians equals the Super Bowl in excitement and importance), the final match will be played. "Klaas doesn't mention it," Mares confides. "Darn," says Klaas, "that's right; maybe I'll go. But wait a minute, we have the British Open at the same time. I love to watch golf."

"Klaas is not as close for Fryslân anymore," Mares decides.

Why did the cattle breeder, who was breaking all the records in Skalsum, want to start here all over again? In Fryslân, family, friends, and colleagues have an explanation. Friend and fellow-breeder Boyen de Boer from Stiens: "Klaas has the mentality of the American manager: he think in terms of strategies, he concentrates on the most important aspects, sees the larger picture, and seems to have the golden touch. He knew that he could succeed in Fryslân. And then comes the urge to tackle a new challenge."

Minne Blanksma, former neighbor and cattle breeder: "In Skalsum he did indeed have something of the sports-champion in him that brings home the gold, then breaks both legs, makes a comeback, and wins the gold again. And then he looks around to see if there are other fields to conquer. Klaas's livestock became infected by [the cattle disease] leucosis. Some of the stock had to be killed. A cattle breeder's disaster, but Klaas fought back and later made it back in the winner's circle. I mean, it's not the dumbest that leave the country, you know."

Ieme Bakker from Lollum, with whom he once closed a legendary transaction: "Around 1975, I had twelve excellent heifers. I wanted to quit, and Klaas came on the scene. He was just a boy then, really, but he bid eighteen thousand guilders for the bunch. I finally accepted. And then he pulled eighteen thousand-guilder bills from his inside pocket — that was a fortune at the time — and then he drove off the yard with a blush on his cheeks. And he knew better than anybody that he had just made a steal of a deal. That one heifer all by itself, Feikje, was worth the whole sum and then some; he became a national champion with Feikje. Some dealers can see inside a cow; Klaas can scan a cow with his bare eye."

His father, Joris van der Ploeg, at ninety: "He was just a kid, and he was standing there when I sold a cow. I can still see that kid race to his mom. 'O, Mom, Dad just sold his very best cow,' he cried. 'The best cow, isn't that just terrible, Mom?' The little boy was hopping mad."

His mother at eighty-nine, Aukje van der Ploeg-Westra, the daughter of a mill maker, and hailing from Frjentsjer: "My husband was more of a crop farmer than dairyman. And he was — how shall I say it? — he was a bit on the tight side, so he resigned his purebred membership. Klaas, still just a stripling, kept trying to convince him otherwise till we rejoined. From that time on he had just one thing in his head: feeding and milking and breeding and becoming the champion. He was our successor, for we were ready to get off the place. He paid no attention to girls at that time, you see, he had an eye only for cows. And then all of a sudden he saw another creature walking among his cows. Now tell me, who else finds his woman that way!"

Klaas himself: "'Can you use a trainee,' Kees van der Hengel from Oentsjerk asked. 'A Canadian, an agricultural college student from

Guelph, Ontario.' 'If it's a good one, send him down,' I said. It turned out to be a female. She ended up boarding with us and learned to talk Frisian in no time. And let me tell you, good Frisian to boot."

Mares Kaas, born a stone's throw from Niagara as daughter of a Catholic local trucker who emigrated from Leusden in 1948: "I rode into Fryslân. What a land! On the other side of Akkrum I saw under beautiful summer skies a large sail glide through the fields, just like that. A sail, gliding along through fields as level as a putting green. I came to Skalsum, Klaas was the farmer; I thought of him as a somewhat older man whom I looked up to. And there were an old dad and mom. I had the feeling that they couldn't do enough for me. Before long Klaas had to give a lecture for farmers in Madison, Wisconsin, and while he was gone I was to show Feikje 89 at a large cattle auction. He called me afterward from Wisconsin, and I told him that his calf had gone for a record sum of fifty-four thousand guilders, but I think he didn't even hear the amount because we were listening only to each other's voice. In reality, it wasn't just Feikje that was sold, but both of us were too.

"I wanted to speak the language of Skalsum. 'How old are you?' Wybren Stelwagen wanted to know. '*Twaentweintich!*' ('Twenty-two!') I said. That startled him. 'Or are you from around here!' I was, just like our four children now, a sponge that sucks up each new word and hangs on to it. When we got married, they said they couldn't tell I wasn't a Frisian."

Klaas: "In Skalsum our guests came from everywhere, from South Africa to China. Just to see how we ran our farm. But to keep the business humming in the meantime, we too had to travel to find prospective breeding material. Here in America we bumped into our own past: we found the improved offspring from cattle which our own forebears had exported a hundred years ago. It wasn't our intention at all to emigrate. But then comes the moment when you get excited about the new possibilities. America, that huge country, where there's still more to be accomplished. Regardless of how merciless the economy can strike you here, the dynamics of the States can't be found on the other side of the ocean."

"As if by providence, one evening in 1990 the telephone rang in Skalsum. It was the automobile-importer and farmer Wijnand Pon. 'I would like to buy your whole herd,' he said. 'I'm interested,' I said, 'but then I want you to buy everything: quota, land, cows, everything.' 'I'll be there at two o'clock tomorrow afternoon,' he said.

"I set the 2,816,000 pounds quota price at four million guilders, the 150 acres at that time went between 14,000 and 16,000 guilders per acre, and the cows I would sell at a premium price. Wijnand came at two o'clock, and at three o'clock I was no longer the farmer."

Pon, the born entrepreneur, did not succeed in reaching and maintaining the top position with the purebred material of Klaas van der Ploeg. After all, the latter was born not only as an entrepreneur but also as a first-rate breeder of pedigreed cattle. Pon did have to pay royalties for years afterward for the use of Klaas's champion bull, Feikje's Rocket Chairman, nicknamed F16. That's how the percentage-take of more than a hundred thousand F16 services were deposited in Van der Ploeg's Dutch business bank account. "Enough to pay for some subscriptions," according to Klaas.

Klaas and Mares went to Ontario, New York State, and eventually to Michigan. There, close to Ithaca, they purchased a quality farm with nearly seven hundred acres of good land and 240 high-producing cows. The challenge began. After a few years the place had transformed into one worth ten million dollars. It's almost time now for Klaas and Mares van der Ploeg to ride to the neighbors and to town in a genuine Frisian gig or sleigh, pulled by a shining star-mare with bells tinkling from its harness.

Ruft Hill

Ray Piso from Arlington, New Jersey, USA

N ot in Heech itself, but in Florida there was still someone, hailing
from Heech, who had seen Age Lourens Wildschut stumbling with
very short steps from the Poorhouse to the Syl, the street along the town's
quaint little harbor. Rinze Piso from Arlington, New Jersey, spending his
winters in Holiday, Florida, still has a sharp memory of that tragic figure.

Ray Piso, one out of the tens of thousands of snowbirds from the
north part of the States: "Age left for America in 1923 sturdy and strong,
and as a poor wretch he came back to Fryslân. America is no land for the
unfit, it is a land of tremendous opportunities and at the same time of dev-
astating tragedies."

Sitting right across from me is a ramrod-straight, slender man of
eighty-three, still well over six feet tall. A healthy complexion, dark-blue
eyes, a perfectly trimmed silver-gray moustache. A spitting image of the
French statesman Pétain. Before turning sixty-five, he was for almost
twenty years a kind of host in the stately skyscraper on the corner of Fifth
Avenue and Central Park, in the heart of Manhattan, New York. In that co-
lossus of a building, the restrooms were larger than the whole first floor of
the little annex store on the Skatting Road of Heech. But, of course, the
apartments were owned by the rich and famous.

The American vice president and millionaire Nelson Rockefeller took
Rinze Piso in his confidence. The renowned of the world lived right above
him. Sometimes the desire for greatness proved fatal; then Ray and his
personnel would find the body smashed into oblivion on Fifth Avenue.

Jumped out of a window, for a pile of money is nice to have, but it doesn't save your soul.

Since Piso's wife died a few years ago, life hasn't been the same for him. There's no longer a sharing of good times, no longer a sharing of a bit of homesickness for Fryslân, but only loneliness for her, Saapke Valkema, a baker's daughter from De Gaastmar, and later from Aldegea-Wymbrits. She was a brave woman to the end. She had been a steady and stabilizing force in his life, especially when the complexity of his work in the center of the New York metropolis would sometimes raise his insecurity or his temper. Together they had shared their love, adventure, and success, and thus had overcome the first difficult years.

They had spent the first two years in New Jersey; he had initially regretted that he had left the store on the Skatting Road in Heech. But what happens when as husband and wife you take over your father's electric business together with a brother and a sister-in-law? The sons already run on different voltage, and the women have different amperage. All right, as the Frisians say, let's not quarrel over a tuft of hay but just get rid of the goat. In other words, one of the two households emigrated.

"We made it, and there was even a bonus," he says. "For fifteen years we have been able to enjoy the winter months in Florida. One April, as we came back to New Jersey, Saap began to talk about the need to buy a gravesite. That's when the last line in the Frisian 'Folksferhuzerslied' ('Immigrant Song') hit us, as it does nearly all immigrants: 'Give me a grave in Frisian ground.' But at the same time you bump into the dilemma that the children and grandchildren make your ties with America unbreakable. Besides that, the village reunion in Heech in 1987 was a high point for me, and the one of 1993 a disillusion: the old people were gone in '93, and the young were absolute strangers to me.

"Saapke and I walked the cemetery in Sussex and noticed all the Frisians buried there, in their own Frisian corner. There was one site left, and that's the one we bought. 'Then this is our Fryslân,' Saapke said. Not so long after that, I had to take her to that last resting place."

As an electrician from Heech, he was able to refine his craft in New Jersey and the city of New York. And when he reached sixty-five, he and

Saap headed for the sunshine land of Florida before the first autumn storms hit. Early in the morning, two days later, they saw filtered sunlight pushing through their bedroom curtains. They were in Florida, and they were sold on it. They acquired a second home, a spacious and comfortable bungalow, and even though it couldn't stand in the shadow of their palatial home on Lake Hopatcong in New Jersey, there were no cold winds here to stiffen their joints.

"Kind seeks kind: the Frisians from New Jersey hang together here in Florida too. Even stronger, the Frisians that came from the southwest corner in Fryslân look for each other here." So it wouldn't be unusual that on a mild evening under the orange trees in Ray and Saapke's backyard, a gathering of Frisians practiced real Frisian *gesellichheid*. The conversation wouldn't be limited to the southwest corner of Fryslân, of course. Sometimes nostalgia raised its head, and then the talk would switch to the tough times and struggle of the first few years in Sussex, New Jersey. About discovering later that the soil there was not as fertile as for example in Vermont. There would be farm talk, the map would be hauled out, and discussion would focus on yet another move.

"Owen Aukema from Aldegea, I mean old Oene, went to America before the war already. In the fifties he had three farms and had one *grifformearde* farm laborer after the other come from Fryslân. So, large families landed in the big house on the hill that Owen owned. Eventually so many diapers were flapping on the line on that hill, that the surrounding neighbors called it Ruft Hill, or in English, Diaper Hill. That's how it is still known."

Frisian immigrants. Wouter Nop from Drylts, the Talmas from the area of Appelskea, the Greidanuses from Tsjom. In Fryslân their living consisted often of some odd jobs and semi-poverty; in Sussex they became big farmers. The children would move farther west and add much more land to their holdings. Some of them had no idea that once there were poor toilers who had kept a family with ten children clothed and fed on the income of mowing a narrow shoulder of a narrow road.

"But they really flourished here! They formed close-knit Frisian friendships in New Jersey, as well as rivalry. We often helped each other out, especially in farming. Take men like Willem van der Eems, somewhere from Wûnseradiel; Bill van der Eems eventually built factories, and then I would do the electric work, Klaas Veenstra from Nijlân the construction work, another the plumbing, and yet another the landscaping. They called us the 'Frisian mafia' sometimes.

But pretty decent people. Take old Teade de Groot who came from the Lemster Road below Follegea. And Andy (Anne) van den Akker who came from the area of Jobbegea. And not to forget, Wytse Falkema from Aldegea, who would become the cookie king of the States. And Oense, I mean Andrew Plantinga from Ginnum who was a hard worker too. Wouter Nop, who had emigrated from Drylts to Eastersea first, once said: 'For the average Frisian it's quite a step to emigrate from one side of the Lemster Road to the other. But when a whole big ocean lies between the two, he rises to the occasion!' And that's true; I know only a few Frisians who with heads hanging low went back to Fryslân."

The Frisian immigrants that were such a close-knit group are fewer now. Their conversation lately is less often about America, and more often about the past in Fryslân.

Ray Piso: "In the time of mobilization of the First World War, Dad landed up under the spell of electricity. When he came back to Wymbrits, it was as if he was literally full of electricity. As a child I saw him climb the electric wire poles with those huge hooks on his heels. The installation of electric lighting had begun."

He found himself dreaming more and more lately about his Frisian past. Especially when he had been telling his grandchildren about it. About the outbreak of the war on May 10, 1940, only a few days after his marriage, and the orders to report in the Chevrolet autobus of his brother-in-law Boate Westra from Heech at the municipal hall of Wymbrits. About being sent to the Enclosure Dike to drive people from the east across. A lot of chaos, a little bit of heroism.

"The one prayed, the other cursed, yet another called for his mom." The buses were wheeled into the locks of Koarnwettersân. Rinze and his buddies fled along the sea posts to Makkum and on to Warkum. Then through Nijhuzum and the Gaastmar to Heech. The Germans were already in control.

"Halfway through the twenties — Age and Ytsje were going to leave

— innkeeper Moeke Swop from Aldegea sent Dad a letter. It was addressed 'To the Man of the New Light in Heech.' The letter said: 'Would you be so kind to stop by, we are thinking about installing new lights.'

"Around that time, Dad installed the first radio in our place. Grandpa Tsjemme lived two houses from us, so a wire was strung across the roof of Jaring Fortuin's house to Grandpa's house. That evening, the old man stood on the Syl bragging about 'our Rinze has the radio and I have the loudspeaker!'"

The evening that Rinze dug back into the more and less recent past, he coaxed me along to Buddy Freddy's Country Buffet. Long tables were loaded with dishes, snowbirds busily plying forks and conversation. We first looked around us for others we might know. Nothing but old people. "Waiting-room for heaven," Rinze mumbled.

The first years of Rinze and Saapke in New Jersey. In his own country, Rinze would dramatically tell his wife and children stories from the Bible, here he was lost without a language. Back there he would be reading the prose of Jan Jelles Hof, alias Jan from the Gaastmar, and he would sometimes even write some verses himself. And now, suddenly, he felt himself illiterate.

"Back at home I had a couple of guys working for me; in Paterson a young fellow, who didn't know half of what I knew, would grab me and try to explain something simple to me. I was blind, deaf, and dumb.

"'Take it easy,' Saapke would tell me at night, 'you're his superior when it comes to electricity.'

"When after a year or so I had managed to make some progress, I got a call one evening from my first big American customer. I picked up the phone, covered the mouthpiece, and called out to my four boys who spoke English fluently already: 'And you keep quiet!' You want to learn to do it on your own, you know."

Ray Piso built up a flourishing business that was later taken over by Marten van Loenen, who had immigrated from Dokkum. He himself became a project manager for a construction firm, eventually had nearly eighty workers under him, was sometimes a construction supervisor for three projects at once, earned a lot of money, and was on the go nearly night and day.

"One night I came home — we lived on the thirteenth floor of a high rise — and Saap said: 'Enough! You've got too many irons in the fire, this way you're going to land up in a nuthouse.' It's funny to say this, but that woke me up."

Somebody he knew — and by this time he had a lot of connections — told him about a special opportunity: a unique job in a unique place in the world. "They were looking for a director of the technical and domestic services in a skyscraper where the Upper Ten of the States hung out. In the bowels of that huge skyscraper was a room loaded with so much technical stuff, it looked like the control room of an ocean liner. Not long after that, Saap and I lived on the corner of Fifth Avenue and Central Park in a luxurious apartment. Our boys could take the subway to school. In the palatial units above us lived the jetset of the States. It was my job and the thirteen employees under me to make their life as comfortable as possible.

"Not only the very rich, like the Rockefellers, but also big-name artists, such as the top people from Warner Brothers, were there. And of course film and TV stars, current American actors and authors. Coleman Dowell was carrying on with a man on the seventeenth floor, but one night he must've had enough for he ended up sprawled out on Fifth Avenue. That meant the need for some special arrangements. When one of the main lawyers from the Nüremberg Tribunal died in my apartment, that generated a lot of tension too. It took hours to determine that the man was not murdered but died from a heart attack.

"The gynecologist Dr. Feldman lived right above us. Among others, he had Jackie Onassis and Saapke as patients, but we never got a bill for Saapke. 'It's better to take it from the top than from the middle,' he said in so many words. And then you had Mr. Lindsey, the man who became mayor of New York, and big bankers like Charles Gordin, and a CEO of a big American airline company who left his wife behind on a beach in Florida so he could mess around with the divorced wife of the boss of Seven Brothers. So the elevator went from the twelfth floor to the third, or the other way around, and we had to pretend ignorance, of course. One day lover boy lost his thick billfold in the stairwell of the emergency exit; it had his business card in it. So I stopped at his apartment. 'There you are, sir. Found it on the twelfth floor.' 'Impossible,' he exclaimed, and gratefully accepted the corpus delicti.

"One summer night, Saap and I met Jackie Kennedy and her new lover while out for a stroll in Central Park. They frequently visited our building. 'Good evening, Mr. and Mrs. Piso!' 'Good evening, Mr. and Mrs. Onassis!' Or Saap and I saw Queen Juliana out for a walk with Marijke's children, who lived very close to us. 'That lady too likes to simply be a grandma once in a while,' Saap said. There was no one in the Netherlands who had an inkling that grandma had sneaked away for a short visit with one of her children.

"Old Nelson Rockefeller had a son and daughter-in-law and some nieces and nephews who lived above us. Now and then he'd remind me: 'Take care of my people, my fellow! And watch Spencer especially, because our kind can get in bad trouble sometimes.'

"When the Rockefellers moved in, security was stepped up considerably. A doorkeeper by the main entrance, surveillance at all the other entrances, alarm buttons by and inside the elevators, always one of the security personnel along in the elevator, special locks on the doors of the Rockefellers, and a direct line to the police station.

"From the outside, the building was like an impregnable fortification. Not till the seventh floor from the bottom were there any side-windows. Next to the apartment on that side was the world-famous Guggenheim Museum of Non-Objective Painting, which also defied any break-in attempt. Next to that a church with walls higher than those of a prison.

"We never had trouble with break-ins, so on Old Year's Day I'd always have a pile of dollars waiting for me as a bonus. Enough to buy a sailboat with or, if you needed one, a new boat dock in front of your house on the lake in New Jersey.

"One morning one of my men came with the message that the domestic help of the rich couple on the seventh floor couldn't get in. I immediately suspected something wrong. The couple was in France on vacation. On the seventh I met the completely trustworthy woman who had been asked to water the plants. She said that she couldn't get the key into the lock. We discovered that there were toothpicks inside the lock. The head porter, with the support of others, steadfastly proclaimed that no unfamiliar person had been admitted to the building during the night.

"I managed to remove the toothpicks with the help of a propane torch. We opened the door. You can't believe what we saw: all the contents of the drawers dumped on the floor, everything of value — and that was quite a bit — taken. Even the small safe with who knows how much cash. From the side window, seven floors high, hung sheets that had been tied together.

"First call the police. In no time I had a bunch of detectives around me, but by then it was already clear what had happened: from Fifth Avenue they had been able to watch the place and notice that on the seventh there were no lights on at night. And of course they were well aware that a new roof was being installed on the church next to the museum. They must've pretended to be part of the installation crew. In any case, they had located a giant ladder, found a lot of other useful stuff on the roof of the church, put together some kind of scaffolding to get across the Guggenheim Museum, then made that into a very long ladder to reach from the Guggenheim rooftop to the side-window of the seventh.

"Now it was a cinch to get inside. They punched some toothpicks inside the lock to keep anybody from catching them in the act. The sheets were used to lower the gold, silver, and other valuables out of the side-window. On the Guggenheim rooftop, one of the men stood ready to haul in the loot with a long hook.

"I came downstairs and said to Saap: 'There were guys here that really did a number on me.' I immediately set out to design an even safer security plan. And there was old Nelson already. 'I'm almost glad it happened,' he said, 'because now you've devised a much better security system!' 'Yeah, Mr. Rockefeller!' I was able to show him and explain the new plan right there. 'You're my kind of man, Ray,' he said."

Leaving the Spinnensteeg

Frits and Anne Newland from Richmond, Ontario, Canada

C anada gasps under a heat wave. The countryside of rolling hills past Richmond in Ontario shimmers beneath the hot summer sun. "You should come here in wintertime, when the hard winds are blowing off the northern lakes. You can live with this heat, but I can't take the biting cold anymore. When you get close to eighty, it's like your skin gets porous or something."

Canadian stories told in air-conditioned comfort. In the front room of Frits and Anne Nieuwland's attractive home in Richmond, images of a half-century ago rise to the surface. A bus came riding that brought Frits and Anne with their two children from the Spinnensteeg in Aldeboarn to Rotterdam.

When years later they returned for the first time to the village on the little river of Boarn, they were momentarily disoriented. The river, the streets and lanes — all of it had shrunk. The village tower was leaning even more, the houses along the Boarn looked punier, and the distance to Akkrum was much shorter. It was as if they had been longing for something other than for this village.

Why did Frits Nieuwland and his sweetheart Anne Berger, from the neighborhood known as Zestien Roeden near It Hearrenfean, stand waiting by the Spinnensteeg for that bus in the first place? There's hesitation before the answer comes.

Frits: "During the first years we felt no urge to see Friesland again. Even though we almost froze to death that first winter up north, what was there for us in the old hometown? No, I wasn't going to give in. And you weren't either, Anne. We weren't coming back with the tail between our legs."

"Still, you simply can't cut yourself loose from your hometown," she says. "Around the month of September, when the procession of gondolas is held in Aldeboarn, or around the time when there would be another school or soccer club reunion, you'd find yourself tossing in the night. So, why don't you explain now why we wanted to leave Aldeboarn."

Frits: "Slowly but surely we felt ourselves being squeezed into a corner there. After the war, business was simply dead. The economy had been crippled, rules all over the place, you couldn't do a damn thing as an entrepreneur. I was the last barrel maker in town, and there were practically no orders. Okay, there was that incident with Policeman Monkel too. There always has to be a last straw to break the camel's back."

November 1952. An absurd tax bill, an aggressive village policeman, in short a period of bad luck. And on that certain evening, the weather was rotten too. Anne prefers not to talk about it after all, and instead talks again about those first years in Canada, about that severe winter, the gnawing homesickness there in the endless hell of the far north. "We were nearly blown out by the draft in the wooden shack that was supplied by the farmer I first worked for," adds Frits.

Anne: "Sometimes I was so lonely, I just stood staring out of the window. Well, not really, because I couldn't see anything because of the frost on the window, but I did feel that smarting pain of homesickness in my chest. At night my pillow was wet with tears. I would lie there motionless so as not to wake Frits. He had to work so hard."

Frits: "It was a tough transition; we had left our social village life in June. Not long after that we arrived in the frosty forsakenness of northern Canada. There was an absolute law for the male immigrant: first you work for a farmer. I had hurriedly learned to milk in Mid-Fryslân, but already then I had never felt very comfortable behind cows' tails. I wanted to be involved in a trade. Making furniture, carpentry. Something like that. That was eventually to become my business here too."

"And we didn't have a car yet," Anne remembers. "That makes for loneliness too."

Frits: "The car came later. A 1935 Ford. You had to walk an hour to get to the nearest decent road. It was close to Christmastime, and we badly needed to take the children to town for some shopping. The two boys needed to get off the yard for a change. But how? That's when I made a sleigh out of the heavy kitchen table. The table upside down, tie a rug around the four legs, and hitch the horse to it. That's how we had a sleigh for the kids to ride on. Oh, man: such snow, such cold, such a trip."

There's silence, with only the sound of the clock's ticking. Frits is choked by sudden memories. Tears run down a weathered face.

"Still, we were happy," comes quietly.

Anne: "This isn't homesickness anymore, by any means. But something strange lingers inside of you. It can push all kinds of emotion to the surface just like that. Maybe that happens also because of age."

Frits: "You were homesick, you suffered, you had the feeling that you had left your mother, I mean old Mrs. Berger, so pathetically all by herself. You were always so close."

Anne: "One Sunday morning we biked, with the kids on the back, from Aldeboarn to Mildam. Mother, who'd been a widow for years already, lived there in a small house. We had to tell her, it wouldn't be right for her to hear from somebody else that we wanted to go to Canada."

Frits, interrupting her: "And what did your mom say to that, Anne? She said: 'My oh my, that's really something. But I'm also glad for you, Frits, and the children, because on the other side of the world there must certainly be more justice.' That's what my mother-in-law said at that point. And those words did make it easier for us to say good-bye."

Anne: "Frits had taken over the barrel-making business in Aldeboarn from his dad. But after the war there was hardly a farmer anymore who still used wooden buckets. The housewife wanted to get rid of the wooden washtub, and the human-waste barrels also lost their popularity. 'Everything is turning to tin,' exclaimed Jan Nieuwland, 'they want a hollow sound nowadays.' At that time there were still seven bakeries in Aldeboarn. But there came a drop-off in customers and a struggle to keep your head above water. Frits was a tremendously skillful cooper; what his eyes saw, his hands made, but business was dead in town."

And what was that incident with the village policeman? What happened on that windy November evening in 1952? In the home of Frits and

Anne, on the corner of the Schoolstraat and the Spinnensteeg, the curtains had been drawn early. That's how you could save one piece of turf a day. The two boys slept like roses in their bedroom upstairs. Downstairs Frits and Anne had finished reading the paper. "It's getting bedtime," Frits observed, and started to undress. "Come on, Anne, let's get in!" He stood there in his long underwear, she turned off the light, in the dark he opened the curtain just a tad, and both could now see by the dim light of the street lantern the wet snow sliding off the windows. The town slept; there wasn't a dog to be seen in the streets.

She remembers it all exactly: "Frits usually got a little impatient around bedtime and would get on me: 'Come on, Anne, let's get in!' It was as if he wanted to push me ahead of him up the stairs. At that moment, there was a vicious knocking on the front room window. I was still dressed, so I unlocked the door, and there stood Policeman Monkel.

"Go upstairs," I said to Frits. He couldn't stand Monkel, who had unnecessarily fined him because the light on his bike wouldn't work. That was all. And it had happened on the forsaken Sminia road. 'The dynamo can't cut it because of all the mud on the road, Policeman Monkel, but normally it works fine!'

"'It's not working. Law is law,' said the policeman.

"So, around bedtime, Monkel at the door. 'What's going on?' I said.

'That front room of yours looks like a showroom window,' I heard him say. 'It is forbidden by law to advertise goods in a living room. I could see a completely new shuffleboard [a popular game for children in Fryslân that includes a table-board and disks], a little doll wagon, and two inlaid tea trays.'

"'In a couple of weeks it's Santa Claus Day,' I said, 'and we hardly get any orders from the creamery anymore. I can't make it without some supplemental income.'

"'Frits doesn't have a permit for this, and besides he doesn't have any certificate that qualifies him for this kind of work,' he said. At that moment I heard Frits come down the stairs. 'You, upstairs,' I hollered, but it was too late.

"'You!' Frits screamed, 'you are right, I don't have diplomas for this kind of work and no permits either to put together a shuffleboard.'"

"Monkel: 'Let me cite for you, Frits J. Nieuwland, from the 1937 Law for Small Business Establishments.' And then began the recitation, the whole gospel of the postwar bureaucracy. It was as if he had first memorized the whole thing by heart.

"'If this isn't enough, Nieuwland, then I will read you the Regulation for the Trades-People as well. That one goes back to the wartime, but it's still in force.'

"By now they stood face to face, Monkel in his impressive uniform, Frits in his undershirt and long underpants. I felt the floor under my feet shake, that's how angry Frits was getting. 'This is going to be trouble,' went through my mind. So I slammed the door shut on Monkel. Bang! Slide the lock in place. Monkel stood outside, and it was quiet for a moment. Fortunately the man was wise enough not to knock again. We went upstairs, lay awake for hours. And all of a sudden I heard Frits say: 'We're going away, Anne, we're going to emigrate.'"

Frits, almost fifty years later: "Did I really say that *then*? And did I say it *that* way? No, no, you're wrong, I said those words the evening of the day that I delivered that shuffleboard to a customer. I had brought the thing on a bike to a farm in the neighborhood known as Sodom, and also had to drop something off at a place with a lot of kids on the Braksdyk. When I got home around bedtime, I discovered that blue letter. Tax notice. That year I had done less than 4,000 guilders' worth of business, but I was assessed 2,200 guilders. That's when I said: "I'm leaving. To America, or to Canada, or to I don't give a damn where!"

Anne: "Then it must've been that night when at a certain moment I missed Frits in bed. I downstairs, and there he sat in his underwear, writing a letter. In the middle of at least ten failed experiments that were scattered on the floor. 'But now I've got it right,' I heard him say, and he sounded satisfied. He had asked a question of his cousins in America and Canada: 'If there's more freedom where you are than there is here, we're coming there. How much freedom do you have?'

"First a letter came back from the Van Zinderen cousins in America. They wrote only about nice weather and long days. It was Frits's cousin Klaas in Canada who reported that it was precisely freedom that made living so worthwhile in Canada. 'It's going to be Canada,' Frits exclaimed at once. And he began to attack all the necessary paperwork. Not long after that, we sold our house. And would you believe that at that moment, W. G. de Jong, director of the creamery, came to the door with so-called good news. De Jong announced: 'Frits! Business! The American army in West Germany needs butter, so I'm going to need lots of small butter barrels.'"

Frits: "I almost went through the floor; I didn't have the guts to tell him that I would be leaving with wife and kids on the boat to Halifax in the first part of June. I said something to the effect that he could figure on me. From that hour on I was over my ears into my own handicraft: making barrels, day and night, and making good money at it. For the first time in my life, my work was too much for me, I couldn't sleep at night. I lost my appetite; my pipe didn't even taste good anymore."

Anne: "Saying good-bye."

"We don't have to talk about that," he says curtly.

"You were overwrought at that time," she says. "When we left Aldeboarn, you were as skinny as a rail, thin enough to change your underwear behind the stovepipe. Tell us how everything went."

Frits: "All right, I'll tell it. In Rotterdam, the *Waterman* lay ready for our departure. The rowers already went into action in the harbor, for it was getting time to cast off, but it turned out that our papers had been lost. So I was hauled off the boat while Anne stayed on deck with the kids.

"In some office somewhere, everybody was in a dither: questions, considerations, somebody even picked up a telephone. Well, my head began to spin from all this tension, and I began to lose it. I was inside somewhere, heard the sound of the *Waterman*'s horn blast across the Rotterdam harbors, all of a sudden didn't feel any ground under my feet anymore, and then sure enough, somebody was coming with the papers. 'Nieuwland, everything is okay!' I was rushed back on board. As un-traveled as I was, I had the feeling that only by the grace of God was I still able to go along."

Frits Nieuwland stands up, walks restlessly up and down the room for a minute. Wet eyes. "I feel I'm getting old now. I can't even bear the tension of a half-century ago anymore. Anne, you tell what happened after that."

"Frits and I stood on the deck with the two boys between us. Behind us stood a woman with two daughters, two really pretty girls, one sixteen, the other maybe eighteen years old. The mother, we found out later, was the widow of a baker from the village of Lúkswâld, just east of It Hearrenfean. She was moving with both daughters to Canada, to a butcher in Ontario with whom the mother had fallen in love already in Fryslân."

Frits has regained his composure and can handle the memories again. "The last hawser was cast off, and at that moment we heard the mother scream: 'Stay here, you! You stay with us!'

"The youngest girl was trying to get away, and was held by her skirt. But she tore herself loose, climbed over the rail, and tried to find her way down. The mother moved heaven and earth, but that child was as lithe as a monkey, was already on the gangplank, which just at that moment was being pulled onboard. She jumped, landed on the pier, got up, and took off.

"That scream of the mother, from the depth of her soul — I have never heard a woman carry on so as the baker's widow from Lúkswâld. The image will never leave me, of that crowded pier with people waving one moment, and then suddenly nobody waved. The girl ran right through the mass of people across the quay. It turned out that a young man on a motorcycle stood waiting for her. She jumped up behind him, and in a cloud of dust and smoke they disappeared. Around the corner and gone."

Anne: "The widow from Lúkswâld, after the captain of the *Waterman* and a harbor authority and a boat chaplain had become involved, ended up traveling to the butcher in Ontario with one daughter. It wasn't till years later that the girl resurfaced. She's now living, with that motorcyclist, in a village on the Veluwe (a scenic nature region of dunes and woods in the middle of the country)."

Frits: "There's more that happened with emigrant children than you think. In the spring of 1921, in the village of Oppenhûsen near Snits, one of a family's seven children hid a couple of hours before departure. The villagers searched for that boy for a whole night and the following day. The boat didn't wait, so that family's trip had to be postponed for a month. They later found the boy half starving in a haymow at an uncle's place."

Anne: "Our children were fortunately very small, they became real Canadians, and are grateful to us that we went."

Frits: "We really do have a good life here too. It turned out well. But on the way over here, I wanted to hide just like that boy in Oppenhûsen. Once

I was on the *Waterman,* I never left my cabin. Anne went with the children to the upper deck, while I stayed behind in pitch darkness. I hardly ate or drank anything for a week. Now and then a slice of apple, that was all. It was on the sixth day that I had the feeling I was going to die. That's when I told myself: Frits, boy, you're going to die here, or you're going up to the deck right now! In short, I washed and shaved, changed clothes, and ventured up the steps to the upper deck. I had no strength left, I could hardly walk. On the way up I discovered a bar. I ordered a drink, only one, and downed it. After that I went in search of Anne and the kids. 'I'm back,' I said. That night Anne and I were back together again for the first time in weeks. We were very happy. We always say in our Frisian way: 'You have to reach the worst before it gets better.'"

Frits Nieuwland becomes emotional again. "We were still happy," he repeats softly.

She laughs, wants to stay in control of emotions. "Those first years were hard, all right. Sometimes it froze so hard that at night we had to stick our feet in the ash pan of the woodstove to stay warm. We lived far beyond where the world ends, and it was lonely. But we don't have to cry about that anymore. We had each other, and that brought us very close."

The name Nieuwland was changed to Newland, but Frits and Anne in their successful quest for more freedom remained themselves. "We got ahead here and are quite content. All we have to do is look at our beautiful garden and at how well the children are doing."

The Broken Village:
Tsjummearum Left, Tsjummearum Stayed

Tsjummearum was liberated, the flag was flying from the tower, the music moved through the neighborhoods. Marches resounded from all sides, from the non-Christian as well as the Christian side, from "Crescendo" and from "De Bazuin." The two groups met each other between the coat of arms of Barradiel and the church. For half a century they had avoided each other, but now both bands played the same march and in the same tempo. Never in this bloody twentieth century here in Tsjummearum had there been such a harmonious and massive sound.

That night there was a concert in the huge potato warehouse. The liberation concert. Potatoes out of the same soil; celebration out of the same dish. Harmony won out over discords and differences.

But in the spring of 1945, Tsjummearum and all the other villages and towns were actually far from this spirit of liberation and unity: one day later everyone sang his own song again, and a week later each band played its own tune.

Here's an episode from the history of a village that since 1846 had survived three waves of emigration and this time was balancing on the top of the third wave. This time Tsjummearum would wave farewell to almost 200 of its 1,600 residents. Wave farewell with a hand half-raised, for it was a matter of out of one's eye, out of one's heart. Each time another busload of happiness-seekers pulled away, the village acted as if it hadn't lost any children. Those left behind just kept on going. The Franeker *Courant* of April 1, 1949, informed the public that skirts were getting shorter, they could now be raised from 11.5 to 12.5 inches from the ground. And that a pair of Robinson shoes cost ten guilders.

Here and there was a hole in the heavy clay of Tsjummearum, the places where adult and also young plants had been torn out. The pain of tearing loose was felt especially on the other side of the ocean. In the village left behind, the holes were filled, for on the same spot something new would have to grow.

This is the story of a village whose residents lived next to each other in three parts but didn't live together. Three segments, for apparently no agreeable middle road could be found between the completely unchurched, the completely *herfoarme* (Reformed), and the completely *grifformeard* (Christian Reformed). It was all so "completely."

What the postwar wave of emigration brought about in Tsjummearum is perhaps best told through the experience of the Christian music society "De Bazuin." In a couple of years' time, the brass band lost so many bugles, trombones, and baritones, that the band no longer dared to march through the neighborhood. And the way that core pieces fell away from the band, in the same way core pieces fell away from the village community. Its harmony had left.

In Tsjummearum, the postwar exodus assumed the character of a nineteenth-century group emigration. As if there were a leader who talked everyone and everything into leaving. In this one episode, the *grifformeard* congregation alone lost 167 of its confessing members. Each emigrant had a main reason and a cluster of secondary reasons. They clarify the deed and the consequences.

Every time you turned around, another group of people would be standing on the square by the Skûtebuorren neighborhood, waiting for the Labo-bus that was picking up another load in Barradiel County. Sometimes it was a large household of eleven children that stood ready to go. Their moving crate had already been shipped ahead. The painter's son, Kees Jouwersma, had painted the new address on it in huge capital letters: "FARMER BURT WILSON, 14 RIVER RD, GREENVILLE MI USA." The household goods of the *grifformeard* farmhand from Barradiel fit easily on a farm wagon. And now the rest also fit inside of one crate from the Rotterdam Lloyd of the Holland-America Line.

A group of emigrants from Tsjummearum, waiting for the bus. "It's coming, Dad!" one of the children hollered. Momentarily the bus was hidden behind the row of homes on the *Seedyk* (sea dike). It stopped there apparently at the Kampioen neighborhood, to pick up Reinder and Jetske Kamstra. After that it made another short stop for the family waiting by the gas factory. Now and then the squeaking of the brakes could be heard in the Skûtebuorren.

A curtain moved, a baker on the way to his customers got off his delivery bike and concluded that once again Tsjummearum would have fewer mouths to feed tomorrow. Aged parents stayed on the little bridge, waiting for a last look. Only when the bus had almost reached Frjentsjer already, both of the old folk turned around and waddled, shoulders drooping, back to the house. It was as if the population here was contaminated with a virus, as if they suffered from some disease that had flight as side effect, as if these church folk were in the grip of some force to which they were thrice as susceptible as others. And there were as many reasons for emigration as there were people in Tsjummearum. Some wouldn't discover their main motivation until a half-century later.

The Canadian with the Tsjummearum accent, Jelte Posthumus, tries to articulate those motives on the other side of the ocean.

"Gé and I already had the two little boys, and lived in with my old mother, the widow Steven's Tryntsje. One evening at suppertime, the old woman asked, 'Would you read the Bible tonight, Jelte?' All right, I grabbed the Book.

"'The promise of God to Abraham, Jelte!' she said. Fine, so I turned the page to Genesis 17, verse 8. . . . 'The whole land of Canada, where you are now an alien, I will give as an everlasting possession to you and your descendants after you.' . . . Of course it didn't say Canada, it said Canaan, but I misquoted.

"'You have your mind set on it,' she said. Then I suddenly realized that I should've said the word earlier. 'Yes, Mom, we're leaving too.'

"I wanted to leave the land of the dogcart and the small profit margins. They had promised us that it would be a different world after the war. But when I finally got rid of the dogcart, there still was no money for anything better. Time to go!

"Everything the poor woman had — her only son with wife and two grandchildren, were going to the other side of the world. I can still hear her that evening during mealtime explain Genesis 17, verse 8, in her own words: 'Yes son, this can only be God's will, because here in Tsjummearum there will be nothing special prepared for us.' That's how she resigned herself."

Jelte Posthumus walked that same evening with a heavy heart and the copper bass horn on his shoulder to the rehearsal hall of "De Bazuin." He came too late to play the chorale, the opening song to praise the Lord and tune the instruments. He hesitated in the hallway, listened to the chords, and observed that "De Bazuin" had never sounded so thin. When the bandleader and farmer Jan Goasses Terpstra threw his baton down on the stand, Jelte entered with the e-flat horn and headed for his chair. He noticed from the empty seats that the band had lost more members. And now they had to find out tonight that Jelte from Steven's Tryntsje would also leave to cross the ocean.

It all happened a half century ago. In the garden behind his small house on James Street in London, Ontario, Jelte Posthumus says: "At the end of August in 1951, I went to rehearsal for the last time. They wanted to say good-bye to me by playing a chorale. But Marten Terpstra who played the big bass horn had just that week gotten his new set of uppers, so he wasn't there, and the baritones and trombones were all overseas in Ontario, British Columbia, and Michigan, USA. It sounded so miserable that I just joined them in playing my own farewell serenade: 'Praise God from whom all blessings flow.'"

A couple of weeks later at the conclusion of the rehearsal, Jan Goasses Terpstra announced in a shaky voice: "We've lost our core. The best players are gone." Those who were left just sat there, heads down."

It must've been hardly a year later when Ale Travaille, post-office manager and alto saxophone player, came home from the annual meeting of "De Bazuin." His wife was already in bed. Ale had just been elected as chairman of the band. When he slid under the blankets next to her, he mumbled, disheartened, "I became a captain on a sinking ship."

Of the thirty-five "Bazuin" members, only nine were left a short time later. So many instruments were missing now: the cornet of Jan Haagsma, the bugles of Ale Zondervan, Sieger Post, and Harm and Houke Steinvoorn, the tuba of Tsjipke Postma, the trombone of Berend Stelstra, the soprano saxophone of Jabik Roorda. Then the Sideriusses and Van der Burgs left Tsjummearum with their very musical families. The evening that Willem de Vries announced that he with his wife and thirteen children were going to leave as well, the cofounder Auke Walda exclaimed: "We can't march with the band through the neighborhood any more this way!" Then he threw both drumsticks to the floor.

The village that left, and the village that stayed. Sybe Sybesma and Sytske Sybesma-de Groot stayed. Years later they are sitting hale and hearty in the front room of their home on their street De Tolve in Tsjummearum. The story of two solid natives, she seventy-nine, he eighty-six. For them an outing on the motorbike to Gaasterlân was far enough. "Wait a minute!" Sybe exclaims. "In those years I wanted to leave too. I was sick and tired of being dependent, of all the slaving for the farmers here. But Sytske didn't want to and dragged her feet." Sybe Sybesma was no musician, but he did go out to collect money for "De Bazuin." "One time a little woman came to the door and said: 'What did I hear, Sybe, you can't get Sytske to go along to Canada!' It was just as if they wanted all the *grifformeard* people in Tsjummearum to go to the other side of the world."

And what about the other side of the ocean? Jan Haagsma who played the second cornet is now a retired Canadian, but sometimes still takes a ride in one of his trucks to Toronto. Or he drives over to his brother Sies to lend a hand, while whistling old familiar tunes. "'De Bazuin' after more than fifty years is still important to me," he concedes. "I was barely seventeen when I told Jan Goasses Terpstra one evening that it was my last night in the band." A day earlier, his wife Hanny Martens Terpstra, also from Tsjummearum, just happened to have polished the old brass instrument that is now proudly on exhibit in their Canadian home: an art object that symbolizes the disharmony from a destructive time period.

"We went back to Tsjummearum for a visit," he reports, "and I attended a rehearsal of 'De Bazuin.' It was beautiful, they just played their hearts out!"

A couple of hours to the northeast lives Sippe, son of the wooden shoe dealer of Tsjummearum, Frans Harkema. From the deck of his spacious villa he has a view of a motionless Lake Louchiching. This has to be one of the most beautiful homes in one of the most beautiful spots in Ontario. Over the huge lake, small clouds of flies hover here and there. "It's going to be another beautiful summer day tomorrow," forecasts Sidney Harkema.

The man sitting here looking at the lake is not only musical. There's a preacher and a businessman in him as well. From the stories told on both sides of the ocean, one may conclude that Sid inherited both from his Dad. Frans Harkema, the wooden shoe dealer, was known as a man who could talk you into a new pair of clogs while preaching.

Sid suddenly remembers. "When I turned in my trombone, Jan Goasses said: 'I knew that you'd be one of the first to leave. You have restlessness, business, and a missionary spirit in your system!' Terpstra was right: Sippe, son of Frans the wooden shoe man, was not the kind of guy that would play the same part in the band for fifty years.

Another living witness of the exodus from the postwar years is Sippe's uncle, Steven Sippes Harkema. At ninety-four, blind and mostly deaf, he lives in the American town of Jenison, Michigan. But to honor his guest from the old country, he poses as the man with a flawless memory. In Tsjummearum they think that Steven Sippes and "De Bazuin" never had any trouble. "Think again!" he exclaims. It must've been in the fall of 1949, during a regular Tuesday evening rehearsal. Jan Goasses Terpstra lay the score of the Wilhelm Tell overture on the music stand. Rossini. A bit worldly, yes, but it would pass.

During the break, Terpstra discovered that another family of band members was going to take its leave. This time it was the Van Steinvoorns. When Terpstra walked home after the rehearsal, he was bitter. Reaching the Kade street, he saw that Steven and Rinske Harkema still had their lights on, and without another thought, he walked up to their place and knocked on the door.

"I let the farmer in myself," Steven Harkema remembers. "'Let me tell you something!'" Terpstra barked. "'With all your nice stories about Canada and America, you've got all of Tsjummearum going crazy, you're tearing the whole village apart!'" I realized right away where Terpstra was heading, because as a board member of the Christian Emigration Central, it was my job to point out the advantages of emigration. 'You,' I said, 'you yourself emigrated from Menaam to Tsjummearum. But that doesn't put you in charge around here!' Then he said: "'If you're a man, why don't you emigrate yourself, get your whole household on the boat!' I said: 'The gentleman farmer's wishes are my command, we already have the papers.'"

"'Good!' he exclaimed, 'then we're rid of the trash.' And then he took his leave."

The ninety-six-year old Reintsje Haagsma-Pasma landed a thousand kilometers to the northwest, in Ontario. She remembers that Steven Harkema practically preached emigration. But even without him she would have left with her husband, Auke Haagsma, and ten children. "Auke was a small truck farmer and one fall, right after the war, he dug up diseased potatoes. They said that there had been strange creatures in the seed potatoes: potato eels. They called it 'Potato fatigue.' Mansholt was Minister of Agriculture and decreed a new law for agricultural and truck farmers. The law would allow us to plant potatoes in the same soil only once every three years. The large agricultural farmers had enough land to vary their crops, but the small truck farmers received a deathblow."

The truck farmers constituted a social middle layer between laborer and farmer. One could try to become a truck farmer by renting an unattached piece of land. And there were plenty of such pieces after the depression in the 1880s had dissolved a lot of farms. But what happened? Stiff competition among the truck farmers. Consequently, they ended up paying high rent for land that was now in high demand. When one could no longer keep up the rent payments, five others stood ready to take over. When after World War I the competition went out of control, the Union of Land Renters was founded. That occurred in 1922, in the city hall of Tsjummearum, well before there was a rent law. In this way the truck farmer tried to gain more influence, power, and status. The administration included confident, rather nationalistic Frisians who were sympathetic with the CDU (Christian Democratic Union) of Fedde Schurer and

Hindrik van Houten. One of the founders was Germ Harkema, who was also a Frisian nationalist. During the war the union proved rather cooperative with the occupiers. Understatements were heard, such as "some during the war were not altogether happy."

"And that's how we followed the Irish," exclaimed Auke Haagsma, "the Irish who almost all left for America. One day the envelope with the papers for Canada lay on the fireplace mantel. There was no turning back." The Haagsmas played in the band; before long, they too were treated to a farewell chorale.

Not everyone who left Tsjummearum went overseas. Dozens of young men left for the mines in Limburg, the textile industry in Twente, the blast furnaces of Ijmuiden, and the new Northeast Polder. Polder immigrant and trombone player Piter Pasma fifty years later: "When the moving van drove up, there were few left in 'De Bazuin.' It went downhill so fast, the members became demoralized. Tsjummearum became a village without ambition. What was the use of rehearsing for a music competition when there was no chance of winning a prize? That was the prevailing attitude." Piter Pasma, with other "Bazuin" members who, because of potato blight, had also been forced to leave, would start another brass band in the Northeast Polder: "Melody of Luttelgeast."

Boukje Boonstra-Harkema, sister of Steven Sippes, stepped onboard the *Rijndam* in 1952 to sail to America. "My husband, Piter Boonstra, didn't have much musical ability, but everybody tried to learn to play an instrument. He did too. We married in 1936, but our store that sold a little bit of everything didn't exactly make us rich. So we left for America in 1952. That was a bad mistake."

Eleven years later, Piter died in Grand Rapids, and in the eighties Boukje returned to Tsjummearum. "As I said, Piter was not so much a brass band player, he was a dreamer, a reader. He was knowledgeable about all kinds of things, but he was no businessman. He ended up working for a painter. As I said, we should never have left Tsjummearum. But that store of ours, you know. A woman would buy a doormat for the kitchen for $3.50. She came every week to pay off twenty-five cents on her purchase. When after three months or so she had it finally paid for, she bought a new teapot, again at twenty-five cents a week. All that penny stuff meant an awful lot of bookkeeping for me."

Sybe of Ale Travaille was a boy of fourteen. Later he would study psychology and settle near the Belgian border in the Kempen. "Yes, I was proud of Dad that he was chosen by the village council as president of 'De Bazuin.' But the following morning he repeated his conclusion: 'I've become a captain on a sinking ship.' I'm not sure how the unchurched and *herfoarme* groups experienced those years, but among us *grifformeard* people, there was a latent feeling that the band would never again become what it once was. Later I realized as an adolescent that I had been dreaming not about the future but about the past. It's unfortunate when for young kids the ideals lie in the past and the concerns in the future."

Jacob Lautenbach, about the same age as Sybe Travaille, was another who had been sucked away in the Frisian brain drain and knew that depressing feeling personally. Lautenbach studied economy and sociology. Sometimes he sees himself sitting in the *Grifformeard* Church again. "Then I hear the organ playing again. As if the devil himself was messing with it, that organ made such a poor sound. I looked around me on that Sunday morning and missed my best friend. Emigrated. Would the son of Hamersma now become my friend? Or the son of the butcher Ourensma? But then I found out that the Hamersmas were going to go to the steel factories of the Dutch Steel Company and the Ourensmas to the Philips factories. The rest of *grifformeard* Tsjummearum stayed behind in despair."

When the very dogmatic Rev. Schelhaas left toward the end of the forties, his mild successor Freark Jansen set himself to the formidable task of preaching comfort. Jacob Lautenbach would always remember one of those sermons. "Another emigrant family sat across the elders bench for the customary farewell. The organ began to play, wheezing like a sick patient. In front of the elders stood a father, a mother, and a long row of children. There was no informal, personal word of farewell, not even an opportunity to shake hands with anyone. Only the minister shook hands. A reading of Scripture, then singing with organ accompaniment. I believe that Klaas Keizer began the singing, very loud and harsh. What I heard was not singing but shouting. The people were shouting their singing to control their tears and doubts and questions. As if there were a punishment for emotions. Psalm 134, verse 3: . . . 'Jehovah bless thee from above, in His boundless love, Our God, who heaven and earth did frame; Blest be His great and holy Name.'"

The father of Jacob, Ulke Sieses Lautenbach, lives in the New Bethany Rest Home. A wise man of ninety-four years old. "I helped to send them off, those emigrants; as a boy I helped bring them to Harns. That must've been in the spring of 1914. With a bag on his back, that's how my older brother Pyt took his leave, never to return. It would often be the larger families among the farm laborers that were the first to leave. Following in their wake would be the small shopkeepers. A steamboat lay ready in Harns to take them to England. There they would transfer to a larger boat that could cross the ocean. America! How terribly far away that was in those days. Place-names like Ohio, Massachusetts, and Wisconsin buzzed inside your head as if they were the names of planets. Now and then I still see the images of the people who left before my eyes. And the farewells by the harbor of Harns. Tears were not yet in fashion then, I think."

Is it a matter then of the tighter one's place against the Wadden Sea dike, the more stifling it becomes? And also the more tedious the working of the land? Unlike the work on a dairy farm, the farm laborer on a crop farm works the soil, and that soil is tough and cold and wet. During a rare hour of leisure, this laborer reads the tempting letter of a brother-in-law in America. Once a five-dollar bill was found in the envelope. Kees Jouwersma took the magic bill along to Ljouwert, exchanged it at the bank, and came back with more than twenty shiny guilder-coins, the equivalent of a week's wages for seventy hours of hard labor. Oh land of dreams and wishes, what in heaven's name are we waiting for?

The people in Barradiel were besieged by pressures, trends, and single-minded motivations. One was the unpleasant climate here versus the impression of a sunnier climate there; another was the dependence on the farm crop seasons, the agricultural organization and consequential rise in unemployment, as well as the diminishing fishing industry. There were also the problems of overpopulation; the ominous devil behind the iron curtain; the rise of the supermarket; the increase in taxes by

Lieftinck; the lingering postwar depression and war bureaucracy; the fear of an uncertain future for the children; the potato blight and its dire consequences for the small truck farmer; the stifling compartmentalization that made the world for young men and women even smaller and more restricted than it already was; the increasing pressure from the government to leave; the information from emigration centers, employment bureaus, and other institutes that was often colored by propaganda.

And that isn't all. What did the people in Tsjummearum read in the Bible about migration? Whatever they wished. It already began in Genesis 1, verse 28, . . . "fill the earth and subdue it" . . . and it ended in Hebrews 13, verse 14, . . . "For here we do not have an enduring city, but we are looking for the city that is to come."

What did Hindrik Algra, managing editor of the *Frisian Daily*, tell his readers about emigration on Thursday, November 13, 1952? He's all for it, but not just to improve one's material well-being. One ought to be a pioneer not only for the sake of the dollar, but also for the sake of Jesus Christ, Algra proposes. "The Lord's promises are good everywhere, there are fields everywhere, and the seed is the Word." Algra also warns the readers who have emigration plans about "the terror of the purely materialistic labor union dictators." Each must ask himself as he walks up the gangplank: "What do I plan to do with my spiritual inheritance?" And "Is my heart filled with the concerns of earthly prosperity?"

Anyone who could read the hearts of Algra's departing reading public would detect but one answer to that last question: "Yes, my heart is also filled with concern for earthly prosperity." The Frisian *grifformeard* people weren't then so world-denying and pietistic anymore as to be indifferent to the prospect of making a better living. They wanted their children to be better off than their dad and mom. However devout their life would be on the other side of the big pond, they wanted to succeed. And succeed they did.

What then may have been the motives of Sybe and Sytske Sybesma to stay behind with their six children in Tsjummearum? Didn't this energetic *grifformeard* farmhand and his sturdy wife fit the profile of the emigrant from the Barradiel area perfectly? "Sybe really pushed for it," says Sytske, "but I didn't want to." In this case, the wife pulled the long straw. It was often the other way, Sytske knows that too. "Many *almost* stayed home, but ended up *just* leaving. With us it was a matter of *almost* leaving, but *just* staying home. The big decisions in life often hinge on very small things."

Sybe: "I saw the shadow side all right, no doubt about that. When my two sisters, Gryt and Tsjitske, boarded the boat with all their kids, Dad and Mom took it hard. Then came the terrible homesickness, especially Gryt. Her letters were clammy from the tears. I think it was Gryt who once wrote: 'I wish that Columbus had never been born.' And here at home we had had that tragedy with Evert. One day before the liberation, the Germans shot him. By the North Bergum gas station. No, that liberation celebration was no feast day for us. It would've killed Dad and Mom if Sytske and I with the kids had left too."

"And yet, Sybe, there came a time when you wanted to leave too," she said. Sybe Sybesma concedes that the push to leave couldn't always be suppressed. Maybe among the labor population here, he speculates, there was a hidden rancor. What had been done to their parents? What had those poor wretches experienced in the flax sheds? The child in Sybe sees the kerosene lamps again, swinging in those stuffy places. Moving shadows. He listens to the flailing and beating of the flax, he notices the draft from the doors forever open in wintertime, he hears the rattle in the throats of the old workers in the flax shed. Lungs clogged with dust. The pain cuts through his soul. Here and there were preachers who would rather not see these damaged laborers in church on Sunday. The coughing and wheezing of the flax shed workers spoiled the sermon. Images of a broken village. There were gaps, gaps between Christians and non-Christians, rich and poor, between the influential and the powerless. Scars that keep smarting, from Tsjummearum to Toronto.

"Real life was elsewhere, that must've been the feeling," Sybe Sybesma thinks. "I too had been a farmhand long enough, so I tried it with a fruit and vegetable wagon: a fox-colored horse in front of the undercarriage of an A-Ford with a box on top; you made a nickel profit on thirty oranges, and then you still had to put up with harangues about an occasional spoiled one. One day the whole business in the ditch, the soaked labels came off the vegetable cans, I couldn't tell anymore what was in the cans, so it turned into a kind of Surprise Show for the customers, and the next five weeks I got bombarded with their complaints.

"So, back to the farmer, and preferably not as an occasional laborer, because that would give you the reputation of not being very reliable."

"In that wet fall when we lived by Pyt van der Schaar in the Tsjummearumer Mieden," she interrupts, "it hit me one late afternoon. You got to his farmstead at four o'clock in the morning, came home on Saturdays at 6:30 in the evening, your clogs heavy with mud."

He: "Home? Our house belonged to the farmer. We drank the farmer's milk, we ate the farmer's potatoes, we ate out of the farmer's hand. Of course, the milk and the spuds and the rent for the house were all deducted from your wages. Pyt van der Schaar was not a bad guy, but our total dependence all of a sudden got to me. I wanted to leave!"

She: "And early Sunday morning, when he had just taken his bath the night before, Sybe's week started all over again, heading back over that same mud path."

He: "By fall-time, when Sytske would leave for the Women's Society 'Pray and Work,' you almost needed an army to maneuver the poor woman and her bike onto the paved roadway: Sytske in her wooden shoes, I in my clog-boots, pushing her bike through the sludgy wagon tracks, trying to deliver the whole business dry if not clean to the civilized world."

She: "How about that evening when you came in, your mind made up?" He: "'We're going to Canada,' I announced. I think my voice cracked, I was so excited. 'No way,' she said."

She: "'I'm here too,' I said, 'and I will never go to Canada!' I wanted to nip it in the bud, had been through so much grief with my parents, with Dad falling through the ceiling of the cow barn and dropping dead on the stone floor beneath, and Mom left in poverty."

He: "We were young, were happy together, so I gave it up, and was able to get a steady job as farm laborer for Wiggele Anema. Anema preferred, like all other farmers, a married man who was likely going to stay around awhile."

She: "Anema made it a part of the deal to have me come on Fridays to wash windows and clean up the yard."

Sybe: "Then, one Friday afternoon, Wiggele Anema said: 'I see that your wife is pregnant, Sybe.'"

"'You have a good eye,' I said."

"'Soon she won't be able to do the work anymore,' he said, 'which means I won't be able to keep you this coming May!'"

Sytske: "But later Anema had a change of heart."

"Why, of course!" And a bit later: "And that's how I ended up staying here, right under the shadow of Tsjummearum. One time we got a letter from Ate and sister Gryt in Ontario. On the bottom of the letter was a P.S.: 'And you, Sybe, you stay so close to home, when you move you could probably easily move everything with the wheelbarrow from one place to another.'"

Why is it that there were so many *grifformeard* farm laborers among the emigrants? According to Sybe and Sytske, that could have been because the ordinary *grifformeard* workingman didn't have much faith in a strong labor movement significantly improving his lot. That's what the socialists believed, and for them often a reason to think twice about emigration. Sybe concedes that his own thinking sometimes leaned in that direction. "Sometimes almost a little red." In addition, the shift to mechanization in working the heavy clay resulted in more unemployment, while on the lighter soil the new agricultural techniques led to a more extensive land use. So, more land, higher income through more fertilizer use, and the need for more workers. In many places where the soil was lighter, the public-land use also resulted in less extreme social contrasts. "The often poor relations between farmer and farm worker certainly promoted emigration in this area," Sybe admits honestly.

"Not just the small farmer on the sandy soil, but also his poor farmhand managed before long to acquire a small piece of land where he could keep a couple of goats. It seemed like that was begrudged of the farm laborer in North Friesland. Those who had a small piece of land in Drente had the opportunity to seed and harvest it. When fertilizer became available, he began to get ahead. When you harvest the fruits of your own soil, you feel the bond to the place on which you live. But what bound the ordinary farm worker in Barradiel? He had nothing, nothing to sow, nothing to harvest."

"The relations have improved a lot," observes another non-emigrant, Kees Jouwersma, "sometimes it seems almost like a completely different world." Jouwersma was the man who as son of the painter decorated the moving crates with their exotic addresses. "Our community brass band 'Crescendo' was founded a hundred years ago by nine independent farmers. Today it looks like it's only the 'laborer' who is still interested in becoming a member of the band."

When the Tsjummearum folk walked to the emigration bus waiting for them at the Skûtebuorren, was that a protest with their feet? An analysis by former Tsjummearum residents now on the other side of the ocean suggests a mix of motives.

Jan Haagsma who played the piston in the band, now living on River Street in London, Ontario, says: "It was not a protest for me, rather an adventure. It was different for Mom and Dad: that potato blight got them in trouble. The requirements were too high and the selection too stringent to become a farmer in the Northeast Polder. At least too high for Dad. One evening I heard him say: 'The fact is that in Canada I will have six big boys who can help get us on our feet.' It must've been in the beginning of 1947 when Jappy as oldest son was likely at any moment to get a draft notice for service in Indonesia. Dad was not very colony-minded, and Jappy apparently not either, for in that same year he left for Canada to pave the way for the rest of us. Jappy's first letter from Canada arrived, and I can still see Mom slitting the envelope and handing the letter to Dad. He should be the first one to read it. When he had finished reading, he said: 'Encouraging, Reintsje!' To me, at that moment, there was nothing that could keep us in Tsjummearum anymore.

"Only in Canada did I finally discover what had been one of Dad's strongest motives for emigration: he really wanted to make farmers of all of his sons; he wanted to achieve the status of a large landowner who had more land than Wybren Oosterbaan in Tsjummearum. And here in Canada I've never seen him discouraged in the pursuit of that ideal. Eventually he did admit to Mom that the farewell had been the hardest. Yes, the farewell. In the early afternoon the bus was going to come from the direction of Easterbierrum. First, though, all twelve of us were going to have a meal at Grandpa Jan Pasma and Grandma Brechtsje. But Grandma was so out of sorts, she couldn't manage to prepare the meal. 'That's all right,' Mom said, 'the kids will pick up a big pan-full of sauerkraut and beans.' No one dared to declare out loud that the sauerkraut and beans were as salty as the North Sea. It became a final meal that stayed in our memory for a long time. The old people wanted to accompany us to the bus stop. Their daughter, their son-in-law, their ten grandchildren — each one had to shake hands with Grandpa and Grandma for the last time. In the final analysis, that to me was the toughest moment of the whole emigration experience. Let me say, a moment of real heart pain. That's how it hits me again even now. After all, not much later their other two children, Gerrit and Tsjipke Pasma, also departed with their offspring.

"Tom Patric was our first boss. A month later, half of our family came home with a decent paycheck. Everything went into one kitty. Two years later Dad was able to buy a small farm of a hundred acres, in Ilderton. The old man must've thought that he had almost caught up with Wybren Oosterbaan in Tsjummearum already. The first time he went back for a trip to Tsjummearum, he took some of the best Frisian seed potatoes, Bildtstars, back with him to Canada. It was as if he wanted to establish his own Tsjummearum in Canada."

And also plant and spread the seeds of faith? Expand Reformed church life in other places? "That commission was more or less given to take along with us, but of course there wasn't a *Grifformeard* Church in Ilderton. So, first to the Presbyterian Church. The minister nodded in our direction with a satisfied smile on his face: the twelve of us filled a whole church bench.

"When Mom's brothers Gerrit and Tsjipke came too, the group was large enough to start our own Reformed service, in our front room. Reinder and Akke Kuiken and all the others from Tsjummearum came too, so Sundays felt almost like a village reunion. Faith and the liturgy were means of binding us together, and the togetherness was the remedy against homesickness. Before long, a *grifformeard* minister from Michigan crossed the border. One day the building plans for a new *grifformeard* church lay on the table.

"No Canadian farmer was able to simply borrow money from the bank, but the Frisian farmer with his small army of hardworking sons and daughters could get all the money he wanted to invest. There was a farm of three hundred acres and some woods for sale in Ingersol. Dad took the chance. Our first Frisian purebred cow was named after Mom: Reintsje. Now there was no stopping: a Reinstsje II followed, a Reintsje 20, a Reinstsje 40. Those were the years when the people back in Tsjummearum found out that Auke and Reintsje had done well in Canada."

The solidarity of "everything in one kitty" one day reached its end, of course. Several kids of Auke and Reintsje Haagsma became farmers; others found work in transportation, in construction, in industry. Most of them successfully ended up in business for themselves.

Jan: "In 1954 Hanny Terpstra from Tsjummearum came here to visit family. She had promised her parents to return after a year."

Hanny: "And then I saw Jan Haagsma, and he saw me, and so here too Tsjummearum married Tsjummearum. Isn't that something?"

Why did Sippe, son of wooden shoe-maker Frâns Harkema, pack his suitcase? And did he do well? Yes, indeed, even though he agreed completely with Hindrik Algra: earthly prosperity is secondary. But nice to have, nevertheless. Did Sidney Harkema the businessman overcome the preacher inside, or did it turn into a draw? Is it possible for both the businessman and the preacher to be in control within the same person? It appears that way in Sid's case. "The Lord has blessed me abundantly in everything," he says. "Me a multimillionaire? Well, in any case, each year I'm able to contribute a couple of million to a good cause. For example, to bring a couple of planeloads of Jews from the Ukraine to Israel. So that God's Son will sit on David's throne.

"In Tsjummearum I painted wooden shoes for Dad. As immigrant I was obligated to work first for a year by a Canadian farmer. Fifty dollars a month, I think. Well, that doesn't earn you a roof over your head in a hurry. One afternoon I saw what looked like an almost new wooden shoe on the small farm of an orthodox Mennonite, a clog with nice flowers inside hanging next to the front door. 'Oh, how beautiful,' I exclaimed to the Mennonite. 'Yes,' he and his neighbors responded in chorus, 'if you should ever make a trip to Friesland, to the land of birth of Menno Simons, please take such a beauty along for me too. I'll make it worth your while!'

"Lots of Mennonites lived there, so that same evening I went to the post office and sent off a telegram to Dad with the message, 'Send me as soon as possible a thousand pairs of wooden shoes.' The old man must've seen business potential in me, because he didn't even send a telegram back wondering what I would do with all those shoes. A couple of weeks later I received delivery of a thousand pairs of clogs. Business boomed. And those Mennonites were so grateful."

Sid Harkema sold those thousand pairs not as pairs but as singles. First the left, then the right. "Before the summer of 1947 came to an end, I had pocketed seven thousand dollars. More than enough reason for Dad to come with the whole household, because for seven thousand dollars you could buy a pretty good piece of land."

Before his fiftieth birthday, Sid Harkema owned one of the biggest international freight-trucking companies in all of Canada and America. His fleet of trucks thundered over the highways from Montreal to Vancouver, and from Boston to Los Angeles. But when the business was worth tens of millions of dollars, and the labor unions called a strike for higher wages, Sid sold the whole outfit just like that and started something new. "No labor union dictators in control! I learned at least that much in Boys Society."

What's left of those kinds of judgments in Tsjummearum today? The people there can hardly remember that village of 1948, but in the memory of many an old immigrant on the other side of the ocean, the images are still razor-sharp. The tragedy of the old immigrant on his last trip: he searches for the village that no longer exists.

Jelte Posthumus, who was so enchanted by emigration that he read "Canada" in the place of "Canaan," still sees the village of Wednesday morning, September 5, 1951, clearly before him. He boarded the Schiphol bus with Geke and the two small boys, then turned to take one more look. That was it. So many Frisians left in that one KLM-Dakota, that the Frisian national anthem came booming through the loudspeakers. How does Jelte, the man who insisted on leaving, explain the tears that came? How does he explain what drove him to emigrate? Was he so sick and tired of it all that he as only child of the poor widow Steven's Tryntsje could gleefully play along when the band played their farewell chorale? The small shopkeeper he was then cannot talk about it now without eyes tearing up now and again. His wife, Geke Ypkes de Haan, calmly tries to control the thread of the conversation. That's how the two managed to keep their heads above water in Ontario: when one gave up hope, the other gathered courage.

"One fall — when the cold winter of 1929 was already in the making — Dad said to Mom suddenly: 'I can't do it anymore, this is killing me.' Mom was on the potato field, crawling next to Dad on her knees. She had something wrong with her neck, caused by a drunken doctor who had tugged at her head too hard at birth, so that the head was now permanently twisted to the side. As she crawled beside Dad, her face automatically pointed in Dad's direction.

"On the day after Christmas in 1929, when I was nine, my dad died. From that hour it rained for three days and three nights; sometimes I would hear hailstones pelting the roof's tiles. It was so wet that we could hardly walk between the gravesites, and the casket started slipping when they lowered it into the grave. The men were trying to hang on to the ropes, but they couldn't hold Dad back. Then I heard the casket smack into the water on the bottom. It made me sick, I hated it, I hated it!"

"Now, now, Jelte. The farmer treated you and your mom well. Wybren Oosterbaan was your dad's last employer, and that could've turned out worse, for Oosterbaan came every Saturday evening to your mom to deliver a whole week's wages. And you were able to live in his hired man's house almost free for a while."

"I had wanted to go to school to learn a trade, and now I had to quit school and help Mom. Going around through the countryside, selling stuff from a cart. Mom wasn't so strong and couldn't handle the cart loaded with goods all by herself. So there we went, over the Old Dike and the Sea Dike, through the Meadows, then the road all the way to Minnertsgea. After a while we got a dogcart. Sugar, tea, coffee, and depression. And then you'd hear: 'Just give me a half pound of salt, boy.'

"Happy as a lark I would go on with the dogcart. Nero, that was the dog's name pulling my cart; nobody in Tsjummearum was better than Nero."

"But things started looking up a bit later on when you got a three-wheeled cart you could peddle yourself," she says. "That's when the war came," he says. "That's when Frâns of old Sippe Harkema stopped me and told me that I should store up some sacks full of salt. But Mom didn't like to do things that way, to her that was hoarding, that was black market. She was so pious and honest. 'We are just ordinary folk,' that's how she always put it. Later on in those war years you could get a thousand guilders for a sackful of salt."

"Right after the war you couldn't do much with hard cash," she observes, "black market dealers got caught. Honesty is the best policy."

"Dishonesty can get you pretty far too," he says. "The honest shopkeeper was hit by a two percent tax increase, and we were not allowed to pass the cost on to the customer. Some liberation that was! The Canadians and Americans rode off in their powerful vehicles, and the government would just as soon have us start all over again driving a dogcart. When the news came about that tax increase, I knew that I couldn't stay there."

"When Dad heard about our plans, he didn't know what to do," she says. "He stopped Rev. Schelhaas when he met him on the bridge. 'Why, pastor, why do we have to lose our Gryt now too!'"

"We arrived here, and the first thing was just like somebody slapped me in the face." His voice falters for a moment. "We were traveling with a Frisian couple who were going to be picked up from the train station by family. We had to go in the same direction, and there was plenty of room for us in their big car. But the man behind the wheel said: 'Family comes first, over here each has to take care of himself!' And he was a Frisian too."

She: "We hung around that station with the little boys for a long time."

He: "That was a moment of great loneliness. We didn't know the language. I wondered if we had undertaken this trip to go from bad to worse, it felt so terrible. We hadn't slept a wink in three days and nights."

Geke remembers that they ended up late that night at Reinder and Anne Kuiken's place, also from Tsjummearum. "That was in Mt. Brydges, in a tobacco-growing countryside. 'It looks like it's going to freeze,' said Reinder, 'I have to go take care of my plants, what do you say, Jelte.' So Jelte went to work right then and there."

He: "Norman Mar was a farmer of Scottish descent, a decent kind of guy. Seventy-five dollars per week, free living and free milk. It was a good deal."

She: "Jelte never had a day off, we didn't have a car at first, had nothing really, but Jelte did not want me to go to work. 'If I can't earn enough for the both of us, I'll go back,' he said."

He: "I landed in a laundry, fifty-four dollars a week."

She: "Seventy hours a week. At 5:30 every morning on the bike to the cleaners."

He: "When the boys were old enough, we tried farming. Bought a place for too much money, and then the times changed and the values dropped drastically. Had to sell the whole works."

She: "Jelte always enjoyed his work a lot. With our son John he spent thirteen years as a school custodian for some additional income. Always at night. John still has that job.

He: "I was seventy-four years old, and I had to have the gallbladder removed. That's when I quit cleaning schools."

She: "When son John got married, he made a speech and said: 'I want to thank Dad and Mom for always doing their best, and for all they've done for me.'"

He: "So, we have reason to be satisfied."

The other witness of the postwar Tsjummearum, the ninety-four-year-old Steven Sippes Harkema from Amsterdam Village in Jenison, Michigan: "I'm not doing too well lately." The children took him out of the nursing home because there the nurses wanted to be in control. "The only thing wrong with me is that I'm blind and mostly deaf and I can't walk anymore, but my mind is good. So I figured that my offspring could help me out; it's not for nothing that I have six healthy children, thirty-four grandchildren, and sixty-three great grandchildren."

When Steven Harkema came to America in 1950, he had never handled a paintbrush in his life, but that didn't keep him from starting a painting business. "The kids were free to pursue whatever they wanted to. There's one who has a chain of supermarkets and a fleet of semis, with our name on them. I myself was doing fine in Tsjummearum too, I had a good income for that time, working for the plant disease service."

When asked about his reasons for leaving, irritation surfaces. Yes, why did some in that village laugh about his arguments for emigration? As board member of the Christian Emigration Central, he had already warned toward the end of 1946 about the rising threat of the pagan Bolsheviks. According to him, the Soviets were flying all their spy planes above Friesland. Then, in addition, the news came that the Kremlin had the atom bomb as well. "The German was, after all, still a Christian, but the Russian was an anti-Christian, a barbarian. When the Red Army would soon come, it would first of all persecute the Reformed Christians. And the Frisian language would die too. Just look at what they did to the minority languages in the Soviet Union."

With his fear of Communism, Steven Sippes Harkema from Tsjummearum influenced a lot of aspiring emigrants at the information evening sessions of the Christian Emigration Central to make the big jump.

But hadn't there been trouble between Steven Harkema and Rev. Schelhaas? "The minister was well educated, but his sermons were as dry as dust. Besides, Schelhaas was as bossy as a bantam rooster. When the man would walk through the neighborhood, swinging his cane and wearing his high hat, the *grifformeard* villagers shook in their boots. If he'd come across a common laborer in dirty work clothes, he would ignore him. That's how high he rose above ordinary creatures.

"I wasn't so dumb myself, but was involved in the Frisian Movement with men like Hindrik Twerda and Sjoerd Bonga. Because of my Frisian-mindedness and as president of the church's youth group, I could hardly avoid banging heads with this character. The man insisted that no Frisian be used in the young people's meetings. 'Let me tell you something!' I said. 'We're going to use Frisian as much and as often as we want to! Whoever undercuts the Frisian language here, undercuts God's Word.' From that time on, it was war between us. Even though I'd come to church twice on Sunday, Schelhaas never again paid any attention to me or the rest of the family. It was the same Schelhaas who saw to it that I never became an elder. For years he gave me nothing but trouble.

"At least in America we were free to honor God's Word in our own language too. I ended up on the Board of a flourishing Frisian society with men like Bernard Fridsma. In Grand Rapids we would have Frisian services with at times at least five hundred in attendance. Those were high points, in which emotions were released that no pen can describe.

"Unfortunately, Christian morality is on the decline everywhere, even here in Michigan. Women in the pulpit, that's of course way off the mark. They even want to make the blacks equal to the whites. That's wrong too. It says in Genesis 9 under 'The Sons of Noah': 'Cursed be Canaan. The lowest of slaves will he be to his brothers.' That's where God decided on the position of the blacks, I'm certain of that.

"I'm not going to get as old as Noah, I'm going to put my head down before long. But when the Resurrection comes, there will be more nationalism than now. Except that we will get a better world then."

In 1948, Harkema, with a minority of the Christian Emigration Central committee, tried to organize a group of emigrants who saw the devil lying in wait behind the iron curtain. "Faith and Frisian identity were already an issue in 1947. Our purpose was to have a whole shipload of Frisian likeminded emigrants, and then to settle somewhere as a group. We were well on the way, but then it failed because too many *herfoarme* members on the Committee objected. That derailed the whole business. They simply refused to see the dangers of Communism."

There are also some encouraging signs, according to Harkema. "When in the summer of 2000 Frisians from all over the continents return to their fatherland with their offspring, that will be a Sign. Just like God is returning their land to the Jews, so God will also return the land to the Frisians."

"You're getting tired, Dad, you better rest now," daughter Tryntsje says caringly. Tryntsje was eleven when she rode right through a storm over the Ofslútdyk to the HAL-wharf in Amsterdam with her dad, Steven Harkema, and mom, Rinske Hoitema, her five sisters and one little brother. "The weather was so bad, it was lightning near Harns, and I said, 'It feels like the journey of Moses through the desert, Dad.' And then Dad answered, 'If we make the other side, we will be saved.'"

It's a half-century later. The world has changed from an immeasurably big planet full of unknown places to a well-traveled territory with well-known distances. Farewell serenades have fallen out of fashion, but in the life-stories of the old immigrants from the Barradiel area, the endless distances have not been forgotten. Men and women, with children in their wake, ventured into endless space. They had little idea of their final destination. Those left behind experienced the final farewell as a live burial. For the emigrant it sometimes turned into a watery grave. For didn't the wooden shoes of the Dutch emigrant once float before the coast of Virginia?

Tsjummearum, summer of 1998. The village is celebrating, and two banners decorated with gold, silver, and brown lead 'De Bazuin' and 'Crescendo,' but the two brass bands are now combined into one. The children of Tsjummearum who have been on a school outing together, are being serenaded. It's like an ode to youth and a serenade to the future. The music resounds through the neighborhood as a celebration of liberation.

This was the century of the broken village. The century of Reintsje Pasma, Ulke Lautenbach, and Steven Harkema; of Sybe Sybesma, Jan Haagsma, Jan Goasses Terpstra, and all the others.

Whether they left Tsjummearum or stayed, ever and always they carried with them the place that hurt them and that they loved. In the holes that had been dug, new flowers bloomed; voices that had fallen away were replaced by new melodies. "De Bazuin" grew into a first-rate brass band with almost sixty members and went on to win first prizes in the superhonor division at the World Music competition festival. Albert, son of Tjitte Bonnema who played his bugle so well and remained a faithful villager, that Albert is now singing in Wagner's "Die Meistersinger von Nürnberg" for the Semper Opera of Dresden. That's how one of the children from the homes against the sea dike found his own way as tenor to the Great Podium.

And on the small square by Skûtebuorren, a bus stops again. Not to pick up the children of Tsjummearum, but to drop off asylum-seekers. The pain of displacement is plainly written on their faces.

Churchgoing

*Dick Boersma and Henny Sikkema-Boersma
from Brampton, Ontario, Canada*

Is it possible that one can tell by the weather that it's Sunday morning? The morning sun casts its glow on the beautiful colors of rolling hills and woodlands this morning, and yet nothing is exactly radiant. There are no church bells calling, no churchgoers with Bibles in their hands who are all heading in the same direction. Is it possible that in Norwal on a Sunday morning only the birds will have a sermon? And is there no singing, just for variety? Not a cloud in the sky. The summer morning, maybe just because it's Sunday, is holding its breath.

High up on the hill stands a villa. A garden gate swings open, and Durk (Dick) Boersma and his wife Henny Sikkema appear. They can choose from three cars that are parked behind the swimming pool on the yard, gleaming from last night's washing. They're going to take the new minivan simply because Dick had left his cassette tapes in that car. On the way to church the couple sings in Dutch to organ accompaniment the beloved sixty-eighth Psalm: *"Gelooft zij God met diepst ontzag."* ("Give praise to God with reverence deep.")

"We are not really fanatical; at least we hate it when people pretend to be more pious than they really are." His words sound like an excuse. "But we just love to sing."

"The fact is," she says, "that Dick has a great passion: he's crazy about organ music, majestic organ music. Just like that he invested a hundred thousand dollars in a good house organ from Pennsylvania. And he's got a great many tapes and CDs of famous organists."

"Organ music underscores the Word, maybe that's it," he says.

Henny: "But it could also have something to do with a religious inclination."

"But that doesn't have to make me special," he says. "No, I don't like to be considered fanatical or dogmatic. When it became obvious that two of our children didn't believe in going to church anymore, my world didn't collapse the way it often did with other parents here in our Christian Reformed Church. The important thing is that they're persons of value, persons who love their neighbor as themselves."

A car that's large enough to hold six persons rides ahead of us on the hilly Creditview Road. It looks like a car from the eighties. Its rear end moves like the rump of an oceangoing yacht that sails away over the long waves. Everything on the Creditview Road moves like a stately procession in the direction of Second Christian Reformed Church in Brampton. In order "to be built up in the faith, and then try to live accordingly."

And to visit with each other after church, like they used to do in Fryslân when they would visit each other in their home. "The church here is also the reason for the social contacts," he says again. "When everything is the way it should be in the church, it means there is also a congenial atmosphere, or what we called *gesellichheid* in the old country. There's no word for that in English."

The ride to church has its own liturgy. That's because the distances are considerable and Dick drives slowly. As it does with a boring sermon, time seems stretched out. Henny, to the accompaniment of organ music, gives an account of her husband's life before she met him. That's when the church meant little more to Dick than a kind of bar, "a kind of refuge place for lonely immigrants."

"When I came, I was nineteen. I would've been even younger if I hadn't had a hernia that had to be taken care of first in Fryslân. Yes, I felt lonesome here. A soldier has an identification number, an immigrant has nothing. In Fryslân you could say, 'I am one of the kids of old Durk Boersma of Rinsumageast, you know, Boersma from the Christian Farmers Association.'

"How would I get to meet anybody here, how would I get a girl? Boatloads of bachelors came to Canada, so of course we got an oversupply of men. As a single young man, I lived in a shabby room near London. On Sunday mornings I attended what was then still a small CRC (Christian Reformed Church), for the sole purpose of meeting a young woman. I'd get there at least a half hour early, and I'd still be hanging around long after church, hoping that I would meet some folks who happened to have a good-looking daughter and would maybe invite me over for coffee. But again and again I was out of luck. So, on Sunday afternoons I'd drive in my beat-up old Dodge pickup to the small church in Chatham. No luck there either. Well, then on Sunday evenings I'd try the church in Sarnia for another chance. But my prayer went unanswered."

She: "People who had a daughter sometimes did invite you to their house, but that usually went nowhere!"

"I needed a buzz," he says in self-defense, "I mean, there's got to be a spark, you know. Arnold de Vries, also from Rinsumageast, took me home with him after church once. I thought, now we're going to have some action, because Arnold had eleven sisters. Mrs. de Vries, she did the best she could and she was a fine, generous woman who had baked a large cake for me. But those eleven daughters: I didn't feel a buzz, you know. Later on I boarded here with a cousin, and went after church for coffee at the Sikkemas, and that's how I met this daughter of theirs."

"And that's when you felt a 'buzz.'"

We drive onto the parking lot of the church, and he turns off the engine and the tape with the background music. Then he tells the last anecdote before the sermon. "We had just finished designing that large house on the hill in Norval, but I was worried about a source for drinking water. There was an old well, but I didn't quite trust it. There had to be a perfect spring somewhere on that large property, but exactly where? I drilled, searched, but found nothing better. Then I had a drawing made of the house and the two and-a-half acres around the place, and, when we were in Fryslân for a few weeks, I took it to Hessel Wiersma in Rinsumageast. I asked him if he would eyeball the drawing and put a check at the spot where he thought the spring would be. Hessel had been known for his knowledge of electromagnetic radiation; he placed some small but mysterious boxes here and there to store the rays, and so helped a lot of people get rid of their rheumatism. Well, Wiersma put my drawing right in front of him on top of the plush tablecloth, fingered the paper, blinked his eyes a few times, and said: 'There!' I got the drawing back with a pencil mark. When I got home, I went and drilled a well right on the spot he had indicated. And now you have to go far in all of Canada to find a better water-well than we have in Norval.

"When Dad came here later on and heard about it, he said: 'Hessel just has a bit more on the ball than the average Joe.' Dad already went to Wiersma for his rheumatism when I was just a boy. Mom confided years later that the old man had come home with a short piece of wire. Mom sewed a small pocket on the inside of Dad's underpants, and that's where Hessel Wiersma's cure had to be worn, 'day and night,' according to the quack doctor. Just for fun, Mom once secretly removed the wire. A couple of days later the trouble started: the rheumatism in the leg was back."

The last fifty yards of churchgoing. The women in comfortable dresses, but not too short; the men for the most part with open collars. Not many young people between ages fifteen and twenty-five. It's vacation time, but still the rounded House of God fills up completely. According to Dick, that's because of the new preacher, Nick. That's how he's identified on the bulletin, so apparently the last name doesn't matter.

Nick preaches his heart out. He weaves in the reading of Job 31, verses 16 through 25. Of course, it's in English. But I spy a Frisian Bible to my side, grab it, and impatiently search for Job. I read in Frisian what the preacher has just read in English: . . . "If I have raised my hand against the fatherless, knowing that I had influence in court . . .": the church as language practicum for the emigrant who on the boat didn't know more than five words in English.

An opportunity is given during the service to shake hands with those sitting around you. I look around, shake hands, and see the same faces I can expect to see in the churches of Tsjerkwert, Tsjerkgaast, Burdaard, or Burchwert. The faces strike me as a bit more sober than the faces I saw last week in the Neland Christian Reformed Church in Grand Rapids, in the USA.

I'm shaking hands. "Jack Miedema." Others around me are the Tilstras, Praamsmas, Riedstras, Dykstras, Drielsmas, and Joustras.

A black young man plays "Let All Things Now Living" on the trumpet. "Those guys have the lungs, I tell you!" whispers Dick in awe. Yes, a bit of a swing sneaks into the liturgy, and some are beginning to move to the music during the singing. But the Praamsmas and the Riedstras stay frozen in their place as immovably as their faith. Between New Orleans and Nijemardum, the same Word is proclaimed, but there's still an ocean between the two.

After church during coffee time, some comment on that one statement of Pastor Nick. It seemed as if he had attacked people who have dollar signs in their eyes. "The fact is," I hear someone say, "people are becoming more materialistic all the time, and I can point them out to you without any trouble: people who spare no effort to get on their feet, but then don't know how to quit when they've become filthy rich. For some it's 'never enough,' but the pastor put it so well: 'It's better to want things you don't have, than to have things you don't want.'"

Post-sermon discussion is an old hallowed tradition, but it's not likely that sermon-talk this Sunday is going to win out over the telling of old stories. Take the story of Wolter Veenstra from Lytsepost above Stynsgea; in 1948, Wolter's departure from the homeland and arrival in Canada was hardly typical. But Wolter did well: he built up a million-dollar business with Dick Boersma. D&W Transport has more than a hundred forty-ton D&W semis roaring through Ontario and bordering areas in Canada and the States. The freight business is linked to economic activity. And that activity flourishes in Brampton, a small city close to the heavily populated city of Toronto. It's only some five hundred miles to the metropolitan areas of Chicago and New York, and the Toronto airport is less than a half hour away from Brampton. "Toronto is the national hottest economic 'hot-spot,'" a regional paper exclaimed in a front-page headline only yesterday.

"I was eighteen," Wolter Veenstra begins, "I wanted to go to Indonesia in the worst way. To fight for queen and fatherland. What else was there to do? A future? There were six boys in our family, and Dad had less than five acres land. None of the six boys were interested in school. When I think back on that, I can't help but think that we must've become sort of fatalistic. There was seemingly only one way out: join the military action in Netherlands East Indies. A couple of my friends were already en route. When I saw them off in their uniform, their adventure and ethical sense of responsibility just choked me up. When I would talk about it at home, Dad would silently turn away from me. That silence: I didn't understand that at all. There were two girls, the oldest one was twenty-two already, and she said: 'C'mon, brother, quit talking about it, can't you see that Dad can't stand it?' But how was that possible, for going to the East Indies was a common thing to do, and in the *grifformeard* church most had no trouble with it. One evening when it was already getting dark, Dad wanted to talk to me. 'Come along!' I can still see him walk ahead of me to the old shed behind the house. There he stood next to me, his cap pushed back a bit. He had a twig in his hand, and I thought what's going to happen now! He used the stick to point to his cow that was standing near the gate close by, and then he pointed to the couple of other animals that were grazing on our little meadow, and he said: 'Do you see this nice piece of land, Wolter? Do you see those cattle? What would you think if strangers came here and said: this little corner of land with those few cattle no longer belongs to you, but to us!'"

"'Well, I wouldn't like that.' I must've stammered something like that. And I don't exactly remember how Dad reacted to my answer. I do know that that moment, there by the gate between the old shed and our little meadow in Fryslân, that is going to stick with me till I die. Because what Dad said there was profound in its simplicity.

"It became gradually clear to me that the old folks couldn't stand to think of one of their boys participating in a war. Both feared that the Russians would come. That feeling of threat began right after the war already. The coming of the Red Army with those hordes of anti-Christians, that was their bogeyman. That's why we came with them this way on the *Cota Inden* in 1948 already.

"Later on you think, what a remarkable decision for two people pushing fifty: with eight children, to exchange forever and always the old and familiar for an uncertain future. It was in April of that year when we were on the train from Halifax to Belwood, Ontario. Hour after hour, the lifeless landscape of Nova Scotia and New Brunswick passed by the windows.

While Dad and Mom had been silent maybe for an hour or so, I for some reason had to make a grumpy remark: 'Are you looking around you, Dad? We've landed here in a place where an old crow can't even find enough to eat!' The silence after that became even thicker.

"When I try to remember the atmosphere on the train to Belwood, I see a Dad and a Mom who knew what they wanted. You could see in their faces that there was no doubt, but an overflowing sense of trust and confidence that somewhere far away there would be a better world for them and the children.

"That trust was rewarded. Before long they were able to buy a farm of 240 acres. But I have to explain how that came about so soon. It was their eight children, half of whom were already grown, who worked the first two years only for that first farm. All the money they earned went into Dad and Mom's kitty. Don't misunderstand me, I have no resentment, but my own children — I see them as the privileged second generation immigrants — don't have a clue about those kinds of sacrifices.

"After a long train trip, we arrived with the old folks, all worn out from the whole ordeal, at the farm of Dad's first employment. When we stood there, circled around Dad and Mom, I felt suddenly a strong sense of loyalty. Why was that — because of our common enemy, which I, after all, defined as uncertainty?

"I got a contract for $45 a month to work for another farmer, and that included room and board. Dad gave me $5 along, a silent hint that I should bring all my wages home. When I had put in the first four weeks of work for that farmer, I wasn't paid. He wanted to make sure that his new hardworking hired man would serve out the whole year's contract.

"When the year was finished, I collected twelve times 45 dollars. "Look, here is the money," I said to Mom that night, and I laid the whole amount of $540 on the table. And I still had seventy-five cents left of that $5 pocket money that Dad had given me a year before. It was on a Saturday night. 'I don't think you've been a spendthrift,' Dad said. Of course, the others had turned their earnings in too. And that's how Dad could buy that 240-acre farm so soon. The price: $11,500.

"In the fall of 1950, Dad gave me some pocket money again, this time $21. I bought a bus ticket to Toronto, which at that time cost me $3.50. I got a job in the city for a consortium that was putting in a subway system, but I still had to find a place to stay. After wandering around for a day and a half, I found a small, plain room. 'Fourteen dollars,' the lady said. 'Including board, of course,' I said brightly. And that's what we agreed on. I was below the ground, preferably twelve hours a day to earn more money. But it turned out that I couldn't get used to the different shifts; my biological clock got all out of whack. So I looked for and found other work: scrap iron, driving truck.

"That's how I met Bartele Huizinga, who came from Twizelerheide. Bartele wanted work that had more people contact, and that sounded good to me too, so together we got a job at a large bakery, going on the road selling bread and cookies. It was a steady job plus commissions.

"In Canada they didn't really know about the old country ways of selling goods on the street or door-to-door, especially not bakery goods. But a day or two later, I drove with horse and wagon through Toronto. The regular pay wasn't too bad in itself, but the possibilities of commissions really looked good to me. So I got busy ringing doorbells, pushing my wares, and if need be, talking the customer into a purchase. When the first week was past, the bakery boss was astonished. 'How can this be!' he exclaimed in alarm, 'You mean I have to pay you forty-six dollars? For one week of work?' He had never seen anything so absurd. 'But I sold accordingly,' I said. Well, I did get my wages and commission, but not with a lot of goodwill. The boss told me that from now on I was not to push the bread and cookies on the people. 'You are to stay on the street with horse and wagon, and let the customers come to you.'

"Later on I found out that Canada still had an economy at that time regulated from the top. That system gave me plenty of conniptions at first. A salesman's blood flows where it cannot go. At least that was true in my case. I had had my eyes wide open while working in the scrap iron trucking business, and I had felt then that there was a future in transportation. And so I met Bartele Huizinga, the man with whom I started D&W. It could've turned out a lot worse."

Coffee time after church. Frisians all around now. When Sam Tilstra was still just Sybren, son of Douwe Broers from Wûns, and began to think about emigration, "I didn't even know where Canada was. Dad had a pretty good-sized farm, but if you projected your future fortune, you had to remember that the number of cows would have to be divided by the number of children. And there were nine children. When the Depression had passed, the war broke out, and it seemed that it had hit Wûns especially. They shot the farm right from under us. Twenty of us found shelter in Wiebe de Witte's cellar, and right above our heads the racket was so violent, you thought the world was coming to an end. In the cellar, all of us were equal: the farmer, the domestic help, and the farm hands.

"Suddenly it became quiet. The tension hung in the air, as between lightning and the thunderclap. We hardly dared to breathe. Then I heard Atsje Wiersma, the domestic help, announce frankly and openly that she had to pee. Well, there was a chamber pot, and I had the task of holding a piece of curtain in front of her, and that's how I saw her take down her panty, squat over the pot, and pee. Strange that that scene and sound from the war stayed so sharply etched in my mind. I remember that afterward it made me feel sinful.

"You must wonder what that little war tale has to do with emigration, but it's perfectly possible that it was one of the reasons to leave Wûns. The Germans shot a Halifax bomber out of the air by us, and that was a bad experience. I found a boot with the foot still in it. Now there were in and around our town not only Frisians, Hollanders, and Germans that had died, but also those who wanted to liberate us.

"All the shocks and tensions, all the human suffering was included in our prayers. I remember that it was around the same time that on Sunday mornings a group of separated *grifformearden* would bike to Makkum to go to church. They said that they had been 'liberated.' Each thought he was right, but it was still very much a sinful world, a world of crime and punishment."

Nanne, son of Egbert de Boer, returned alive from the Grebbeberch [the place of the fierce but losing battle between the Dutch and Germans after the invasion], and walking along the *Ofslûtdyk* (enclosure dike), looking in the direction of Wûns, he noticed a gap in the skyline. Nanne failed to see the red-tiled roof of their barn. The whole barn was gone. Nanne walked the rest of the way with a heavy heart. The place was gone; he didn't know where in Wûns he should go now. He stumbled past the smoldering remains, and a short time later stood at the backdoor of his parents' home. He knocked. Old Mrs. De Boer had thought her son a casualty at the Grebbeberch. Even their pastor had made an official announcement: "Nanne, son of Egbert de Boer, has fallen in the battle at the Grebbeberch."

When Mrs. De Boer opened the backdoor, she saw her son who was supposed to be in heaven. This could not be real, this had to be a bizarre dream. The poor woman slammed the door in her son's face, the son she had assumed dead.

"It was all crime and punishment in Wûns. Not long ago I was at Dick and Henny Boersma. Talking. Dick suddenly dashed for his Pennsylvania-organ. He played and played, he made that huge organ roar, and everything from my years in Wûns came to the surface. Hymn #16 from the *grifformeard* psalm book: '. . . Behold our sin, our guilt within, from our trespassing/Behold our guilt, our heart hate-filled, for we have sinned.'"

It's getting close to lunchtime, but the coffee-story time is extended today. The men are in no hurry and eager to unload yet another story. But the women feel the urge to head for home, knowing that the meal will be expected to stand ready and waiting.

Auke Huizinga was resident of Lytsegast till September 1948, when he emigrated to Ontario. For nine years he tried to find a good wife. "I have to admit, I couldn't get a bite." Still, Auke was known as a pleasant, good guy.

"I was eighteen in 1948, and I didn't want to go to the East Indies. Well, maybe they could've gotten me to go, but Mom was dead set against it. Dad had been in the service at the beginning of their marriage, in the mobilization of World War I. 'Dad didn't make a dime in 1914–18,' Mom explained. 'That's one of the reasons we couldn't get on our feet. As far as I'm concerned: that will never happen again, so you're not going to Indië, and that's that!' She would much rather have me emigrate to Canada, so that's what I did. That was also one way of getting out of going to the East Indies. Though it did mean that I couldn't go back to Fryslân for the first five years. They would've collared me immediately and at the least stuck me with two years of military service. So I just couldn't go back to revive an old flame.

"The first farmer I worked for lived way out in the bush, and I was working all the time, so there wasn't much of a social life. I hardly ever saw a young woman. That was a good place to work otherwise. Aloy Trudeau and his wife were French in background, but they were first class people. And then she died suddenly. The old man was so out of sorts, that he lasted only thirty-seven days after that. I brought both the farmer and his wife to the cemetery, in fact, *carried* them. I considered that an honor and a duty.

"It was a time when a woman didn't yet meet a man more than half-way. Eventually, it began to bother me so much that I couldn't sleep well anymore, and then I put an ad in the paper. Something like '... Frisian Canadian would like to meet Christian lady living in Southern Ontario ...' A letter came shortly, and the romance didn't take long to bloom."

That's how Auke Huizinga hooked Boukje Faber. And now Boukje really wants to go home, because the Sunday dinner should've been on the table long ago. But Auke still wants to say that in the meantime he's been working for D&W Transport for thirty-three years already, as a driver. At seventy, he's still free to drive as much or as little as he chooses. "Where are you going to find a better boss than that!"

Behind the long tables with the by now mostly empty coffeepots, a woman says: "In the first decade of the immigration wave, let's say in the fifties, the after-church coffee time was in a lot of churches like a prayer without end."

Henk de Weerd says: "It's gotten shorter now. It seems like everybody is busier now, even in their free time. And don't forget, the immigrants of the forties and fifties have grown children now. So on Sundays you now have the grandchildren underfoot. There's more in life now than just the church."

Henk de Weerd is a son of a skipper from Eastersea, who came in 1954 with Shirley (Sytske) Bergsma from Warkum. "Dad was captain of *De Onderneming,* an inland eighty-ton cargo boat. There were nine children, so we weren't exactly floating in gravy. I don't mean to say that we lived in poverty, but the quarter for the drawbridge operator was turned over at least three times before Mom let it drop in the wooden shoe that dangled before her on a piece of rope. No, I didn't want to become a skipper. A new adventure in a new country appealed more to me."

It became an adventure with the wind in the sails. When later the first snow fell in Ontario, Henk and Shirley would already be underway in their fifty-one-foot sailing yacht, *Seaquest III,* from Lake Ontario to the mild temperatures of Florida. A skipper after all, but then just for the fun of it.

A half hour later, the parking lot of the church is empty. Dick and Henny Boersma drive back home through the rolling countryside. He points to the screen of the digital Guidance Positioning System. It's a kind of compass one simply cannot do without of course on the straight roads of the forsaken Canadian hinterland. "'What do you need something like that for,' Dad in his old age, when he was still with us, wanted to know, and he pointed to the small compass of those years. 'That thing tells me that I'm lost,' I answered. After a while, he said, 'and there, in that mirror, you can see *who* is lost!'

"Dad was born in 1883, and remained sharp in his old age. He had studied to become a schoolteacher initially, held out for two days in front of the classroom, and then knew for sure that he might be better at farming than at teaching. He became a kind of *'Dichter und Bauer'* ('Poet-Farmer'), and spent most of his time reading, philosophizing, and writing articles. He wasn't the kind of dad who walked the fields with his sons to talk about nothing but cows. Because of his philosophical bent, a kind of distance remained between father and son. At times he also had that certainty of a rock-like faith. However, I left. When I told Dad of my decision, it seemed like he turned into a different man. 'Durk,' he said, 'I want you back here again after three years!' I said, 'After three years I'll come back for a week or two.' He was obviously relieved to hear it. And I kept that pledge."

We're riding past the head office of D&W, and decide to make a stop. Dick discovers that a fax arrived in which an oral agreement is ratified. D&W is again permitted to haul loads of roofing materials across the North American continent. Dick reads the first part of the fax on the run, and then puts it back on top of the fax machine. "Yes, we do quite a bit of business with Jews. As one from the Wâlden [the woodland area of Fryslân], I kind of like those people. They have your number already before you even open your mouth. That keeps you alert."

But the story soon returns to the dominant factor in the son's existence: his father. "He wrote stories, postulated theses, held readings with titles like 'God's Wonders in the Universe.' Long before the war he predicted that around the year 2000, one would be able to travel from Ljouwert to Amsterdam in half an hour. I remember one time when I went along to a farmers night, and a Christian Farmers Association farmer stood up and asked: 'What do you think, Boersma, will we make it to the moon?' The man who asked the question was really only interested in hearing a loud, principled 'no.' Dad must've felt that too, for he chose a compromise: 'We don't know, Dykstra, but I think we'll come a long way.'"

It's getting on toward evening, a Sunday evening, and a very peaceful one on the large veranda of the mansion on the hill. The sun with perfect self-control descends into the woods. Below, in the deep valley, the Credit River has to find its way through the dark-green foliage.

"In that river you find so much salmon sometimes, you can walk on their backs," Dick says. "But our boys prefer to take their fishing gear to the big lakes, and then they like to go out quite a ways. A lot of people need challenges, challenges that each time take them a little further.

"Take myself, for instance: I stood thumbing a ride on the 401 in my new herringbone overcoat and a suitcase in my hand. One vehicle after the other rushed past. Finally, a compact car stopped with three great big guys inside. I was offered a seat in front. After riding awhile, one of the men in the backseat asked: 'Do you love the Lord?' I didn't know what to say. 'Sometimes, not always,' I said.

"It turned out that they were Jehovah's Witnesses. The driver stopped the car on the side of the road, and all three began to pray for me. It took a long time, and I was eager to get going.

"They took me another thirty miles, where they needed to be. Back to hitching a ride. This time a Chevrolet stopped with a man and his wife inside. I got into the back seat. The guy saw me in his rearview mirror, and his eye fell on the paper the Jehovah Witnesses had given along with me. 'You get out or you get rid of that Jehovah junk!' the man snarled at me. So I cranked the window down and threw the paper out. Because I was determined to go a ways. Well, it didn't take me long to catch on that in order to reach your goal you had to be ready to roll with the punches a little bit.

"One time we got back from a really exhausting trip — Big Harm Dykstra, Little Harm Veenstra, Arnold de Vries, and I. Our goal: to harvest the beet crop from a rented piece of land. It was on a farm near Belmont. The farmer turned out to be a real swine, a troublemaker with two wooden legs. 'Fortunately, a good piece of that scoundrel is in the ground already,' Arnold said that same evening.

"The farmer had promised us a good place to sleep. And for the first week the food would be free. Well, he opened the door reluctantly when we came and indicated with a shrug that somewhere at the end of a dark stairs there would be sleeping facilities. What we found upstairs were some dilapidated beds in the middle of an unimaginable pile of junk. Big Harm screwed up the courage to holler down the stairs that we were hungry. That night at ten o'clock we were trying to eat four-day old porridge.

"Early to work the next morning. Harm always had a sense of humor. 'I dreamed last night that I could buy this place, man!' 'That dream could turn into a nightmare,' I said. And that's how it turned out. We slept with our caps on and didn't taste a potato in the half year we spent there.

"It didn't take long for me to go and try to make cornstarch for the others. A bucketful of water went on the stove, and Harm was going to stir. But it didn't work, and it made us ornery. So I wrote a postcard to a Frisian lady in Toronto asking how to make cornstarch. It turned into starch with lumps, but Big Harm bragged about our Canadian *potstro* [a Frisian dish of thick, solid gruel served with molasses and bacon fat]. He almost ate himself into a stupor.

"Whenever Wooden Leg could give us a hard time, he would. One early morning he turned off the water. It was an act of revenge. From that time on, it was open warfare. That same day we stuffed a burlap bag into his kitchen chimney. We found out the next morning that we had smoked him out. When he had recovered a bit, we watched a man go crazy. I had never known that a man could run so fast on two wooden legs. Furious, he went rushing inside the house, and it was a good thing that all four of us were Wâldmannen [Frisians from the woodlands, reputedly known for their fighting spirit], otherwise we wouldn't have caught on right away that he was getting his gun. So, when the first burst of buckshot raked the yard, we weren't standing around and waiting. When he ran out of ammo,

Big Harm grabbed Wooden Leg, carried him up the stairs, and set him on a chair in our palace. 'First calm down, fellah,' Harm said in Frisian. 'And then promise that you will never do it again!' Little Harm said, 'He doesn't understand you, you know.'

"'But he knows what I mean,' said Big Harm.

"It was a hard, rough life there by the wooden leg farmer, but it was good money. After awhile, though, Harm couldn't stand it anymore and wanted to pack up. 'The Lord has given and the Lord has taken, I have to go somewhere else,' he said one early morning. Before he left, he changed clothes. All of a sudden, there he stood at the foot of the stairs in nice striped pants. It looked almost as if he was wearing a wedding suit. Then I remembered: Harm had been going with a nurse from De Geast. They were going to get hitched, but apparently somebody threw a monkey wrench into their plans, and the wedding was canceled.

"'I'm leaving in peace,' he said, kind of choked up. 'I understand, Harm,' Arnold answered seriously, 'you want to start a new life, and I can't blame you for that.'

"Not long after that, another Harm made himself known at the wooden leg place: a letter from Harm Dykstra, a son of a teacher from Rinsumageast. This Harm had learned to milk at my dad's place, and now he too was in Canada. The letter said that he would just 'come by' at such and such a time. I had a strong feeling in my guts, though, that Dad had sent Harm Dykstra to check up on me. My parents wanted to know, of course, if Durk was taking care of himself, if he was living a good Christian life, and how far he was getting toward buying a farm.

"The first thing I did was to clean house, but Harm arrived before I could finish. We didn't even get such a bad review, I found out later, but at that moment the poor guy didn't know what he saw when he had a look at our little room and the kitchen of the wooden leg farmer. Not long after that, we had a visit from a minister, Reverend Gritter, who had come from Grand Rapids, Michigan, USA, to establish a Christian Reformed Church in our area. 'A cup of coffee, Reverend?' Little Harm was the kind of guy who wants to make a good impression. The Reverend had been looking around with a turned-up nose, and he decided not to take advantage of the offer. Later I thought, 'So, some kind of communication line runs all the way from Rinsumageast across Michigan, USA, to London, Ontario. Before long, the whole bunch of us attended catechism classes in London.

"It's a lifetime ago, that adventure at the wooden leg farmer in Belmont, but a year or so ago at the Frisian Day in Paris I met Big Harm again, and it was just like time had stood still. I thought that I had good news for him; I said: 'The wooden leg place isn't there anymore, Harm, the whole joint has been demolished and cleared off.' 'Yes,' he exclaimed, 'the other day I drove two hundred miles out of my way, looking for the place, when I discovered there was nothing left of it. And I said to myself what the Scripture says, that the place thereof shall know it no more.'

"Time went on, we grew roots, and the church asked me to become a deacon. In that office I encountered a lot of people with grief, also among the immigrants. I won't mention names, but you may be sure that not all the immigrants enjoyed success.

"At the Frisian Day, you seldom bump into the sad cases; in fact, you rarely meet them. It's as if they disappeared and with all their trouble simply dissolved into the landscape of this huge country. Some immigrants soon saw how the wind was blowing and sailed or flew back to the Netherlands. There was 'Jan,' for example — not his real name, of course — who I worked with during the first years on the assembly line for General Motors. I found out that he hadn't paid room and board for sixteen weeks and was heading for trouble. Eventually he tried to make do with just a dirty little room. Late at night I couldn't find him there. Then I would just shove a couple pieces of bread with a thick layer of margarine under his window. The next morning, the food was always gone. The diaconate of the church finally bought him a return ticket.

"One day I came into contact with an older immigrant woman. She was at her wits' end. 'Elder Boersma,' she said when I was leaving, 'Canada not only gave me severe winters, but also severe summers.'"

Frisian Day

*Lút Miedema and Freerkje Miedema-Haagsma
from Waterloo, Ontario, Canada*

It's nice weather in Paris, Ontario, on July 1, and that's the way it's been for twenty-eight years already. And each year on this day Frisians flock to this town. Some come from thousands of miles away, by plane from Nova Scotia, and by car from Michigan, USA. Indeed, whole families all the way from Manitoba, Iowa, and the Far West descend on Paris for this occasion. Because here you can catch up on conversation. You can talk about the rough life during the last years of the forties and the beginning of the fifties. Or about the Depression- and war-years before that. It's like time standing still for the moment.

When the first of July falls on a Sunday, the Frisian Day is held on Monday. "If they weren't so Christian Reformed here, Paris would've long ago been a place of pilgrimage," the former butcher Lút Miedema laughs, one of the original organizers. "Thirty-five hundred people coming together for this event, the largest Frisian town celebration in the world." "The Butcher of Waterdown" is having a ball today, because the annual party, from bag racing to rope pulling, is again a smashing success.

This Miedema (born in 1925) must've had a potent dose of Frisian spirit to turn the idea of holding a Canadian-Frisian Day into reality. When he was still living with his parents in Bûtenpost, he didn't feel like such a strong Frisian. "And I wasn't at all a man of the Frisian Movement [a cultural-political activist movement on behalf of Frisian rights to their own language and literature]. After all, Mom was a *Grinslânner* (one born in the province of Groningen) who wasn't at all interested in such Frisian farces. I caught my Frisian-mindedness here in Canada, and I suppose that happened because at first I was as homesick as a cat. With us the situation was in reverse: my wife was never sorry that we took the big step."

Did the old butcher want to create a new Fryslân around him? Was "Paris" really only a kind of therapy for his longing for a Frisian identity? If that should be the case, then it wasn't therapy for him only but also for thousands of others.

"Look at these people picnicking here together, look at them having fun and socializing together. Some look forward all year to this one special day. And the nicest thing is that in the last few years more and more young people come to Paris. I think it's beautiful that the second and sometimes even the third generation wants to maintain the ties with the old country. My wife and I made sure that in our case too there are possibilities for that: we have fifty grandchildren and eight great-grandchildren. And I believe that is only a beginning, because we found out that several more are on the way. I hope they will become good Canadians, but that at the same time they will also stay a bit Frisian."

And so for one day a year, a Canadian town functions as an alternative to a country that at one time was so far from ideal for these folk that they turned their back to it. How could that same country later, from such a distance, awaken such longing! It's a mystery for which Lút Miedema has no answer. "Paris" is emotion, idealization, and illusion all at the same time.

"We hadn't been here very long, when I had Abe Brouwer, the author, come over. I had gotten to know Abe under rather unusual circumstances, during the war. The Germans had caught me along with a few other fellows in a razzia and locked us up in Glimmen. A couple of young men were killed in that encounter. And who should I meet in that jail in Glimmen? Abe Brouwer, our Frisian writer, the author of *De Gouden Swipe* (*The Golden Whip*, a famous Frisian novel), but now in the function of paymaster. It occurred to me that he stood sort of between the enemy and us. And that wasn't quite right.

"There were some seventy of us there, and one of the men asked if Abe Brouwer would read to us from *De Gouden Swipe*. I think that was the second night we were there. 'I sure will,' he said. There was kind of a strange, tense atmosphere in the air, but the language made it seem at once as if Abe Brouwer was one of us. He also stood up for us. What's more, I was glad that it was he who was our paymaster. I still remember that I was very, very impressed with his stories.

"Maybe that's why I later let Abe Brouwer come here to Canada. It was the first night that he was with us, and I thought, you're going to be better off here than we were in Glimmen. During the meal, I said: 'I met you before, Abe, you read to me once from *De Gouden Swipe.*

"'Where must *that* have been,' he wanted to know. 'In camp,' I said, 'the Germans had locked us up in Glimmen, and that's where you were paymaster.' The old man was plainly shocked, really shocked. He didn't have much to say, and we never touched the subject again.

"On the occasion of his visit, three Frisian get-togethers in different places had been organized. Of course, he would read from his *De Gouden Swipe.* That title alone dripped with farm-romance. Who of our generation of rural emigrants had never dreamed of winning the golden whip in that great perennial Frisian horse race? With Abe Brouwer we would feel as if we were back home again for the moment.

"He attracted a full house wherever he went. But now it became apparent to me that he was not a talented speaker. He wasn't able to make it compelling; it was all a bit humorless, and his stories lacked good organization. I think the women liked it better than the men; Abe was good to look at.

"With the years, Frisian-Canadian societies in several places began to stage Frisian plays on their own. Some had so much success with their comedy pieces that they went on the road with them to places sometimes five hundred miles away. I participated too, now and then in the main role. That was a wonderful time. They've said to me, 'Lút, you missed your calling, you should have been in theater.' And I think they're right.

"So Abe became too old-fashioned: Canada had long exhausted his *Gouden Swipe,* and the members of the Frisian groups were eager for something different. Then I had little Teake van der Meer [a very popular Frisian comedian] come here three different times. Performing in the churches, because those easily have room for four hundred people. Teake is of course a *Westereinder* (from an area of Fryslân that a century ago was impoverished and whose denizens were considered roughnecks), so before we let him loose, I had to have a talk with him: 'Not too rough, mind you, not too suggestive, keep it decent, these are good church people here.'

"The first time we had the church so full, there was standing room only, and we laughed ourselves silly. Some laughed so hard that by intermission time they were in need of clean underwear. But what we also found out, it was too much for some of the more uptight among us. That's why the church wasn't nearly full the second time. That's when we had to give Teake a piece of our mind again: Not too uncouth! The last time he was here the church was filled to capacity again.

"All those Frisian activities here in Canada — sometimes I wondered why I try to bring so many nice things from Fryslân over here while I myself left Fryslân with discontent. Maybe it is because in Bûtenpost there was a time when the cable got too many kinks.

"Dad had a good livery stable, we had plenty of flour, fertilizer, and potatoes. The depression years were merciless for us, but that wasn't the end of the poor times — a war followed. And that one hurt! Our parents could've made it all right with five older children, but in 1943 my brother came back from Germany with a bad case of TB. My dad and sister caught it too. In one fell swoop we were marked: a TB family. Before long all three were consigned to a tent.

And it was wartime; I was hardly eighteen, a dangerous age, and I took risks. In everything. Big risks, in fact. I worked for Dad in the livery stable. We had eight horses and used quite a few carriages. Then we also contracted to haul the mail from Ljouwert to Grins by automobile. Later on in the war years, we had a kind of furnace in the front of that postal vehicle that burned the strangest kinds of stuff. It furnished the power for the engine to run on.

"One morning I went with my brother Durk and Harm, the son of Jelle van der Valle, taking the mail from Ljouwert to Grins. Harm was sitting on the right fender to scan the skies for British fighter planes. Those 'Tommies' shot at everything that looked the least bit like German transportation.

"Just before Briltil, Harm screamed: 'Tommies!' I braked hard. We raced into the field like idiots and dived into a gully. The machine guns did a good job on the postal van: first they took care of the front, then the back, and then both sides.

"'Are you still alive?' Durk was the first to utter a word when the airplanes left. Yes, all three of us were okay, but the Tommies had done a bang-up job. The furnace-generator in front of the cab was shot to pieces and . . . the mailbags were dripping blood. Yes, we had hid fresh meat among the mailbags, for war or no war, our business of course had to go on. 'Oh, this is too much,' Harm exclaimed, 'there's a corpse in one of the mailbags!'

"'Germans are coming in the distance,' Durk yelled. That's when we took off, as fast as we could. With six pounds of meat. And they didn't nab us. At least not that time.

"In the meantime I had met Freerkje Haagsma, who lived close to the town of De Koaten. My parents weren't very excited about it, because she was from rather simple laboring folk. Dad and Mom would rather have had me come home with a farmer's daughter. What's forbidden is always beautiful of course, so it turned into a serious relationship with Freerkje.

"'You better become a little less bold,' Freerkje told me one night. She meant that the Germans were watching me and I was totally reckless. Her warnings fell on deaf ears, for not long after that I got nabbed in that razzia. We should've stayed inside as Bútenpost young people, but we didn't. Big mistake. That's how we got caught under German crossfire. It went terrible; as I said, some got killed. The Landwacht (Home Guard, serving the German occupation) was behind the betrayal. So that's how I landed in Glimmen. It could've turned out a lot worse.

"When I was let go, Freerkje was waiting for me. We were hardly eighteen and as green as grass. 'I'm pregnant,' she said a couple of months later. I said, 'I only need to look at you, and you're pregnant already.' We had to get married! Well, that was no small thing, we were grifformeard and it wasn't acceptable to slip up in those things. Now, if Freerkje had been the daughter of a farmer with twenty head of cattle, that might've made a difference.

"In short, first I had to bow my head low for my parents, then for the in-laws, and then I had to kneel before the minister, and after that once more before the church council. That position didn't exactly sit well with me already then — on my knees — but I did feel that I had no other option. And Freerkje wanted to get married in church, so I put up with it.

"The minister came over. And everybody praying. And that preacher coughed up a prayer you wouldn't believe! By golly, there wouldn't be much left of Lút the way he was going at it. Was I such an evil creep? Both of us had just turned eighteen, were crazy about each other, so just what had been my awful sin? The flesh had been willing and the grass dry.

"When the preacher said 'Amen,' and the people in the circle opened their eyes again, one was missing: this boy had left. When the preacher later that week asked me about the how and why, I said: 'Such an evil guy as you prayed for, that's not Lút Miedema!' A couple of days later, Freerkje had a miscarriage. I didn't want the minister to hear about it before our marriage, because then he would be sure to proclaim that this was God's punishment.

"We ended up getting married outside the church. And there came the preacher again. 'What did I hear, Lút, didn't you *have* to get married after all?' 'We don't *have* to do anything!' I said.

The war was nearing its end, and Mom said one early morning, 'Throw the wheels of all our carriages in the canal by Dr. Keizer, because today we still have to ride for the Germans, tomorrow maybe for the British or Americans, and that way we never get a turn ourselves.' Mom was, what they called, 'war-weary.' It must've been early April 1945.

"When three sets of wheels lay in the canal by Dr. Keizer, the Germans came racing up our driveway. They shot in the air and requisitioned everything that was still capable of moving. And one of us had to come along. I said to Mom, 'Can't one of the younger ones go along, I'm a married man, have been picked up so often, and have already been away from Freerkje for so long.'

"'One who's just married,' she said, 'is at his sharpest and will survive the longest.' The next day — it was running toward evening already — I took off under orders of the Wehrmacht with a column of some fifty Germans to Donkerbroek. The wagons were loaded with weapons. I had it all figured out: that's how I would be driven with the *moffen* [a derogatory term, like "krauts," for German soldiers] into the hands of their enemy, an enemy who for everyone else here would be the liberator. I waited for the chance to escape.

"We had three wagons from our livery and a manure wagon along from Edse de Haan from Bûtenpost. And three teams of horses. I had old Hylke Boorsma with me as fellow-driver. Hylke had lived for years already as steady hired man by Jabik Kuipers near Bûtenpost and had gotten this message along from the farmer: 'Even if the world is going to be leveled, Hylke, you're coming back with both of my beautiful horses!'

"The third driver was a young farmer from *Grinzer* background whose name was Rinkema. The other team of horses was ours.

"They were really just kids, those *moffen;* the oldest, an officer, must've been just twenty or so, the rest were between fifteen and eighteen years old. The boys were so scared of the British fighter planes that they dared to travel only by dark. But the days were getting longer, and it turned into a long, miserable trip.

"The destination was altered from Donkerbroek to It Hearrenfean, but past Gordyk already the first Canadian tanks came to meet us. The Germans fled to a nearby farm, and we landed with the whole shebang in a deep ditch. Then the shooting started, enough to make you sick, so the horses clambered out of the ditch and took off like wild animals. Dragging pieces of wagon behind them. And old Hylke Boorsma had lost a wooden shoe, was still standing in the ditch, and screamed: 'This is crazy, men, this way I'm going back to Jabik Kuipers without the horses.'

"When the young Germans had surrendered, they got cigarettes and chewing gum from the Canadians. And I can still see old Hylke standing there up to his waist in that ditch by the farm. He got nothing, because they didn't see Hylke: he was totally covered with duckweed as an effective camouflage.

"Everything was gone or had taken off, so, thoroughly soaked, we walked with the three of us back to the farmer by the tollhouse near De Sweach. That night there was more shooting. We dug ourselves deeper and deeper into the hay. The next morning we found two young Germans lying dead on the cow-stall next to us.

"How we got home, on foot and sometimes by bike, I'm not sure anymore, but I can still recall a couple of things. It was a beautiful Sunday morning. Freerkje stood high and dry in the garden, crying from happiness; yes, she was pregnant then with Aukje. And old Hylke, he hung around for a while, because the poor man dreaded like the plague coming back to Jabik Kuipers's farm without the horses.

"The Netherlands was liberated, but as a young man with wife and child I got the feeling that it didn't apply to me. I wasn't free: to Ljouwert for the medical board, and then to Indonesia. The norm was: To Indonesia! Heroes had come to conquer the Germans and to liberate us, and now we shouldn't behave as cowards ourselves. As soldier to Indonesia; it was the norm for everything and everyone around me, including the church.

"'We have to accept it,' Freerkje said. I can't deny it: that's how I saw it then too. But for the medical exam not everybody thought that way. A boy of Broersma from Gerkeskleaster hit himself, just before the exam, on the knee with a hammer and was rejected. He could've hit a bit less hard, though, because he remained a cripple for life. Eppy Wynstra, who later had a potato business in It Hearrenfean, tackled it with a little more shrewdness. He had already been called up, when one evening he told me: 'I'm going to pee in bed, Lút, then they won't send me away.' I said, 'Then you should do it right away tonight, otherwise they won't believe you.' 'I want to sleep dry,' Eppy said, and he peed on the side of the bed. That's how he handled it, and he got rejected for duty in Indonesia.

"I had to go to Indonesia with the first conscripted division. There you are, stuck on that boat for thirty-one days. I became a tank-driver, and once I got over my ears into the first political action, all fear drained away. I had a wife and kids on the other side of the world, but it was just like the mischief-maker was reawakened in me. But that changed in the second political action. It became a matter of survival at all costs. Haaije Helder was in a tank ahead of me, crossing a bridge. We heard a terrible bang, and he was gone just like that. We lost our sergeant, Frederik Pol, the same way. Another one, an officer, lost his life in quite another way. When that man saw a nice-looking brown woman, he'd get all carried away. There was a young woman who got him so under her spell that he never noticed that she mixed female hair into his food. Female hair that had a spell cast on it first and then been dipped in poison.

"One night, the officer joined us. He was as yellow as a dandelion. 'I come to say good-bye, I'm going to die,' he said. Two days later he was in the ground. In the official papers he's listed as killed in action.

"The wet monsoon hit us, more and more got killed, we had to travel through dangerous places, and I wanted to return to Freerkje and our little girl, but I was stuck as if I were imprisoned, as if the net of death got pulled around me tighter and tighter. By now more than thirty men of our battalion had lost their lives.

"One early morning we had to lug heavy rocks from a pathway, and all of a sudden my back gave out and I could hardly move. My left leg had no feeling. They transported me to the hospital in Batavia. 'You're faking it!' snarled both doctors who were in charge of me. And they left me as so much garbage. But the problem didn't go away, and I persisted. With each new examination, I got the same reaction: they said that I was role-playing.

"'As medical staff of the hospital, we've come to the same diagnosis,' the specialist in Batavia informed me one morning. 'You need surgery at once! It's going to be a serious but necessary operation.'

"'And who's going to do that,' I wanted to know. 'I'm going to do it myself,' he answered. It sounded hostile. There was no way that I wanted to be operated on by these bunglers, so I didn't give my permission.

"The gentlemen at last couldn't do anything but send me back to the Netherlands, but they would have the last laugh: on board the *Volendam* they had me put in the boatswain's storeroom, all the way in the bottom, where some space had been cleared for me in a dirty, pitch-black corner. As if I had been doomed to an isolation cell, it couldn't be worse. I lost all sense of place and time and was in constant pain. It made me depressed. At last I lost my appetite. Every once in a while someone would bring me some water.

"It lasted an eternity. Then it felt like the ship had stopped. I found out that we had only made it to North Sumatra. It was the same night that a captain came to see me. It was so dark, I could hardly make him out, but when he had sat awhile with me, I noticed that he was missing a leg. It was a captain-physician from Frisian background. When I think back to that moment, I know that it was this doctor who saved me. In fact, the hour that this Frisian doctor came on board there in North Sumatra has always remained a sign that reminds me: when it comes to crunch time, the Frisians are there to help each other.

"While the doctor lit a candle, he said: 'You're going to die here, Lút, you have to have light. And air. Let me read the letter they gave along.' I hauled out the sealed envelope, which had been under my pillow for an eternity already. He carefully opened the envelope. 'It says here that upon arrival you should be placed on a board on which you must lie for three years. That would do you in, Lút. Let me give you some good advice: to-morrow morning, before they come with food, you try to crawl up the stairs. Tell them that you're going berserk down here. And remember, I've said nothing and seen nothing!'

"And that's how it went. I somehow struggled my way upstairs, a couple of days later I could sit in a chair again, and after that I never had a bad day again.

"There was a guy from Brabant who had stepped on a landmine and had all kinds of things wrong with him. I sat with that boy all the time and taught him how to play checkers. When he learned to play it a bit, he all of a sudden got very sick. After a couple of days he caught on that he wouldn't make it. They gave him a sea-burial near Malta. One, two, three, in God's name there he goes. In a sort of bag with rocks in it; a lot like Grandpa in Bûtenpost would drown the scrawniest from a nest of young dogs.

"The *Volendam* had not yet anchored in the Netherlands when the "*Wilhelmus*" (the Dutch national anthem) already resounded across the water. But we had to wait a long time before the bus came to bring us home. Not serious, for I could run again like a deer.

"Even though I had been in Indonesia on behalf of Her Majesty, I never thought of her for a second; I thought only of Freerkje and our little girl. When the moment came at last, when she came to meet me with the little girl by the hand, well — I will never forget that moment. Aukje was now a child of four and talked a blue streak, but she didn't quite trust that strange man, in fact she was dead scared of me. That hurt.

"It was now 1949. And now, I thought to myself, I will never, never leave Fryslân again. I was home, I threw my hat through the door, Freerkje sat down on it, and then she was pregnant again. Apparently, a lot of resin had been smeared on the strings, for this time it turned out to be twins.

"'You can take over the business,' Dad said. We had just finished coffee and together stepped into our clogs, when he surprised me with that.

The man had been sickly, wasn't very strong, had gone broke twice, was just now beginning to feel somewhat better and getting back on his feet. 'Then we better do that right away,' I said, 'I'll take over the business.'

"'With joys and sorrows,' he complained. But I hardly heard the last part. And what happened? The sorrows came thick and fast, and I had to search hard for the joys.

"The first year I cleared 3,500 guilders, and I thought this is pretty good. But then the first cat came out of the bag: those 3,500 guilders went to pay off old debts. And then came the tax bill: exactly 3,500 guilders. So I grabbed the bike and raced at once to the revenue office. 'Now I'm trying hard to get on my feet and you guys push me like a kitten under water and choke me to death before I can drown!'

"'We're going to make it 350 guilders,' the inspector said after much deliberation. I thought, as long as I'm here to yell, I'm not going to accept that. At last they reduced it to 35 guilders. On the way home, I all of a sudden got fed up; they were just fooling around with taxes. To me it was suddenly as clear as daylight: we were liberated, but the new government wanted to twist the neck of the little guy. The taxes stuck in my craw, for my business was practically broke and the competition became worse and worse. How would Freerkje and I get up on our feet this way?

We began to talk about emigration. In my heart I was resisting it; after all, I had sworn that I would never leave Fryslân again, but a kind of grumpiness came over me. What kind of world did we live in, anyway! And Freerkje was willing.

"A year after I returned from Indonesia, I sat with wife and three children on the boat to Canada. To become a successful farmer, that's what I wanted. And Freerkje would like to show our parents in Bûtenpost that she was born to become a first-rate farmer's wife.

"Like almost every immigrant, I had to take a job on a farm first. I ended up with a very strict Baptist farmer. I would rather have had someone a little more fun, but we got along fine. And what was even more important, I made good money.

"So on a Saturday morning, I walked up to the farmer calm as a cucumber and told him proudly that for Freerkje and the kids I had found ten pounds of beautiful horse meat. 'Look at this, such wonderful horse meat.'

"That made the man furious, he was spitting fire, it was enough to scare you.

"'Don't you know it, then,' he hollered, 'are you a pagan? Don't you know Leviticus 11? There it's written that you may only eat animals that have a split hoof, and then hoofs that are *completely* split. And besides, the animal has to be one that chews the cud!' The farmer was pale from anger and disappointment. 'I'm asking you straight out,' he went on, 'have you seen a horse with split hoofs? Did you see a horse that chews the cud?'

"'Not so far as I know,' I said.

"'If my wife hears this,' he fumed, 'if my wife finds out that you eat horse meat, I won't be able to keep you on, and then you'll have to leave to-night yet.'

"I was of a mind to leave him, but then he said: 'I'll make it right with you: you promise me that tonight you will read in the Bible about clean and unclean domesticated animals, and then as a Christian I'll give you a heifer and two young pigs. I won't subtract that present from your wages either, no sir, and when the animals are full-grown, you butcher them for yourselves. But promise me then that you will read from Leviticus tonight, and that you will take the Word into your heart!'

"'Okay, boss!' Well, what do you think, I was plenty agreeable because I had gained a heifer and two pigs for ten pounds of horse meat. I paid special attention on that farm to my heifer and two pigs. That fall they were ready for butchering. I had learned that skill pretty well in the war already, but now I became an expert butcher. I didn't tell the farmer that I peddled the horse meat after church behind our Christian Reformed church. *Ja*, the same way that clean meat would find its way later on to the Frisian immigrants.

"What did life in Canada bring me? I'll make it short: a very big family and enough happiness and income. The first years were hard. But as I said, Freerkje was never homesick.

"And I?

"At first, miserable every day. You wouldn't believe that of a man like Lúts Miedema, but that's how it was.

"I hit some rough spots in my life that took me off course, but now I've come to a place that brings me peace: a whole assembly of some fifty healthy grandchildren. And, as I said, there are more on the way."

Nightflight

Frisians in the Holland Christian Home
in Brampton, Ontario, Canada

A mild evening in early summer. The low sun paints a deep glow over the forefront of the apartment buildings. From top to bottom the balconies bulge with flowers, making it look like the geraniums are taking root in the joints of the redbrick walls.

Below, there are tulips, dahlias, and marigolds in the wide borders. Even the dresses of the two old women who're taking their last stroll for the day are covered with flowers.

The day is ending in and around the rest home, Holland Christian Home in Brampton, Ontario. The sprinklers swish and sway, the windmill in front is in the cross-position, and the carillon has been silenced. But tomorrow morning the chimes will play again the old songs learned in the classrooms of long ago and never forgotten.

Holland Home has 437 spacious, well-equipped apartments with large balconies. Even the balconies offer considerable privacy. Most of the people here enjoy independent living, but there is a nursing section with 120 beds as well. The Christian Reformed Church, which also holds services inside the building, is represented by a good 400 residents. Every Sunday night there's a Dutch service; now and then a Frisian. For a large part of the residents are from Frisian origin. And the initiative for the building of this multimillion-dollar project also came from the Frisian immigrants.

When the flow of immigrants began here in 1948, Canada had hardly any social services. When a woman had to go to a hospital to give birth, one would first of all have to deposit eighty dollars to get in. It was the

Frisians who at once began to form a private cooperative insurance. And here too it was the CRC that contributed board members and promoted membership. In fact, every immigrant was eligible for membership.

When the Canadian government introduced a mandatory national health law in 1965, the immigrants were covered under that too, of course. At that point their own plan had more than a million dollars in the fund, money from and for its members. The decision was to build a rest home with the funds. The leaders bought ten acres of land and developed ambitious building plans. The million dollars grew larger when the Christian Reformed churches in the area as well as individuals contributed to the cause. The government was so impressed with the plan that it decided to more than double the amount of investment. "Sturdy Frisians build Holland Home," shouted the local headlines.

Board member Wolter Veenstra from Brampton, born in 1929 in Lytsepost by Stynsgea, reports that they've decided on another million-dollar expansion. According to him, more than ninety percent of the residents are easily able to pay their own way; six or seven percent need some financial assistance. "Those having a hard time tend to be older women who were widowed fairly young. But from the figures I mentioned, you can draw the conclusion that more than ninety percent of the immigrants did well financially."

A new day, a Saturday morning in sunny weather. It's so early that the windmill in front of the Holland Home is still in cross-position, but the first gray-haired couple is already driving out the gate in their full-size Dodge. And then the carillon begins to play a tune that conjures up images of distant dunes whose bright tops gleam in the glow of the sun.

Behind all those flowered balconies, the aged live out their lives. Men and women who, for whatever reason, took a leap in the dark. They did a pile of work, that much is for certain. An old lady said last night: "Let us not talk about the tears anymore, but let me tell you, enough tears were shed here to fill an ocean; people suffered more than a little."

"You ooh'd and aah'd about our nice flowers awhile ago," said Sytse Douma with a wink, "but when you look around inside of these four walls, you'll notice that the flowering days are pretty much over. "Don't listen to

Sidney," a heavy-boned man retorts while pointing his cane in Douma's direction, "people from Anjum are fantastic liars." The men are in the lounge, which in the evening they prefer to the outside. "I spent enough time in the fields, on the grass," says a skinny old man who in the late fifties began with 60 acres near Woodstock and later on milked 130 cows. And the gentlemen are also careful not to look for a chair in the stone-floor section, for that's the domain of the demented residents. There sit the poor souls who have become so forgetful that they can only mumble a few words in their first language. Apparently the roots of the second language didn't go as deep as expected.

"We often have a hundred Frisians get together here for coffee in the morning. The Dutch aren't too happy about that, all those Frisians." Simen Boersema raises his eyebrows while making the remark. His friend chides him: "You Simen, you are half a Groninger, you don't know a thing about it!" "The other day," another begins, "the other day a young man was here from De Jouwer visiting his uncle, and that uncle was me, and that boy couldn't get enough of what he saw here. 'Uncle,' he said, 'I think there are more real Frisians living here in Brampton than by us in De Jouwer, at least they speak a purer Frisian.'"

"And *Bilkerts* [a dialect of It Bilt, a coastal area just northwest of Ljouwert]!" exclaims Jetse Andringa from Ouwesyl. Andringa claims he's no talker but asks his neighbor Boersema to tell the story of the first *grifformeard* farm-worker from It Bilt who in Ontario — still as a farm-worker — was elected elder.

"Well, yes, as an elder the man of course had to lead in prayer when on house visits. And that gave him conniptions — to pray aloud in public. He tried to practice while plowing. At first he ran out of words before he'd gotten halfway across the field, but after persistent effort it became a prayer that took him the whole length. Eventually the man was able to keep praying while plowing all the way around a beet field of ten acres. This looked promising. But when we asked him later how the praying had actually turned out for the family visit, he answered: 'I was barely able to make it from one clod to the next.'"

"The day is too short here," begins Albert Mulder from Ychten, later from Donkerbroek, whose forty-five-ton Mac truck roared for almost half a century throughout Canada and the United States. "Berty doesn't always tell the truth," warns somebody from the sidelines, but Mulder ignores the teasing interruptions. "For a lot of old people here the day is too short because it takes them three hours in the morning to get dressed and three hours in the evening to get undressed."

"I'd rather be here as for example in the Flecke in De Jouwer," somebody says. Others chime in. "In Fryslân the rest homes are old-fashioned." "You have only old people in the homes there who can't take care of themselves anymore." "Everything is the same there." "Dad got me a job in the twenties working for a farmer, and it took me years to realize that a steady farm job meant steady poverty. So we left, but I was thirty-nine already by the time my wife was ready to go. June 1947, the very first emigrant boat to Montreal. I never settled down after that, did all sorts of things, and never regretted that we left."

"Well, I sure had regrets!" Hank Kloosterman, who recently celebrated his ninetieth birthday, taps his cane on the floor to get everybody's attention. "Who dares to say that out loud here? I regret that we came, we were too old when we came on the *Great Bear*. I know that emigration was in fashion. And after all, what kind of life did you have at that time: every day on the bike from Gerskeskleaster to the export butcher business of Foppe Feenstra in Dokkum. When we got married, we emigrated to Dokkum, and that was quite a step in those days. But every day was the same old thing. My first wife was still alive then, and said: 'What kind of life is that, always cutting up dead meat,' and that's when I got the papers in order. I had a neighbor who couldn't be trusted in the wartime, and he warned me. 'In Canada,' he said, 'the communists are going to be in power.' 'As Canadians we'll take care of that,' I answered. I was never more Canadian as then, before I left. When toward the end of the sixties I was back there for the first time, the times in Holland had changed a lot. It shocked us to see how well off they were already then. I worked for a farmer here who had twenty-five thousand chickens, and those critters had to be butchered same as in Dokkum."

A short silence is broken by Yde Straatsma from Rinsumageast: "We aren't all the same. It was right after the war, and my sister started it — she wanted to go to the States. There were twelve of us children — an army of boys — and the sister apparently got the ball rolling. Of the twelve kids, ten emigrated; Dad and Mom came in 1957 with the last two. The old man was almost sixty by then, but he was never sorry he came. 'Where the children are, there is my home,' he said.

"Your dad, Andrys Straatsma, always stayed the same. He had a real dry wit. One Saturday morning he was clipping the hedge — I think that was still in Norval — while a legion of grandchildren swarmed around him. A neighbor lady asked how many children he had. 'Twelve,' Andrys answered. 'Oh, my goodness,' the woman exclaimed, 'twelve children!' And how many grandchildren do you have, Mr. Straatsma.' Andrys went right on clipping and chewing his tobacco, and said: 'Around fifty-three or so.' Then she wanted to know if he knew them all by name. 'No!' was the answer, 'but Mom knows all of them.'"

An old lady walks past behind a walker and says: "Men, tomorrow we eat Apricot Honey and Chicken Legs! The menu for tomorrow is already posted." Some of the men pay no attention to the woman, a few follow her with their eyes, one points in her direction with his cane and says: "If as a single man you're still sound in body and mind and you have a license to drive a car, then it wouldn't be hard to get something going here." "Not you, we never let you out of our sight." "I don't regret a thing," says Frank Bruining from Droegeham mildly, "no regret either that we took the big step." "How often haven't I driven my truck through Canada and the USA," Mulder resumes. "I've seen a lot of the world, and I drove enough to make it at least five times around the world."

"Most of us here have a good pension," Hank Kloosterman tempers his initial declarations of regret. "That's right!" says Yde Straatsma. "Everybody has had times of homesickness. Murkje would sometimes stand by the window in the evening, and I thought that she was going soft on me, but you can't let yourself go, you know."

"You have to go far to find a beautiful rest home like this."

"There are people here who are very well off. Multimillionaires are here; Anne de Vries from Snits lives right above here, and that man built up a furniture business you wouldn't believe."

"There are also those who don't want to be buried here in Ontario, they want to lie in a cemetery in Fryslân. There's a Strikwerda from the

Wûnzer area who in Fryslân used to be poor as church mice, but nevertheless, in his old age he went back with his wife. Just so he could be buried in Wûns."

"Wûns!" Pieter Kuiper from Harns, who spent his life as a foreman in the laundry business, says: "I wouldn't be caught dead there."

"You hear a lot of silly talk here."

"Why don't you come on up," says Straatsma, "to our apartment, then you can see what a wonderful view we have from the highest floors."

"Upstairs!" Hank Kloosterman agrees, who's been getting ready to leave the company since he's said what he had to say. "Let's go upstairs, because when the sun is down, everything in the world looks the same."

Yde Straatsma steps into the elevator and rides up to his wife, Murkje. We find her on the flower balcony. In the west the skyline of Toronto is visible, and far in the distance the white buildings of Toronto's airport seem to pull in the last dash of daylight. In the spot on the balcony where the geraniums cascade a bit less profusely out of the flowerbox, stands Yde's chair. He can't stand up for long on account of a bad hip.

"There he sits every afternoon around four o'clock," says Murkje. "Then he waits for his big bird to come. All day long airplanes take off and land, of course, but for Yde the only one that counts is the evening flight of the KLM. That one arrives late in the afternoon.

"When the wind is northeast, it flies lower," says Murkje Straatsma. "Then he gets up out of the chair."

"That's because our buddy flies so low then, I can almost reach him with my cane."

Good Choice

Jan and Jeep Veenstra Dairy, South Africa

B ooks keep getting published about heroes who through the years took the boat all the way to South Africa. Where are the books about the heroines? There are alphabetized registers in South Africa of male immigrants. There are faded photo books chock full of male faces. Tough faces with or without the dirty Krugerian tobacco-juice grooves in the corners of the mouth. (Paul Kruger, the renowned leader of the Boers, chewed tobacco and was well known for the tobacco juice coloring parts of his deeply lined face.) The captions maintain the distorted notion that it was only the male procreators who in South Africa *"diep spore getrap het op baie terreine"* ("stomped deep tracks in many areas").

But what about the courage, the sacrifice, and the tears of all the women? Where did the mothers go? Where may we read about their support, tenacity, and flexibility? They certainly were there, on the exhausting long journey from Leeuwekop to the roaring shores of Natal and the searing heat of Transvaal.

Take Riemkje Heida, for example, the poor farm maid from the Appelskea area. Make no mistake, she cut quite a figure! She was beautiful. Such attractive eyes, such an engaging laugh, such marvelous white teeth. But what kind of a future did an impoverished girl of sixteen have who as oldest in a family of seven children had already buried both parents? Could this Riemkje still hope for a better life than that of father Jeep Heida and her mother Grietsje Hooisma? She was, according to the ways of that time, hired out as farm maid to little Hindrik Pijlman in the Streek neighborhood near Lúnbert. There was no such thing as sympathy on his farm. Riemkje experienced her employment by Hindrik from Lúnbert as the most hard-hearted phase of her turbulent existence.

Her dreams were shattered, her last hope seemed to dissolve forever. That's how she sat, in the muddy milk-yard below Streek road, under a cow that was tough to milk from the purebred herd of farmer Hindrik. The cow turned its rear toward the first fall rain, which meant Riemkje now sat in the wind. But her early dreams didn't let go; she'd dream of a boy with blond hair and blue eyes in a dark-tanned face. He was riding a wobbly cart finding its way in a land full of sun and adventure.

Was there such a land? Was there such a boy? There must be a boy like that somewhere, but he would surely be unreachable for a poor farm maid from Lúnbert.

She had caught a glimpse of him once. On a Sunday morning by the bell-cage of Lúnbert. He looked in her direction for just a second, and froze in place, motionless. Then he went on, apparently on the way to the church of Tsjalbert, the big church that according to the stories paid its minister one of the highest salaries in Fryslân.

Later one evening, the same boy was standing in the twilight with a bunch of buddies in front of the "cooperative," the creamery in the Streek neighborhood. He was standing by his bike, a pretty impressive one. Oh yes, farmer-son Piter had his own bike already! After all, he was one of the nine sons of Jan Linses Veenstra and Wikje Popkema. Smart people.

Riemkje had to milk the cows of little cruel Hindrik at four o'clock in the morning. But in her imagination she was riding with the blond-haired, blue-eyed boy on a big, wobbly cart across a land of sun and adventure.

Behind a large tree, between the cooperative and little Hindrik's farm, the boy waited one quiet Thursday evening. Piter Veenstra. He had been waiting a half hour for the moment that the maid would leave the yard. There she came. She was startled by her own dream and, too self-conscious now, walked right past him. "I have to go to catechism," she said.

Then he said: "Where you're going, I will go." Her dream began to turn into reality, for it had been a dream on both sides.

The cruel farmer told her: "You better not get off the yard too much, or I'll hire you out to a farmer on the clay!" And one early morning he said: "I want to tell you this: the sons of Jan Linses are going to board an ocean steamer one after the other for the land of lions and tigers, to black Africa. Lúnbert is too small for the nine Veenstra boys. You need not figure on anything."

Riemkje knew that already. Some already were naming the Veenstra place "The Transvaal." There was only one of the nine sons, Popke, who wasn't too keen on a farm adventure far across the ocean; so Popke decided to become a teacher. In Holland.

End of September 1923. Piter ventured up the gangplank in Rotterdam and sailed to that land of sun and adventure. Two nights before that, he had waited for her under the big tree for the last time. It wasn't raining, but everything was wet and clammy.

After she came to meet him, they walked together to the bell-cage.

An iron gate squeaked. Behind the thick hedge, no one would disturb them. When later the iron gate squeaked again, she used the words he had spoken that first evening: "Where you're going, I will too."

Farmer Hindrik intercepted the first letter from Piter Veenstra in South Africa to his girlfriend. He stuck it behind the granite mantel clock in the front room. He didn't want to lose his milkmaid to an impossible love. But it was Riemkje herself who discovered the letter.

"In my thoughts I'm with you all the time." That was Piter's first sentence, and that was all she needed. She stuck the letter in her coat, in her mind looked directly into Piter's blue eyes, and left the farm of Hindrik Pijlman forever. Somewhat timidly she made her way to the Veenstra farm and knocked on the door (actually, according to rural custom of the time, stood by the back door and called out: "*Folk,*" announcing her presence). She kept the letter in her coat.

Jan and Wikje Veenstra heartily approved of this farm maid. The old farmer, when saying good-bye to all of his eight emigrating sons, hadn't said for nothing: "Now watch it when you go chasing girls that you take a Frisian wife, let a Frisian come over to South Africa, and then take along a Frisian purebred bull and some heifers too."

The Veenstra boys heeded their father's advice regarding bull and heifers. Except for two. One didn't care for girls, and the other settled for a

Dutch woman. But that woman learned Frisian so well that even their children and grandchildren were able to speak and read Frisian, besides Afrikaans and English.

Riemkje kept the letter in her coat, against her belly. Piter wrote that, near the Spanish coast, he had run into heavy weather with the yearling bull, Titus Adema, and the four young heifers from the Hartwert area. Even though his stomach was turning, he stayed with his cattle in the stuffy hold of the ship. He was no seaman, but he was a farmer.

Her sweet words of response took a few weeks to get there. First they floated along the West African coastline, then they rattled by rail for a couple of days into the rough countryside of the northeast. "I'm also with you all the time in my thoughts, Piter," he read, with the hot sun of *Wittekopsberge* (Whitehead Mountain) in his neck.

He wandered through the wild, mountainous landscape, her letter in his pocket, and he felt a pounding desire rise up. Sometimes he would hear again the squeaking of the iron gate by the Lúnbert bell-cage.

Against the décor of the purple hills in the east, the farm Welbedagt ("well thought out," or "good choice," in Afrikaans) lay behind him, the farm where he had become the manager. Bull Titus had the first heifers with calf already. Piter dreamed of the future and saw a scene with his own black and white cows in his own fields. Some evening the two of them, Riemkje and he, would walk to their cows together.

It rained in Lúnbert, and Riemkje wanted to leave. And she did leave. On foot to It Hearrenfean, with the tram to De Lemmer, with the boat to Amsterdam. And there the ocean steamer, *Oesa Kuma*, was waiting. A shipful of mostly young people. In Lúnbert, some details had again been taken care of: below deck, in the hold of the ship, a couple of purebred heifers from the Hartwert area were busy chewing cud.

The *Oesa Kuma* bunkered in Casablanca, Dakar, Monrovia, Banana, and Walvisbaai (Whale Bay), and a good four weeks later finally dropped anchor in Tafelbaai (Table Bay). A few days later, the copper-colored Karroo (the semi-arid plateau region of southwest South Africa) slid slowly past Riemkje riding on the train. The piercing sun gave way to a cold moon, and she knew that the stars above were bright. The maid from

Lúnbert wasn't even aware that as many male eyes stared at her as there were stars in the sky.

After what seemed forever, the train stopped all worn-out in the small station of Lady Grey, but it could've been Karingmelkspruit too. Just before they fell into each other's arms, she said: "The heifers are here too, Piter."

On the morning of the 28th of March, when for the first time in about six months snow again glittered on the Wittekopbergen, they married. In a ceremony the way the ordinary Afrikaner Boer (African Farmer, literally, and collectively the name of the Dutch colonists and their descendants in South Africa) preferred it: in the large church of Bloemfontein, with a long sermon. As if the words should resound all the way to Lúnbert. Riemkje was not wearing all white.

Nature took its course. Titus had most of the heifers with calf. Piter, manager of the farm Welbedagt, dreamed of his own "Frisian herd." The old folks across the seas were regularly informed, and the letters were saved: ". . . the blackleg has calved, a bull." And, ". . . we have a leopard . . . the hardly dry calf of Wikje VI was seized and dragged up the high cliffs."

Piter and Riemkje had two worthy advisers available to them on Welbedagt. First there was Piter's oldest brother Linse, who had already landed there in 1909 when he was hardly twenty years old, and had since that time become lecturer at the Glen Agricultural College in Potschefstroom. This oldest son of Jan and Wikje, born in Nij-Beets, would become the biggest name in the dairy industry of his time in South Africa.

The other adviser was Simon Lekuto, the oldest black farmhand of Welbedagt. Simon might not know the day of his birthday, but he knew the secrets of the landscape. The black man was there when Titus was let loose for the first time with the Adema heifers. And he accompanied his new boss into the fields, a white man wearing heavy wooden shoes, a blue work shirt, and a pair of canvas working trousers.

He and the boss, in search of a new water source for large tracts of cork-dry land. They roamed, farther and farther, higher and higher. With a stone, Simon knocked on a rock that looked like the back of a turtle. The old black man licked the moisture of the shards and tasted, looked at the farmer, reflected deeply, and explained that they should have another try higher up.

That afternoon, a miracle unfolded: a little higher up water was flowing down, beautiful water that disappeared into the dark claws of the huge mountain range. Simon was sure of it: there was so much water in these cliffs that a stream could be directed to the dry land that lay diagonally above Welbedagt. "With this water," Simon determined, "grass will grow for as many heifers as there are crickets that call out at night on the yard of Welbedagt." The old man hadn't even struck the rocks with his stick; the water was already there.

The new farmer of Welbedagt later saw to it with the help of his hired men that the water was directed to the dry land.

Simon taught his boss the first words of the Xhosa language. And he himself learned, with his aptitude for language, his first Frisian. So that, when Piter was conferring on the yard with his brother Linse one day, and Simon came past, he said: "*O baas, ek het 't lankal gehoor wat jullie sê: 'de boys mutte de kij ophelje.'*" (A mixture of Afrikaans and Frisian: "Oh boss, I know what you were saying: 'The boys have to fetch the cows.'")

On the farm, Apartheid had already been in place for generations, but then as an unwritten law. At the same time, in everyday life, black and white lived so closely together that they nevertheless formed a kind of unit. Simon showed his boss on the cliffs the spot where the young boys were circumcised. The farmer saw to it that a public shower was installed on the grounds where the boys could rinse themselves after circumcision. The farmer had chewing tobacco come for Simon from De Jouwer, and Simon took the farmer to the secret place where now and then he would get and smoke the dagga (a South African herb akin to marijuana). And once in a while he would let one of his three women come there too. That evening, when the old man with his gray curls would trudge across the yard behind the wheelbarrow, there wasn't much spunk left in him. And that's how each did their own thing around there.

Warm letters floated across the waters to and from the low country too. Always important news: Titus could be credited with the first new-milking heifers, and Riemkje was pregnant. And everything was flourishing.

In the Streek neighborhood of Lúnbert, the old folks knew too that on

Welbedagt the water from the high rocks had been diverted to the dry valleys. "It's a question there by you too of land development," Jan Linses observed proudly. Hadn't they themselves also gotten on their feet by land reclamation?

One time Simon had to alert his boss to the fact that the big game had bewitched Titus. So the boss better be careful with the bull. Titus had seen the "big cat," the leopard, sneak around. Once domesticated cattle get a whiff of big game, they get the "bush" in their system and can never be trusted again.

One day Piter Veenstra wandered in the direction of the mountains.

There was snow already on the Wittekoppen. The farmer was curious how Titus and his large harem of heifers were doing in the newly green valley.

What Piter Veenstra encountered after an hour's stroll was nothing less than an idyllic still life: gleaming black and white bodies against the dark of gigantic heights. White, yellow, and purple flowers were teeming everywhere. He counted the heifers, estimated how many were with young, and noted how the bull calmly ruled his harem. The animal looked up, observed the farmer in the blue shirt, the man with whom he had been seasick on a groaning ship in a storm, and resumed his peaceful grazing. And he kept grazing even when the farmer came through the barbed wire and proudly walked toward his herd.

But then, suddenly, the rage unleashed in Titus that Simon Lekuto had warned his boss about. The bull strode toward the dark figure, eyes wild, nostrils wide open.

The farmer rushed back to the barbed-wire fence, but he was just too late. The bull rammed and rammed. Four times, five times. Until his victim hung like a rag on the barbed wire. That's when Piter Veenstra pleaded: "Lord God, save me!"

The bull, sniffing, backed up a little more. It was preparing for the ultimate attack. At that moment Piter Veenstra twisted to get himself through the barbed wire fence, with two broken legs, a shattered shoulder, eight broken ribs, and numerous internal injuries.

The evening fell; a slice of moon rose above the Wittekopbergen; a wild cat on the craggy rocks called out; and then the folk of Welbedagt found their boss. A small ox wagon pulled by a team of horses came. An uncomfortable ride to the small hospital in Aliwal-Noord followed.

"You have to get well," Riemkje whispered to him in the night.

"I'm going to get well!" she heard. "And then we're going to take a baptism journey; then we will go with our child to the big church of Tsjalbert."

Little Jan was four when Piter Veenstra was almost himself again. The farmer and his wife of Welbedagt embarked on the German steamer *Adolf Wörmann* to the land behind the dikes. It was in the early spring of 1932. They arrived on a Sunday morning. One week later their boy was baptized.

Jan Piters Veenstra, farmer in the Transvaal hamlet of Veenstra Dairy near Pretoria, has, sixty-seven years later, not forgotten his baptism journey. He still remembers how one morning, between his dad and mom, he walked into the Reformed Church. The little boy heard an organ play the way it played in Bloemfontein, but then with a somewhat lighter sound. He noticed that there was a little bird in church that flew from one beam to the other. A bit later he felt the tepid baptismal water run down his cheek, he felt how the warmth of Grandma Wikje's lap rose up in him. He remembers how Grandpa's beard prickled when you touched it, how boys were jumping with a pole across a ditch, how good it was to hold in his cap in his hand for a moment a lapwing's egg that a neighbor carried, how he looked at the land that was as flat as a calm sea, and how he listened to the language which to him sounded as awe-inspiring as the thunder over the heights of Natal. All of that was Lúnbert in the beginning of April 1932.

A lifetime later. The two gray-haired sons of Piter and Riemkje tell of their parents with much admiration. They tell in a musical Frisian about Dad and Mom's mystical connection to the land where they didn't want to stay. However contradictory and incomprehensible, there's still a strong thread that reaches across the seas to that low, wet country. The emotions still flow through that thread, as the sound of voices flows through telephone wires. It goes across continents and through the depths of the sea. Jan and Jeep Veenstra hardly have a realistic image of that faraway country, for they weren't born there. But in ways that are beyond explanation, that connection still has a daily impact on their way of life. The South African descendants of Jan and Wikje Veenstra from Lúnbert — and by now there must be more than a hundred of them — deeply appreciate their unique inheritance.

"I believe that Dad and Mom loved each other a lot," says Jeep Piters Veenstra, retired agricultural engineer. "When they later moved farther north and eventually retired at Groenkloof, Dad admitted one time that they had had a tough but beautiful life. Then he said to Mom: 'You and I have it so good, Riemkje.' Later Mom passed that same feeling on in her own words to the children and grandchildren: 'Our life was like the jacaranda, the tree that blooms so early and so abundantly. And when the tree loses its blossoms, then the leaves are still to come. We live content in the shade of the jacaranda.'"

"That was at Groenkloof," adds his brother Jan, "that must've been in 1964. A year later Dad passed away." At that time Jan had been his dad's successor for some time already and had expanded the little hamlet of Veenstra Dairy. Jan even ventured to mix his Frisian herd with Jersey blood. Oh, that "mingling," how the old man had at first hated it. But it turned out later that Veenstra Dairy did not only produce a lot of milk, but also milk with a higher fat content.

"When years later Mom also passed away, Jeep discovered some amazing stuff underneath the floor at Groenkloof." Jeep remembers the treasure trove. "There was a large space under the floor beneath their bedrooms. Dad thought a double floor was good for rheumatism. First I dug up a wooden box. Their letters were in there. And, not to forget, the tobacco pipe that a very distant uncle had made on St. Helena after the British had put the Boers away in concentration camps. The British who are still deeply hated here. We see that pipe as the symbol of Dad's strong distaste for the British.

"Dad and Mom led the way in our aversion to everything British. In the Boer War they chased the Boers from their own farms and imprisoned their children, thereby trying to break down the Boer resistance. Those

British who destroyed the Boer language the way they destroy so many languages in the world."

Underneath the floor was another symbol of sorts: Piter Jans Veenstra's first pair of wooden shoes to be worn out on Welbedagt. "And I found a Frisian tile that meant a lot to Mom: *'Dêr't God in doar tichtslacht, docht Er in finster iepen'* ('Where God closes a door, He opens a window')."

"You found something else too, Jeep."

"There were a couple of large tin cans that I think had had tobacco in them for Dad and Simon Lekuto. Now it contained the mothballed baptism outfits of their two boys. And what else? Long, knitted socks. A silent hint to the descendants to keep the road open to Fryslân."

Flowering Bark

Willem van Dijk and Aaltsje van Dijk-van Essen,
Durbanville, South Africa

It's a warm October day. The mountains and valleys, cliffs and brooks, farms and neighborhoods — everything bears the name of what it is. The Klapmutsberch is an old full-bottomed lace-cap, the Tigerberch a tiger because against the sand-colored slopes there are dark bushes everywhere. Here the connection between language, nature, and logic still applies. Here runs the Groenrivier, the stream with a green sheen; and when one drives across the Platteklip, it's an elevation on which a giant with a gigantic spade flattened the top. And that's how the trip from the northwest to the Cape becomes a journey through Nameland.

We land on the Hoge Kop, where the Atlantic Ocean stretches below into infinity. On this day the wet giant lies there like a blue mirror in the blazing sun. A narrow silver rim cautiously touches the African continent. Robben Island gleams in the distance. Higher up to the north is the atomic power plant, a shape that looks like nothing else on earth. Hence they could think of no other name for it than atomic station.

The small city of Durbanville. A narrow bypass road. In the dale the water reservoir of the winegrower, large enough for the kids to sail their boats on. Across it, against the slopes, the villa district with short, wide lanes of asphalt that roll in rhythm with the hills. Lanes are wet from the garden sprinklers. Independent-minded houses in red, brown, and yellow. By a tall white wall, a tree with a rough outer bark that features flowering parasites. Red flowers so beautiful that one forgives the plant for belonging to the category of parasites.

A spacious home. A yard that looks like a slice of overseas cradle-land. *"Fryslân Hiem"* ("Friesland Yard") it says in iron-forged letters. The garden doors are open, and on the inside of the house a Frisian clock strikes two o'clock. The young red-breasted thrushes apparently are so used to the strange bird that they keep right on hopping around by the open doors, foraging for food.

The man comes down the path to meet his guest. In tennis shoes. Willem Linses van Dijk. Gray and in good shape, not too short and not too tall, not too fat and not too thin. Ninety years old. He begins with an anecdote about the Easterwierrum from a long human lifetime ago.

His wife who married him sixty-three years ago, Aaltsje Tymens van Essen from Swichum. She's standing beside him now. The blue in her blouse is the blue of the ocean a distance away, the blue of the sky, the blue of her eyes. She announces that the tea is ready. The teapot sits on the single-burner kerosene stove that came with them on *Her Majesty Pretoria Castle* longer than half a century ago and never fell out of fashion. Part of a couple of cratefuls of goods packed in Easterbierrum, the contents that sailed along to the Cape of Good Hope.

The kitchen smells like the Swichum of just past the war, after the day that Jan Piteroalje (John Kerosene) had visited on his dogcart. The door to another room is ajar, and I see half a wall lined with books. Books everywhere. Afrikaans, English, German, Frisian.

"We kept our health," she says suddenly. "It could've been different, like Drys and Ine. The Douwingas. Did you know them? Ine came from the Tútsebrêge, that's between Grou and Warten. The poor dear had just had a baby."

"Drys came here ahead of her," Willem van Dijk recalls. "He boarded with us for a time. Ine had to come alone with the little boy on a crowded Fonteinboat to the Cape, and that wasn't easy."

His wife continues the story. "Drys was in the dairy products business and landed with Ine and their little boy a thousand kilometers away, on the border of Lesotho. Godforsaken little place, not so far from the Drakensberch. Ine homesick, then the baby got sick, seriously sick. There was no help where they lived or good medical advice and support. And then the baby passed away. It was a scene that has never left us: a young distraught couple inside a grubby shack with bare walls. And on the table the coffin with their dead child."

"Ine didn't get old," he says. He stands there as if by the grave, hands on his back, and face down. "Drys is still living there all by himself," she thinks. "Aaltsje writes Frisian letters to him. But Drys is not a writer."

The living room. Above the door a plate with the message in Frisian that the same sun shines on us, regardless where in the world we may be. And *"Hoe fet sopkje oarmans petielen en buormans kij jaen grutte mielen"* ("How lavish another's dish and the neighbor's cows produce lots of milk"). Behind her, above the tea table, a silver-clasped handbag with a thousand beads. A relic from a farm family who through the turmoil of the thirties were swept off their place. The farmer of that time, Tymen Gerbens van Essen, one-time winner of the Golden Violin — an award for those who contributed much to the Frisian Orchestra — the farmer who in his white slacks milked his cows. If he's to be called an aristocrat, then it was an aristocrat who on winter days saw to it that needy families in Swichum would get the beestings from his newly fresh cows. By dark, for no one needed to see his good deeds. That's how the poor fell under the mercy of the man of the people. But the Depression had no mercy. Van Essen ran out of means and lost his farm.

Willem van Dijk's anecdote about Easterbierrum: "It was in wintertime, and across from the ice pub [a favorite tanking spot for weary skaters] on the Dille [the bridge across the Swette, a centuries-old waterway between Snits and Ljouwert] a small barge lay frozen in the ice. 'Well,' the skipper said one morning, 'I'm going to skate to Yfke in Dokkum [a distance of more than twenty-five miles].' In the later afternoon the same skipper was back in the ice pub. 'You're back already, skipper! You sure must've had quite an exhausting trip,' the people exclaimed. 'Let me tell you,' the skipper answered, 'here on the Swette I put my head down, and when I raised it again, I was in Dokkum.'"

Mrs. van Essen says: "Life at that time, the atmosphere, our background — you hardly lose any of that. And really, do you know what I think is especially nice? That our children and grandchildren here also know where we came from. That way they understand something of what we're all about. You have such a nice example of that, Willem."

"When we reached the point of doing pretty well here," he continues, "we took our children and later the grandchildren too to Raerd, Dearsum, Easterwierrum, Wiuwert."

"And to Swichum!"

"And to Swichum! 'Look,' I said to the grandkids, 'my grandfather and grandmother lived here, in this small home. And they were so poor. And here, in Raerd, in this little nook, my father died when he was only fifty-eight. And the letter I so often told you about, the letter that as a young boy I had to take from Raerd to Wiuwert — well, do you see that church tower in the distance? That's where I had to go first, and then to that village over there. On foot, all the way.'

"One of the grandchildren said — it was Anthony: *'Pake, dis vroeg in die dag, ons sal loop so pake die pad geloop het, ons sal hier al die doen en late van pake en beppe in Fryslân voel'* ('Grandpa, early in the morning we will walk the same path you walked, here in Fryslân we want to get a sense of all that you and Grandma did').

"And then they walked that path from Raerd to Wiuwert and back again," she interrupts. "And when the kids came back that evening all excited and couldn't ask us enough questions, it was just like an old chapter had now been concluded. After that we didn't — how do I say it: grieve — as much when our thoughts went back to Fryslân."

In the bookcase in another corner of the room, in a prominent place, are the Frisian and English versions of Shakespeare. Underneath the glass coffee table lies the *Chronicle of a Frisian Farmer (1821-1856)*, the notebook of Doeke Wigers Hellema from Wurdum.

"When our Gabe — grown up here and married to an English-speaking woman — when Gabe goes back to Fryslân, his first stop is the bookstore De Tille. So that's why. Here in South Africa we have all six volumes of the Frisian Yearbooks of 1771. 'From the earliest recollections to the present time.' Isn't it amazing that the people who left get the chance this way to take Friesland's heritage along overseas!"

"It's got a good place here," comments Mrs. van Dijk.

Now and then Willem van Dijk tries to keep his hands out of sight. His hands have been attacked by skin cancer, those hands that built hundreds of homes, turned thousands of pages, that now carefully lower the needle on the phonograph record. Caruso's Rudolfo from "La Bohème." On His Masters Voice. His hands: a finger is missing already, and it looks like he's going to lose others. The hands of a man who for a lifetime, from early in the morning to late at night, labored in the African sun, built up a construction company, and whose property includes the apartment complex visible from here with who knows how many units.

"When we left Easter,wierrum, that was hard." She picks up on a fragment from a long story. "My family was not in favor of it. Maybe I should say it this way: they were dead set against it. But you go anyway. One day the bus stops to take you to Ljouwert. I can still see Aunt Tryntsje stand there on the street below Barhûs waving good-bye. And that was it."

He: "How shall I say it, it's like tearing a bunch of marigolds in full bloom out of the ground. Maybe that same bunch of flowers will manage one day to bloom on the other side of the world, but there's a hole left behind in the ground from which it was torn."

She: "The marigolds did bloom again here."

He: "We were all packed and stood with the small boys in the door with Mom. A very old little widow lady. I still see how she bent down to the oldest of the two, to Linse, and said: 'I hope that you, when you come back, will bend down to me like this.'"

Mrs. van Dijk has her own memories of those last days. "Mrs. Spekman, the innkeeper from Easterbierrum, stopped me the night before. In the middle of the neighborhood. The woman must've felt how I dreaded leaving. 'What all are you taking along to the new country,' she wanted to know. 'All the furniture, Mrs. Spekman,' I said, 'all the bedding, and pretty much everything.' Then she pinched my arm and said, 'Then you will soon feel at home there, Aaltsje, then you'll be all right there!'"

He: "After thirteen days on the *Pretoria Castle*, we got sight of the Tafelberch (Table Mountain). That almost brought some of the people around us in a celebration mood, but I felt a kind of emotion of fear descend on me. I wondered what life there, behind those mountains, would bring us. I was well over forty, and you become a little more sensible. Not much later we found ourselves in a rickety trailer, and I had to bike twenty-five kilometers a day to reach my job. Six, sometimes seven days a week. We had boarders, and sometimes we lived with two households under one roof. We wanted to scrape enough money together to buy a piece of land where we could build our own house. That's how we struggled ahead, with the result that eventually we could provide good work and wages for a number of other households from all races and colors."

"It wasn't for nothing," Mrs. van Dijk concludes. "Later we could afford to take a trip now and then to Fryslân, stay in Oranjewâld [a fairly exclusive resort hotel], and eat on the water at Aldeskou."

"Ja, ja!" His voice is intentionally loud. "We were sometimes given the cold shoulder there too. I remember, we were back for the first time and were biking through the village of Sibrandabuorren, and there was farmhand cleaning out a canal along the road. We dismounted to make some conversation. Almost right away the man asked: 'And where do you come from.'

"'South Africa,' I said.

"'I'll be darned!' the man scoffed, 'Over there you let the poor blacks handle this kind of work, of course.' That gives you kind of a sick feeling for a moment."

His wife is searching for a new subject. The books, for example. And the music. "After his seventieth, Willem's hobbies came more into their own. The literature, the music disks with the famous tenors. Reading and music, it turned out, was Willem's world."

"For me there was only one world and that was the world of work!" It sounds almost irritable. "With my music and reading I'm done. My eyes, my hearing, my hands — they all leave me in the lurch. The worst of all is losing your hearing. The most beautiful music now sounds off-key in my ears. A few nights ago I played the Russian bass Fedor Shalyapin. Shalyapin sings Boris in the opera of Boris Godunov by Mussorgsky. And all of a sudden it sounded way off-key. I can't trust my ears anymore. Shalyapin; that man could write prose beautifully too, and now I'm going to tackle his memoirs, but my reading doesn't go so well anymore either."

"Beethoven in his forty-eighth year was stone-deaf, in his fiftieth he was overcome by paranoia, and eventually he and his housekeeper exchanged only notes," she says.

"Well, it hasn't come to that yet with us!"

A little later: "Aaltsje writes nice letters for overseas. Nice letters in Frisian."

The Frisian clock has already registered the first full hour when he starts about Wiuwert. Willem van Dijk is a man one simply has to listen to. "1908. Dad and Mom were of the poor farm laborers class. Now I sometimes think, what kind of a life was that really! Stuck by a farmer, stuck in a vicious circle of making a living that was almost impossible to escape. That darn hard clay with those darn difficult people. And Dad working his tail off, and Mom making sure that all the necessities were provided for and even saving a few cents. Dad, I'm sure, had his dreams too; he didn't expect to always and ever work for somebody else. In 1910 — I was a boy of two — we emigrated to Germany. Linse and Teakje left with all they had. From Wiuwert to Keulen in those days was considered farther than Kraalfontein is today. In Germany the laborer earned almost double what he could make in Wiuwert."

Willem van Dijk gets up, strides toward a wall lined with books, searches the spines, tries to find a work about Bismarck, comes back without results, and says: "He was probably a scoundrel, that Bismarck, but the working men were going to be well off in his new equality-state. You could still tell that in the beginning of this century. The old fire-eater by that time had of course been pushed out.

"Dad landed in the coal mines of the Ruhr, and one day a loaded dump-cart ran over his leg. It looked grim, he couldn't stand on it, and it took half a year to heal. But during all that time he did get paid and that helped us to squeak by."

Old Mrs. van Dijk had told Aaltsje about it: "Women who were sloppy housekeepers had to pay full rent in Germany, but those who always kept a neat home and well-scrubbed children received a discount."

"That's how the ghost of Bismarck was still floating around," he says. "Well, Mom was so tidy that we ended up finally living there free. In 1914 my parents had saved up quite a nice number of marks. And I'm not talking about paper money. The First World War broke out when I was six and had to start school. Before school in the morning I would see the columns march off. Off to the front lines. To the East front, and to the West front. 'They march with a rose on the barrel of their guns,' Dad said, shaking his head. 'While singing, they're marching straight to death.' 'I'm worried about us,' Mom sighed. 'I feel like looking for work on the farm again,' Dad said, 'because things really have to get bad for a farmer to run out of food.'

"Dad working for a farmer again, I to another school again, another unfamiliar classroom, another unfamiliar teacher.

"As young as I was, I knew what it meant to emigrate. When the teacher would ask me something, in strident high German, I'd stand beside my desk already, at attention. '*Gott straft England!*' ('God punishes England!') I had to call out. What later would become 'Heil Hitler!' was then '*Gott straft England!*' All right, I still had to answer the teacher's question, but because of my fear I had forgotten it, so for punishment I held out my hand. I would get as many slaps as my age. And not to move a muscle, for in my new country there was only room for heroes. As an *Ausländer* (foreigner) I tried to hold my own on the playground. 'You skunk!' 'You damn Hollander!' they would yell. Once in a while I would resist and not do what they commanded. 'Go to the devil,' I'd scream, 'I'm not going to do it!' That's how I learned to take care of myself. Later on I would get spanked with a stick, so one morning I sat in my desk with a bulky folded-together newspaper in my pants. When the teacher found out, I got the licking of my life that I can still feel. Don't think that I was permanently traumatized; not at all. But I learned my German well. To have command of four major languages, that's nothing but a privilege. You learn to work automatically. Child labor? That makes me laugh. When other kids were playing, I was looking for grubs on the cabbage.

"We lived in Steel, a village below Gelsenkirchen, and it was the summer of the Battle at Verdun. In a few weeks' time, there were 100,000 casualties just on the German side and nearly 300,000 wounded. It was a summer evening when I was standing on the quiet side of the train station platform. Right in front of me I saw how carloads of wounded were unloaded. Wrecked bodies, lying on a stretcher; men with one leg hopping on two crutches; one with his head all bandaged, his throat rattling from the gas in the trenches. And a mother who screamed because her youngest son apparently had died on the way back. And I just stood there, eight years old, and it was long clear to me: God didn't just punish England.

"'We have to get out of here, Linse,' I heard Mom say, 'we have to get back across the border.' Mom was a daughter of De Rook from De Lemmer, so she not only had music in her but also a sense of adventure.

"Evenings I would hear Dad talk softly about Wiuwert. The way he would say the name of that village, that strange diphthong slide in 'Wiuwert'! For me the village acquired a heavenly sound. 'But our money,' he said, 'what will my marks be worth pretty soon in Wiuwert.' Mom countered: 'But we have to worry about five growing children.'

"'But that's why we came here, Teakje, for the kids. We did it for the children.'

"'We have to leave here.'"

In Fryslân, meanwhile, they had only heard the war in the far distance. That must've been in the noisy morning of the first of June 1916. Beyond the northern horizon there was a rumbling, sounds carried by the breezes high up in the air. There came a confused account of the Battle of Jutland in which 150 English and 90 German battleships tried to smash each other to smithereens.

"Sipke was our oldest son and could be drafted into the German armed forces and sent to the front. That was enough reason to escape to Fryslân with the whole bunch. But Kees had caught TB and had to stay down. Mom was conflicted, and Dad lost his job on the dairy farm: the farmer, his employer, had become a casualty in the Battle on the Somme. A few days earlier I had seen a couple of women trudge with a bunch of cows in the direction of the butcher. One evening Dad said that he would start working early the next morning in one of the Alfred Krupp factories. And at the railroad station I noticed how older men now would be walking out on the station platform and catch the train to the Western Front. The horses that were loaded on were hardly trained, while others were getting too old.

"When in Verdun even General von Hindenburg failed to subdue the French and allies, things got tough. Now there was clearly talk about *Kinderarbeit* (child labor), and I participated without being aware of it. At home we ate only *Kartoffelbrei mit Wirsingkohl* and *Wirsingkohl mit Kartoffeln* (potato porridge with savoy cabbage and savoy cabbage with potatoes). That same winter we ran out of food. Every morsel was consumed by the war effort. Sipke managed to get back to Fryslân. After that came the winter in which I learned what real hunger was all about.

"One early morning after the hard winter of 1917, Dad and Mom took a chance and traveled back to Wiuwert. As a boy of hardly nine I felt very keenly that this was a matter of going for broke. At the Dutch border — I'm not sure where — you could cut the tension with a knife. I can still see Dad emerge at last from the German border patrol office. He walked with his head down. Without looking at us, he pointed to the gates. Were we allowed to go through? Yes, we were, but something was wrong. Not until much later I understood what it was: Dad had discovered that the seventy-five hundred marks that he and Mom had saved up in those six distressing years were hardly worth half of that in guilders.

"It was late one night when we landed in the little ginger-nut house of Grandpa and Grandma in the Wiuwert neighborhood. What I can still see in front of me is the wrought-iron work of the window above the door and a tight little sleeping space against a boarded roof. For Dad and Mom it was a happy homecoming, but to me it was immigrating all over again. A couple days later Dad reported to a farmer for milking at four in the morning. And on the school's playing ground, they drummed it into me that I was a *smoarge poep!* (dirty kraut). That new boy used foreign words now and then and couldn't even write decent Dutch. And what strange penmanship he had. And who jumped to attention when the teacher asked a question.

"There wasn't enough room in the ginger-nut house, so one day I suddenly found myself staying with Aunt Anne in Mantgum. Now I had to attend school there. And there it became apparent that I was a very good student, and before long I felt safe there.

"I had to take a letter from my aunt to Wiuwert. 'Willem isn't doing so bad; as far as eating goes: where does it all go!' One time I had met the specter of hunger, one time a demanding stomach had plagued me, one time that pounding longing for food had spooked around in my head. This is what it comes down to — I had wanted to use my stomach in Mantgum as a hoarding place.

"When Dad took a job with a farmer near Raerd, we moved there. It must've been around that time when a man came over one Saturday night who seemed to know a lot about money. Somebody who had a good reputation in Jirnsum too. The man's good advice was taken: the money slaved for in Germany was invested in an international fund with an impressive name.

"The man had the guts to return. As a kind of messenger of death. That was a few years later. In short, the bank went broke and the money was lost. That was a tremendous blow for Dad and Mom; I can still feel the gloom that descended on our family. It wasn't just the money that was lost, but the reward for seven years of war and exile was gone to blazes.

"If Dad advised against it or not, I'm not sure, but when I was finished with school it was a foregone conclusion that I should not become a farm-worker. But what else could a boy of fourteen do in those days? Exactly! Work for the blacksmith. Or for the baker or the painter or the carpenter. It turned out to be carpentry. That night when I came home with my own self-earned money — oh man!

"'You're going to get the chance to become a craftsman,' the other carpentry worker assured me.

"But Dad's health deteriorated. 'My strength is waning,' that's how it started. It must've been on a Saturday night, I can still see Mom beat a couple of eggs for Dad. He was so thin, and he had vomited. I still see his large, questioning eyes before me.

"'Dad doesn't feel quite right,' they said. And always getting up in the dark early in the morning, struggling to get his socks on, and coming back home late at night. One day, it wasn't dark yet, he came in and couldn't stand up anymore. He was completely done in. He died a short time later. When I reconstruct the whole business, I think it must've been a brain tumor.

"It was as if by that one blow I became an adult. All of a sudden you're the oldest one at home and feel yourself responsible for Mom and the couple of kids who're still at home. You're nineteen, twenty years old, your desires wake up, you dream of having a girlfriend, but it gives you the shivers at the same time. Why? Let me tell you! Because you're afraid of poverty. And you're afraid of the worst ogre that exists for a child: hunger."

Willem van Dijk interrupts his story and leaves the room for a moment. "It's possible that he's getting a book," Aaltsje says. And a bit later: "When Willem and I met each other for the first time, I discovered that he was eight years older than I was. I was a farmer's daughter, like I said. He was a carpentry worker. When he took me home, I knew right away that he was more than just a carpentry worker; he had character.

"The carpentry business of Douma badly needed Willem: to a large extent he was the man who kept the business going. But there was one thing wrong with Willem: he was not Catholic. So, he couldn't become the manager. That's how the world was at the time."

"There were four Douma sons." Willem van Dijk has rejoined. "Those four were Tsjerk, Jan, Tseard, and Feike. Even though I could do ten times the work of those four, other laws were in force then. The laws of Rome. I put up with it for three years, and then I came to the obvious conclusion. I was thirty-nine. I wanted to start on my own, but I stumbled over all kinds of barriers: establishment regulations for this, a permit for that, a diploma for this, credit ratings for that.

"During the Depression I'd read a lot about South Africa. Not that I had my head full of romantic images; I didn't see myself bump along on an oxcart with wife and kids exactly, but I did hear that many Afrikaners became casualties in the Second World War and that there was a crying need for craftsmen. And then the climate, of course, the space, the freedom. Don't think that it was really a political decision. Once you got South Africa in your head and applied, then you landed in South Africa."

"I didn't want to go," his wife repeats, "I didn't cooperate very much." It sounds like an excuse. "Honey!" Willem van Dijk loses composure momentarily again, chokes up. Then: "This afternoon we went back over our life. It shakes me up now and then. To actually take that big step was hard. But after that, Aaltsje, you were a wonder. What you and I haven't overcome and experienced in these sixty-three years of marriage, that's made me realize, yes, how shall I put it, how even as an immigrant I could never have found a better wife."

Later, when she offers a couple of apples for the trip back, she says: "I'm now at a stage of really wanting to go back to Fryslân, but like Willem said, we *can't* go back. Here are our children who pulled us through, everything is here. And they're not waiting for us in Easterbierrum, Wiuwert, or Wurdum."

They walk down the garden path to the asphalt driveway. She stops by the flowering plant that grows on the rough bark of an old tree, and says: "When necessary, everything that's alive can survive on very little."

Frisian Nick

*Lyckele de Jong and Aly de Jong-ten Boom
from Te Aroha, New Zealand*

D own in the South Island of New Zealand, in the early fifties, on a
wintery Sunday in July. Lyckele Lyckles de Jong, hailing from
Aldeskoat, woke up that morning in Roxburgh and saw that the tree ferns
were coated with white, and he couldn't believe his eyes. Who would have
expected that: winter in the land of tree ferns. And besides, it happened to
be his first free day in his new life.

He had been working night and day in the huge construction project
of the flood control dam, and now he lucked out by having beautiful winter weather. His aged father had been right after all when at the last minute
he slipped his skates into the suitcase. A pair of Vonk-skates, made in
Aldeskoat. That was half a year ago. Lyckele Junior had said that the skates
wouldn't be needed.

"I want to start a new life, Dad!"

But Senior had insisted: "If there are streams in that land, or there's a
small flooded piece of land, and a good freeze should come along, you
would go crazy if you didn't have your skates handy." Then Lyckele let him
have his way. Two Vonk speed skates with new heel leathers in the suitcase.

The dam south of the New Zealand Alps, in the wild Otago region,
had to bring a wild river, the Clutha, under control. It was a masterful
piece of work, that dam. Lyckele was excited about it and put in as much
overtime as possible. And now, after a good three months of slaving away,
he had time off to explore the area. The project guys told him that there
were beautiful lakes a bit farther up. Lakes that had never been sailed and

likely never been skated either. Farther up more wild rivers roared, he heard his co-workers tell, even places where since creation no human had ever set foot.

Suddenly Lyckele got the notion to climb Mt. Whitecomb, with its white crown, the mountain that had now and then looked at him with a challenge in its smile. So he rented a feisty, fox-colored horse and started out.

He made the top in the early part of the afternoon already. There he stood with his mount in the snow. The clear weather provided a sharp aerial view of the valley. He hadn't seen the construction project and the river like this before: a silver thread with a thick knot.

In a letter to his girlfriend, Aly ten Boom, in Sint Jansgea he wrote that the tower of Sint Jut and Aldeskoat would both fit a hundred times into the dam under construction. But, he asked himself in that same letter, which Great Works, made by human hand, would appear great in this impressive landscape of mountains, fjords, and extraordinary flowers and animals. "This land is as if from a different planet, it has its own unique human and animal kingdom. I can hardly comprehend in what kind of paradise I've landed."

When Aly had read the letter, she could hardly breathe from longing. She only wanted one thing: to go to Lyckele and his paradise. To Nick, because that's the name he now had, "Frisian Nick."

Right after the war, he was one of thousands of emigrants who left for New Zealand as single men. New Zealand offered everyone a labor contract, and that's how they got a chance to work for a roof over their heads; and then, after a year or so, to let their great love come over. Aly and Nick lived for that, each on one side of the globe.

It was a week after the climb of Mt. Whitecomb, and now it had frozen so hard that it awakened a very strange longing in Frisian Nick: a nice piece of ice to skate on. After wandering and exploring on his fox-colored horse — some grain for the horse, a snack for himself, and the skates along — he landed between two hills. And then his eye fell on a narrow cleft. Did he see a glimpse of a blue-gray plain? He risked a narrow path, and there appeared almost magically before him a frozen lake, a plain the size of the Tsjûkemar.

He let the horse eat the snow, tried out the ice, determined that it was at least five inches thick, and tied on his skates. Very cautiously he ventured up the lake, but it didn't take long for him to put his hands behind his back. And then Lyckele, alias Frisian Nick, took off.

Above the immeasurable depths, he heard the crackling of the ice. Now and then it intensified into the loud rumble of a warning. But Frisian Nick from Aldeskoat was one who apparently couldn't resist the challenge of danger and skated on. To him there was no more compelling concert than that which arises from the vaults located somewhere under the layer of ice. He immersed himself in the music, of what was otherwise a soundless day, on a bottomless lake amidst the mountains of a remote region. This music had no composer, he thought, or it must be the Creator himself.

He had circled the whole lake, and it was clear that the ice could be trusted all around. And then something happened that to him had all the appearance of a mysterious miracle. It must've been around two o'clock in the afternoon. A couple of figures appeared in the cleft, and they were coming toward the ice. They were carrying skates. Frisian skates. They turned out to be fellows who had been searching for a good place to skate. There was a farm laborer from Akmaryp, a builder from Huzum, and a fellow from Snits who, after he had come out of hiding after the war, had stayed around working for a farmer in Earnewâld, close to Grou, but who one day had quietly taken off.

The men shook hands with each other, said where they came from, tied on their skates, pinched their nose between thumb and forefinger and blew it empty, and together started out. They took off like a flight of geese in formation and floated over the shiny ice, till, against the décor of the purple hills, they could no longer be seen. In fact, there was no one here to watch them. Within an hour they came back, and it seemed like they were skating in time to their own music. They took just a short break to catch their breath, then they felt the skating-urge return. Again they took off. They kept it up till the chill of the evening reminded them of day's end. Then the farm laborer from Akmaryp broke his silence for the first time: "I have the solution to this mystery, men. Just like bees have a kind of radar in their heads to help them find the honey fields, so we have radar in our heads that sent us in the direction of the ice." They agreed: that's the way it was.

It's almost fifty New Zealand years later, and Nick has been a retired farmer for many years, living with Aly in the village of Te Aroha, on the North Island of New Zealand. Now they live much closer to the equator than they did in the deep south of the country, so here the cattle can be outside in every season.

When "Frisian Nick" gets started about those first years in the wilderness of Otago, he has to do it standing up. Then it's like the whole landscape, with all its images and sounds, comes to life.

"It was in the first year, when the Clutha River and I were both still wild. You could hear the sound of the river by night and day. In the summer, during dry spells, the river sang more timidly, something like the choir from Aldeskoat that always started a little timidly when it performed at Tjaarda's in Oranjewâld. But it could change, to the fortissimo of the autumn song, transforming into a wild animal that would end up beside himself. Trees upstream a thousand years old would be torn loose, and the churning waters would chase them as matchsticks toward the Pacific Ocean.

"After the war, New Zealand was desperate for energy and workers. The dam was going to deliver electricity. Night and day, we crawled around that Roxburgh Dam like ants. It was quite a rough bunch, those workers. There were twenty nationalities, most of them between ages twenty and forty, men who in one way or another had managed to survive the wartime Europe of 1939–45. Some of my buddies had survived the invasion of Normandy, others who had also participated in the Korean War imagined that they were still hearing the staccato sounds of the Korean machine guns now and then. Or take Doug McIntyre, who would sometimes call for his mother in the night, or dream of the Japanese airplanes that in the Pacific had sunk the ship from under him.

"Later I heard that Doug made his last misstep when he worked on a drilling platform somewhere below Australia. A misstep in a hurricane, blown overboard, and drowned. Yeah, where did they go, all those ruffians. I know that there were quite a few Scots and Irish who later on started a sheep farm in the Otago. One of my buddies became chauffeur-owner of one of those big trucks that forever and always rumble between the North and the South Island. Not so long ago I met a driver of the cement trucks, who was now a pianist in a trendy café in Auckland. And then I haven't even mentioned the almost thirty percent of the New Zealand immigrants who wasted no time in packing their suitcases and taking the boat back to Hamburg, Liverpool, Rotterdam, Boston, Cape Town, or Melbourne.

"I found out that of the ninety men with whom I came from Rotterdam to the South Island, there were ten who never unpacked their suitcase. Especially men from the big city were no match for the rough Otago."

The home of Nick and Aly is built against the hills near the village of Te Aroha. There's a wooden name sign in the flower garden: "Orangewood." Which ordinary boy from Aldeskoat, which ordinary girl from Sint Jut, wouldn't dream of living in Oranjewâld?

Aly in her garden: a happy woman with beautiful eyes among flowers still in full bloom. Exotic flowers, but also ordinary violets. Next to the woman, Nick: a tall, fine-boned man of age with thick dark-gray hair and red spidery lines running through his cheeks.

In the deep valley a winding little river that runs through the center of town, a town with a straight main street and straight side streets, a white church, a statue in honor of the fallen soldiers from a forgotten war, a golf course ("All of New Zealand is a golf course."); on the slopes farther on here and there a dairy farm. Far in the distance, the vainest mountain in the whole world, the Ruapehu. Sometimes it belches fire while it's snow-capped. Which mountain wears a white hat while at the same time wearing a green spring jacket? Which mountain occasionally regurgitates smoke and fire right through its white hat? Is it any wonder that they call the Ruapehu, which now and then smokes at the top, the heap of lies?

Aly ten Boom: "Nick was in the Otago already, when in Sint Jut the bus of Slof of De Jouwer came for me. 'Well, then it's time to say good-bye,' Mom said calmly. I thought, Dad and Mom are going to take me to the road, but Dad couldn't get out of his chair, he just sat there as if abandoned. 'Dad,' I said, 'aren't you coming to the bus with me?' But he couldn't, he was crying. Those good-byes: When I sat in the bus, later on the boat, busy working with Nick in the wild Otago — everywhere I tasted again the salt of Dad's tears."

While she's talking, her own tears fall.

Nick: "Your dad wanted to keep his only flower with him in Sint Jut. Mother-in-law Geartsje would have liked that too, but she was a De Heij: even-tempered, less fragile. It was a few years earlier, and the old man apparently caught on that I wanted to emigrate. When in addition he realized that Aly and I were inseparable, he became upset.

"One Sunday evening, he took me aside. Face to face; he took me along outside: 'You better not figure on taking her along to such a far country!' Before I was aware of it myself, I threw my strongest weapon into the fray: 'If I want to go, I'll go, and we will see what Aly will do then!'

"It took a moment, and then: 'Well, well, is that so!' That's all he said. He turned around uncertainly and went back inside. Only then did I realize that he had been standing in his socks on the wet path. That's how upset he was. But he stood still in the dark hallway and said: 'Some things can't be stopped, but I want to tell you one thing: I will not let my only daughter go before her twenty-first birthday. That's how long *I* am the boss.'

"It was a couple weeks later, on another Sunday night, and between me and Jan Hindriks ten Boom the friendly relationship had been broken. And then he asked me to come with him to the front room. It was the first time that he called me by my first name, I'm sure of that. 'Lyckele, come with me to the front room.'

"'Don't go so far away, Lyckele.'

"If someone else at that time had said something like that to me, I would've said something like, 'Why don't you go to blazes?' but what was I going to say now? No one at that moment could talk me out of the plans I'd made.

"He reached for his inside pocket. 'Look here! Mom and I have a thousand guilders for you, Lyckele, with that you can get on your feet here too. There'll be work available in De Jouwer, and someday there will be an end to the housing problem.'

'I'm going to emigrate, ten Boom,' I heard myself say. 'Aly and I are going to New Zealand. I've already taken care of the details for myself.' At that point I had the victory over Jan Hindriks. He stood there as a whipped little puppy.

"Another Sunday, a week later. When I came into the house, you could cut the tension with a knife. 'Now you better damn well listen to me good!' he began, while stretching his large hands in front of him, 'with these claws I started as a boy of eleven to work on the fields in the Skar [the low wetlands east of It Hearrenfean, in the past mined for turf]. That was the time when there were no opportunities, but I wanted to make something of myself, I was looking forward to having a family and happiness. And now that we're well off, you come here, you good-for-nothing, and tear my whole family apart. But I'm not going to let that happen!'

"Had he only screamed at me, but he didn't do that. His voice was hoarse and shaky, hardly audible, and that made it hit a lot harder.

"'Lyckele! Look at me! They're going to send you there into the wild forests with an ax, and then leave you on your own. And the country is so far away, once you're there, you won't come back.' He meant of course that he would never see us again."

Nick, older now than Jan Hindriks ten Boom was then, gets up and ambles to the sliding doors. It appears that his own words have touched him.

Aly: "When the bus with Jaap Slof behind the wheel stopped — that was two days before my twenty-first birthday — it was really tough. 'Those two days aren't going to make much difference,' Dad had said."

Nick, his voice stronger again: "That first year in the construction project of Roxburgh, that was a rough place to be. It was a warm late-summer evening; the whole day the sun had been high in the sky above Clutha River. I trudged back to the barracks with a bunch of guys. Farther on, halfway to Cool Creek, some eight hundred men were horsing around. We decided to head there too. They were having a contest. The one who could swim against the current the longest would get the pot. Hundreds of us plunged into the Clutha at the same time. In long underpants or stark naked, it made no difference. There was only one in that whole mass who lasted fifteen minutes without floating backward: Doug McIntyre. The pot went to Dougy. That night we must've consumed a tank-truck full of beer.

"Aly still wasn't there, and then we got that wet fall. Nothing but rain.

The Clutha became wilder, higher, bigger. One night it began to roar. My room was only one of two thousand. It was on the same weekend that I and a few other guys had worked for double pay. I heard something strange; some guys were coming toward my little hut. They sounded loaded. Suddenly I realized that they were talking about Nick, that bloody Frisian Nick who was always collecting overtime and stashing all kinds of New Zealand pounds away.

"They were now so close that I could hear the sucking of their boots in the soft sludge. I don't think I even took time to put my pants on. I grabbed my gun and met them halfway.

"'Get the hell out of here!' I warned them.

"The light beam of their flashlight dropped a little lower now, and I think that two took right off. But there were two more, and I shot close to their feet. The mud splattered against their boots.

"'*Opsoademiterje of ik sjit jim kroandea!*' ('Scram or I'll shoot to kill!') I said it in plain Frisian, and that helped. They were gone.

"The next morning I heard at work that they had just wanted to find out if Frisian Nick had indeed made so many hours of overtime, if he really had so many New Zealand pounds under his mattress, and if he was really a hero or a coward.

"When it was fall in the Otago, it was really fall; when it was moonless, it was really moonless; when the men drank too much, they really drank too much. Even if that drinking had to take place between five and six in the afternoon. The pub wasn't open any longer than that. So it became an art to get stoned in three quarters of an hour. I didn't take part in that myself, because I wanted to save my money. Aly was going to come, and we needed a roof above our heads and become husband and wife."

At last the time had come. The *Waterman*, after stops in Wellington and Christchurch, arrived with Aly ten Boom in Dunedin. Her first memories of Nick's paradisaical Otago: "'That has to be the harbor,' they shouted on board. Nick and I, we hadn't seen each other for a long time, I almost exploded from excitement.

"Disembark. Papers. Waiting for the suitcases. And there he came to meet me. 'Frisian Nick,' they said. He was still the same, tall and handsome, clean-shaven but with some shaving soap left by his temples. We went on our way, and when there wasn't a means of transportation left, there was all of a sudden a beautiful brown horse. 'That's my little fox,' he said proudly."

Nick: "For the last part of the trip, on horseback together into the Otago. Now we were together. I said: 'I have good news!'"

Aly: "I thought, now we're going to have it, now he's going to tell me that he wants to marry me at once, but he said: 'Farther on in the South-land, there's a farm with first-rate soil, but I can't quite afford it yet, so at first we'll have to work our tails off and save. I've found work for you already, for a fruit-grower on the other side of Roxburgh.'"

Nick: "I'll be honest, I told her that I was crazy about her, that I wanted her to become my wife. And those words meant something to you, Aly. Later that day we tied the horse to a tree, nobody was around, and we went a little further than we ever had in Sint Jut. After that she said, boy oh boy, if we can just get a roof above our heads first."

Aly: "In those years, lovers were not allowed to live together here, and especially not in the barracks by the dam of Roxburgh. So first I landed in a room way in the back of the barracks camp. Gray from all the cobwebs. 'Here we can get along fine at first,' he said proudly. Nick had bought me a bike to get to my work, the first lady's bike in Roxburgh. That same day I bought a little gas stove. I didn't think they would forbid me to cook meals for Nick and me.

"The first night. I lay alone in a small hut; in the far distance cement trucks rumbled through the night. The next morning at four o'clock I still hadn't slept a wink, and there was Nick already again. Afterward I said: 'Now one of the two, we get married or I'm going to board the ship again.' He stood motionless in the door. 'Dear God,' he said, 'we are man and wife and we have no house.'

"I to the fruit trees, he to the flood control dam, both putting in long days. I really didn't make much money in my job. At around seven in the evening, I had the meal ready. Then Nick would be there. 'I've got something,' he began all excited, 'a wagon with a kind of house on top of it, everything of steel as far as I know, and they call it a mobile home. For less than two hundred New Zealand pounds, dearie.'

158

"'Where is that thing,' I wanted to know. 'Not far from Ashburton,' he said. I could already see myself with Nick on the brown horse to pick up the mobile home a minute, but it turned out that Ashburton lay three hundred miles north of us.

"'And then we'll put the mobile home on the fruit grower's yard,' was his thought, 'then we'll have electric too, and we'll be further ahead than the folk way back in the Skar by Sint Jut.'"

Nick: "Brian O'Casey was eager to go along to pick up the mobile home. I thought, if Aly and I with Brian O'Casey can't handle it, then nobody can. Brian was something of a slob with a terrific car, a 1932 Dodge. Powerful enough to pull a mobile home. We set out in the early evening to Ashburton, and if it hadn't started to rain cats and dogs, we would've been able to finish the whole thing in a day and a half. Now everything went wrong. While driving through the high areas of Tuapeka, we literally slid over the edge of the ravine.

"'Put on the brakes, Brian!' Aly screamed, but he could brake as hard as he wanted, the whole business began to roll backward down the mountain.

"We tied a rope to the front bumper of the Dodge, and Ali and I hung as rope-pullers before the car. The Dodge started to steam, to shake, and then quit. Now there was no holding us. The car hung over the edge again. 'Get out, Brian!'

"'Hold on!' he yelled back. He stayed in his Dodge like a captain on a sinking ship. He tried to get it started again. A few yards down a hole yawned nearly a thousand feet wide.

"'Let the rope go!' I bellowed to Aly, but she didn't let go. Aly never let go."

Aly: "We spent more than twenty-four hours getting that Dodge back on the road. Three days and three nights later, we had everything in place on the fruit grower's yard. We called our shelter Heavy Metal Mobile Home, because the little stinker weighed a ton. One night Brian came over. Nick and I happened to sit near the open door of Heavy Metal Mobile Home, talking and happy as larks. I don't think Brian went to church anymore, but when he saw us sitting there like that, he said, with three days worth of tobacco juice lining his chin: 'God's blessing gained, all is obtained!'

"That Irish grower demanded so much parking money that I essentially was plucking cherries for nothing. If I took the chance of eating a cherry while working, I would hear about it. Sure, I could have those that had been picked over by the birds. One evening, the woman said: 'Tomorrow it's Saturday, then I'm going to give you some cherries to take home.' So I came the next morning with a half-quart container with me. Don't ask for too much, I had always been taught. And what do you think? She filled that little bowl half full.

"'It's half empty,' I said. Then she added two more cherries. That did it, right then and there. That night I told Nick that I didn't want to be there with the Heavy Metal Home anymore."

Nick: "That same evening we hauled our home off the yard with the help of Brian, and parked it on another, more friendly yard."

Aly: "We wanted to get married, but the Kiwis told us that I would first have to find a bridesmaid and Nick a best man. That didn't take Nick long: Brian O'Casey. I hadn't had time to find friends, so I approached a total stranger. Well, she was perfectly willing to do me that favor. A City Hall? There wasn't any. But you could get married in the post office, where there was also a telephone. Nick talked about a wedding celebration and asked the postmaster to serve coffee and cake.

"'Who do you expect to come to our wedding,' I wanted to know. 'Just wait and see!' he said, 'Brian will take some guests along.'"

Nick: "It turned out to be an unforgettable wedding. There were at least eight guests or so."

Aly: "We were married in less than ten minutes. I can still hear Nick's speech: 'Well, now our life together has more of a foundation.'"

Nick, with eyes wet now, "And what a wonderful honeymoon we had, Aly! Been married less than an hour, and on to Queenstown, a place even more beautiful than Davos in Switzerland. We didn't have a car yet, of course, so Brian brought us for a bottle of whiskey and a couple of packages of chewing tobacco. We sang all the way through the mountain country of the Remarkables, across elevations of some six thousand feet. By eight o'clock he had us there. And he even had a present for us: a copper kettle full of eggs, according to Irish tradition. Twelve eggs: six for Aly and six for me.

PPLJC9GC3bPE

People.

PO BOX 37428
BOONE IA   50037-0428
UNITED STATES OF AMERICA

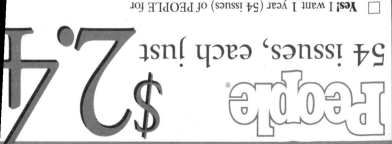

"We had rented a small place at a reasonable price. It turned out to have been built from whiskey and wine bottles. When the mountain winds surged, the whole house began to whistle and sing. In the daytime, when the sun would swallow the wind, we went into the mountains and came to places so quiet and beautiful that you hardly dared to breathe there. There were large and small lakes, we could take our clothes off because nobody came there, and at night in the bottle-home, we could watch the moon."

Aly: "Around bedtime, when the mountain winds picked up again, the little house would tell the happenings of the day. No, it wasn't exactly singing, it was more like humming; we were hummed to sleep.

"One morning, Nick woke up, saw the sun shine through the glass bottles, and said: 'It's about eight o'clock in the evening in Aldeskoat now. It's summer here, but there it's in the middle of the winter. Maybe the old main street is as slippery as a bar of soap and Mom and Dad are skating with socks over their shoes to the widow of Jippe Bouma, to old Martyntsje. It's the night for card playing.'"

"I've never been homesick," he says loudly, "but at first I did think every day about the years in Aldeskoat. Always dreaming about things from my childhood and growing-up years. Sometimes I'd be up to my ears in that terribly cold winter during the war, and then I'd find myself on the old Church Lane tramping back to town. My hands would be so cold, that I'd be all bent over. I must've been about twelve when, at the end of the path where there are all kinds of factories now, I met Gabe Westra. He saw me shivering, and hollered: 'Hey, aren't you one of the kids of Lyckele and Jantsje? You may hold my warm pipe for a while. That'll warm your hands in no time.' And then, with the imagined pipe of Gabe in both hands, I'd wake up. Thirteen thousand miles away from here. But is that homesickness?

"It was in that cold, wartime winter of 1944, and Eit Gaastra had tied a lamb to be slaughtered for Dad to a post behind his house in Nijeskoat. That night Dad had to go get that lamb, and I could go along. There was a curfew in force, so we couldn't be seen outside after eight at night. But Dad took a chance. When we were going to walk the railroad tracks, a bunch of *moffen* (German soldiers; a pejorative term) were coming from Jagtlust, the milk factory. They were striding our way in the middle of the tracks. Dad and I ducked in the bushes next to the tracks. When one of the Germans was very close, the lamb was going to bleat, but Dad tore a piece of string out of his pocket and tied that around his mouth. The *mof* seemed to have heard something, stood stock-still for a long while, then ran right past us.

"Later that night we landed with the lamb in Timen Hofstee's kitchen. 'Let's butcher it right now.' Timen was good at selling wooden shoes, but he wasn't much of a butcher. He had a book of instructions. But he couldn't find his glasses, so I had to read to Timen what the book said to do. Cutting into it with the knife, blood all over, and at the same time the doorbell. Germans by the door. But that last part happened here in New Zealand; hollering and with the smell of the warm, steaming lamb flesh in my nostrils, I awoke from a scary dream. Aly and I would sit on the edge of the bed to calm down. 'You were back in Aldeskoat, weren't you,' she said then.'"

Aly: "I still dream sometimes about those rough years in the Otago. Our oldest son was two, and one night Nick came with the story that in the south there was a seventy-five-acre piece of land for sale. 'Then in one swoop we'll have more land than Minne Wijtsma from Ousterhaule,' he bragged. But at the same time he had to admit that the farm was not in a prime location and condition. We could handle about ten cows there and some fifty sheep. 'Something to start with.' And we would have to buy some cattle too. It was in the time that cattle-buying was still a matter of cash-and-carry.

"The next night Nick came in and I saw it right away: he had made a deal, he'd bought the farm. 'I went in with Kees de Bruin, the North-Hollander, to buy the place,' he explained. I wasn't overjoyed with the deal, but I was ready for moving out of the heavy metal home.

"So one morning we took off in Kees de Bruin's rickety car, deep into the Otago. Raining hard, cold, very windy, deep puddles of water on the road, not a person anywhere. It must've been around eight o'clock that night, when some dreary-looking houses came into view. Oh good, Kees kept driving. A little while later a worn-out old mailbox, then a forsaken house, a skeleton of a cow that had gone to rack and ruin, and a field covered with tall thistles and piles of rock. With each house, I thought: I hope it isn't this one. And Kees and Nick bragging: 'Man oh man, this is really quality land.'

"It was pitch-dark, and we went on and on. At last we landed on a yard. The headlights shone on a mess; I hardly dared to ask if this was it. The outside door had been wide open for at least a month. We went inside. Nick couldn't stand up straight, and I was crabby by that time and said: 'Hold your head up high, you bought it yourself!' All the doors were rotten and ready to fall apart.

"'If we do get into an argument here,' Aaf de Bruin said, 'then at least we can't slam the doors.' I think it's only then that I realized that on top of everything else, we were going to have to live here with two families.

"Nick never smelled the mustiness of that abandoned house, he could only smell adventure on that excursion. We lasted three weeks, and then the bomb exploded with the De Bruins. One morning, Kees yelled that he'd rather get back on the boat with the whole caboodle than to spend one more day in this dirty shack. We could buy him out for a reasonable sum, he said. From that time on, we were farmers on a farm with seventy-five acres."

Nick: "And then it started. There were some eight farmers in the general area. And in the heart of the Otago, a distant neighbor was worth more than a distant friend. I got on the horse and started calling on my neighbors. All eight of us had to band together and try to get a telephone out here. And we succeeded — a kind of party-line. When it rang once, the call was for the Camerons, twice was for old Milton Kennedy, three times for the Langleys, four times for us. And if at night, close to bedtime, the telephone would ring seven times for the first time in fourteen days, it must be news from Ireland for the O'Learys.

"Our first big setback was a rabbit plague. The land was brown from all the rabbits, so as neighbors we went as one man to the Board, let's say to the polder council, to request money for a plan of counterattack. They offered us a goodly sum for each dead rabbit. That sounded good. We flailed away and saved more on those rabbits than we did on all the cows and sheep combined. One night Geoff Henderson called. 'We should make sure that we keep enough rabbits alive,' he said. We were all of the same mind, so we thought of a plan that would go easy on the rabbits for a while. It wasn't long, and the rabbits were in rampant supply again.

"Predictably, government agents came from the South Island to look things over. Consequence: they wanted to put us on a regular salary. We wanted a bounty for each rabbit. Under the leadership of Willy Cameron, we succeeded and agreed to a regular wage plus a couple of dimes for each dead rabbit, some spending money for the use of each horse and dog, and a settlement for each acre we would have to clear.

"My military force gathered against the rabbits consisted of: 3 horses and 36 dogs, and there were 10,000 acres of rabbit territory to cover. Of course, as farmers we needed to be taken seriously, so we started out with rat poison. That kills 80 percent of your customers. But at the same time we told the newspaper people, and therefore also the council and politicians, that the use of such poison endangered the sheep and cows as well. We wanted to keep the public opinion on our side.

"We stopped the use of arsenic. Now we went after the rabbits only with dogs and guns. When we had given that a good run, there was maybe 10 percent or so left. Now we chased them with dogs during daytime and at nighttime we used lights. And then we'd shoot. At last there was something like 5 percent left of the rabbit population. We tried to attack that remnant through special rabbit traps.

"But as with people, so with rabbits: the smartest ones survive. And I wanted to belong to that last category myself. We had had three really good rabbit years, but we didn't want to do ourselves in. In the meantime we were getting a good price for milk, and the sheep weren't doing badly either. Now the rabbits were almost exterminated.

"It didn't take long, or a new enemy made his appearance: the wild boar, a plague for the sheep farmer. He killed more and more of our lambs. I had excellent dogs, including some really tough ones, and for the next half-year or so it became a life-and-death battle between the dogs and pigs. I can still see one of my very best dogs emerge from the woods one afternoon. His entrails were hanging out. As farmers we couldn't go on like this any longer, so we went and stuffed a dead sheep full of phosphorus. Poison. The next day we had the villain in our gun's sight. Bang!

"The toughest and meanest and smartest pig was a huge sow. It had snatched at least fifty of our lambs. Eight of us spent a long time in wait for the beast, but we couldn't catch it. Again we lost a couple of lambs. But then it got a litter of piglets, and we managed to get our hands on one of those. That was the beginning of the end for the sow. Neighbor Pearsy Black had the formula: tie the little pig to a tree, let it scream for its mama, let the old bitch come, and then three times bang! That's how life was in the Otago."

Aly: "You can hear it on everything that there's 'Otago' in Nick. Once that's inside of you, it'll never get out again."

Nick, a bit emotional again: "As cattle farmer on the North Island, I've always been fond of my big herd of cows, but as sheep farmer in the Otago, I was more one with nature. They say in New Zealand: though the Otago-farmer may become as dim-witted as a paper bag, even if he's forgotten the name of his own wife, he will be able to tell you at once the name of his first sheepdog."

Nick and Aly had three healthy boys, who grew into big, strong men with a good dose of Otago in their blood too. "Nothing is too much for them," Nick says proudly. "One's on a big farm here below, each of the other two has a leasing business."

Night falls across the hilly countryside of Te Aroha; the storyteller gets up, stops at the threshold of the night by the open door. A couple of light points seem to be creeping up from the mountains in the clear starstrewn sky. He turns around and says: "We have it good now, but at first we had a lot of hard struggles to deal with. The new decimal system and a new monetary system were introduced; we got only two New Zealand dollars for a pound, and a little later those dollars weren't worth a darn. At first you could make a living with five hundred sheep, but now it takes five hundred cows. There were inflation times when farming was tough going. Sometimes I was almost afraid that everything would slip through my fingers like sand. But that didn't happen."

We're walking into the mild night, stop at a gigantic tree. Nick: "The Maoris claim that this giant is older than five hundred years. They say it's a tree with mana, which means something like wisdom, authority, status. You don't fell an old tree like this, but give it the time to die till its time has come."

Aly: "In Sint Jansgea Dad and Mom became old, and New Zealand for them was always too far away. So we couldn't believe it when we heard that they were coming." There's a pause in the story; we walk by the woods.

"They came together, they saw the strange fruits here, the snow on the mountain, the smoke from the crater, the fields behind the lake, the large farm, our new home against the slope. Orangewood. I still remember, I was going to make coffee, and went inside with Mom. Dad and Nick stayed behind in the garden; they stood there with their backs toward me, and it seemed then that there had never been seven seas between us, as if nothing had ever happened."

Nick de Jong: "The next morning my father-in-law said: 'Maybe I could paint an hourglass on the barn doors, just like the farmers used to do that in Gaasterlân.' What a great idea. The boys picked up red, white, and deep-green paint for Grandpa. The old man stood on the ladder briefly, but died in a way of speaking with the paintbrush still in his hand."

They stop by the old tree with so much mana. Then they walk back to the house.

The Night of Okaihau

Marten Dykstra from Okaihau, New Zealand
Simone Koornstra from Makkum

"What an awful feeling that is! It starts real subtly; at first you don't even know what it is. It's like the beginning of a chronic disease. A terrible disease."

For Simone Koornstra of Makkum, born in the summer of 1970, the years became very difficult. The young farmer's wife fought against this strange malady in New Zealand, didn't want to make a big deal of it, tried to be strong. But it turned into a battle that couldn't be won. At last there was only one remedy left. It was a do-or-die remedy and deliverance at the same time: give up everything and go back to the Grutte Sylsroede in Makkum.

"At first you feel only a vague longing," relates Simone. "One night I'm returning with Marten from the hills by the Bay of Islands, and I see our own nice home and the fern trees before me, and all of a sudden the strangeness of it all hit me again. You think of home back there, the feelings get worse, the pictures in your imagination intensify."

In Okaihau, at the top of the North Island, it's bedtime. A soft breeze from the open garden doors wafts through the whole house. What time is it now in Makkum? Must be about morning coffee time. Yes, at the Grutte Sylsroede they're having coffee now. She sees the parental home before her, clear as glass: the house of yellow glazed brick.

167

In the meantime they're done with coffee in Makkum, for now she sees in her imagination her mom come out of the house, dressed warmly against the cold of winter. Makkum in the season of the shortest days. It barely gets light. Or is there moisture in the air? The cobbled street stones are shining. Farther on the sluice is lit up. She sees a thousand bricks and pebbles glisten, the whole town glowing in the low lights of street and homes. She sees Makkum as a paradise with gold-paved streets, the unreachable paradise.

Mom crosses the white bridge, shopping bag on her arm. She's probably heading for Kluft to pick up some custard buns or maybe pastry. Wait a minute, that's right — they're going to have company tonight. Then she hears Dad telling an old story. And then the strong fisherman's voice of Jehannes Koornstra. She hears a story of the sea. Yes, Dad is home from a long journey, and tonight there'll be lots of talk. It's going to be fun and late at the Grutte Sylsroede.

It's night in Okaihau. She feels again the soft wind of the Pacific Ocean circulate the room. "Dad came home," she suddenly thinks aloud. Her own words startle her and she thinks: this can drive me crazy. But then she starts fighting back. Be careful not to wake Marten, he works long days and needs his rest. No funny business, keep your head on straight! After all, here in New Zealand she has everything her heart desires. She loves the man she went to the cows with just awhile ago — their cows. She didn't fall in love for nothing with Marten Dykstra from Brantgum; she could never be happier with anybody else than she is with Marten Dykstra.

They lie in bed, and in the other room their little boy sleeps like a rose: Jacob Martens Dykstra from Okaihau. "Once you have a baby, you'll get over it," a Makkum neighbor lady wrote in a letter. But the neighbor's theory doesn't turn out to be completely right. Simone is happy and unhappy at the same time. She doesn't understand herself anymore, let alone that another should understand her.

On the Bay of Islands, the weather is mild and great for growing. The cows that are grazing in the direction of Kerikeri find more grass than they can chew. Simone was there when the cows were bred, she was there when they calved, she gave the calves their names, she's crazy about them. Indeed, she has her whole future wrapped around her and under her con-

trol. In fact, if she should want to, she could now — in the middle of the
night — call home, call the Grutte Sylsroede. It's daytime there now. But
she doesn't call; she's sometimes afraid now to face the confrontation.

That wasn't the worst of it, for that was only the first phase of homesickness. At first it subsides a little. But later on it starts all over again and
becomes much worse. Christmas is approaching. And New Year's Eve and
New Year's Day. She now sees everybody at home not only drinking coffee, she actually can smell the coffee. At midnight she suddenly hears the
clock of the Makkum Weighhouse strike twelve. "Then you wake up to the
reality, and it hits you hard. You lie awake and you feel like screaming:
'Marten, it's eating me up!'"

"I can see it," he says the next morning, and he's upset by it. "I see the
dull look in your eyes, oh honey, it's terrible! Where is this taking us.
You're thin as a rail, your skin is breaking out, it's doing you in."

The next day she sees Marten jump on the tractor and thinks: oh my
dear boy, your big plans, your great adventure, your beautiful herd of
cows, your life — I can't stay here. Then she says: "Maybe it's going to get
better." She looks for fault within herself. Is she not a good farmer's wife?
Is it because she didn't inherit that strong bond between the soil and people that old Grandfather Marten from Dronryp sometimes talked about?

That night Marten again notices the dullness of her eyes and thinks:
This could well end up into a terrible mess. Can I just leave the whole business here? No, that's impossible.

One evening Marten says: "It weighs on me like a load of bricks, it's
like everything is turning against us, Simone. Milk prices are falling, the
price of cows is half of what it was, a lot of recurrent expenses are going
sky high. Because of all the rain we've been having, a lot of phosphate has
to be spread. There's three times the rainfall here as in Fryslân. The land is
needier here than I had expected, that's for sure."

In February, with the days gradually shortening, Simone is starting to
do a little better. But then the misery begins anew. Her homesickness no
longer has boundaries. "Marten, this is killing me."

Marten Dykstra, a year and a half later: "There comes a time when you
have to face up to the reality. When homesickness just won't go away,
when nothing helps anymore, not even the happiness of being with the

three of us — because in essence we were — when even a round trip Okaihau-Makkum in between brings no improvement, then you feel hopelessly stuck. Who would've thought in the beginning that this is how it would turn out for us, that we would have to face this kind of dilemma."

Marten Jacobs Dykstra from Brantgum was only a boy when he would think every so often: Brantgum; am I stuck here now and forever? But he was the only son, and his older sister married a non-farmer's son who had a good job in the gas industry. So Marten could slide right into his place as farmer-successor. His father Jacob, when he married Anna Olivier, came from Dronryp to rent the farm in Brantgum, later on bought it, expanded it by buying additional land, and did well. With the wind in his back, actually.

"I don't know what it was with me," says Marten. "I just couldn't stand the idea of settling in Brantgum, I wanted to get away. A neighbor once confided to me: 'My goodness, are you thinking of leaving! The Dykstras of Menameradiel are generally stay-at-home types, that's why there are scads of Dykstras around here. We don't even call Dykstras by their last name anymore; it's "Marten Lammerts" and "Jabik Martens" and "Minne Piters," and on and on like that. In the past one would walk from Menaam to Wier over nothing but Dykstra-land. So what in the world are you, Marten of Jappy Dykstra, thinking of! Where do you want to go? Your Grandpa Marten has always been a leader. He was the psychologist behind the land consolidation, changed the world around here, persuaded the farmers in the Berltsum area to expand their farms; he essentially turned the land consolidation act into a success. And your dad also was a class act as farmer and organization man. So there's a farm waiting for you, and the milk price is not bad either. What I mean to say is: you can put your talents to good use in your own region too, you know!'

"That's what the neighbor said in so many words. But I thought: there it is again, it's just like you're handcuffed here, as if I'm not *supposed* to leave. Aren't there after all more places in the world where you can make a good go of it like my forefathers did here?

"As a student in agriculture school, I became certain that I wanted to leave. It was kind of an ambivalent feeling. I had respect for Dad, as a person as well as farmer. But there were days when I felt that I couldn't get enough air to breathe. Well, a good ten years later I think back sometimes on what was going on inside me then. I was the somewhat playful and adventuresome son of a strong father, of a man who would simply declare: This is the way it is! And heck, most of the time he was right too! But, I would think to myself, for dairy farms like this with plenty of milk rights and financial means the eighties are a breeze. Tackle something different, go away and start over on the other side of the world. In the middle of the prairie, with a young wife and a few cows, and make something happen. Then you're really a farmer!

"There was that restlessness. Dad and I had an argument sometimes, but not real trouble. So I went to New Zealand as a student intern. Maybe he thought, 'Let him go, then he'll be cured for good in nine months' time.'

"I landed on a large dairy farm on the North Island of New Zealand, in the region of Rotarua and Taupo. That farmer milked 1100 cows. Well, you call a farmer like that by his last name at first. Crafter. And what those Crafters didn't dare to tackle! Irish by background. And all that space, that herd of cows, that freedom. I was totally fascinated. I did run to the mailbox every day to check if I'd gotten something from Fryslân, but I didn't spend a lot of time thinking about Fryslân.

"I had almost finished my eight months, and I thought: this is going to become my country, here I want to live my adventure. I began dreaming about my own New Zealand dairy farm. In my thoughts I could already see Dad and Mom come and visit, and I could show off to them how well my farm was doing here. I would've raised all the heifers myself, selected the bulls myself, overcome adversity myself.

"One morning near lunchtime, a letter from Brantgum was in the mailbox. 'Yesterday I bought an additional 170,000 liter quota,' I read. 'Then pretty soon you'll have better opportunities here in Brantgum.' It was like getting hit over the head. Let me admit honestly: that night I cried in bed. Brantgum, there on the other side of the world, began to tear at me again.

"That week doubts began to pile up. I needed advice, needed to talk to somebody. That could only be Grandpa Marten, he had always been a kind of comrade for me. But I didn't dare to call him at first. I could sense even through my wooden shoes way over here on the other side of the world

171

that Grandpa Marten would also love to see me on the Brantgum farm. And he was a man who said what was in his heart. He wouldn't spare you. If I were to stay in New Zealand, I would break a chain of at least ten generations of Dykstra farmers. He had never said that in so many words, but that was certainly what he believed. Yes, I was the big spoilsport. On the Ids Wiersmastreet in Brantgum lay a farm of some 125 acres waiting for me. Grandpa Lou Olivier, had he still been alive, would also have had conniptions. Strangely enough, I had to think more and more about that bond with the past.

"The eight months of internship was over, and now I took four weeks of vacation to explore New Zealand, and then return briefly to the Crafters. I was hardly twenty but old enough to become a farmer, they said. They offered me share-milking at 25 percent.

"All right," I said, but then I want to milk four hundred cows." They accepted. But I thought about it some more, and called Dad. He was totally against it. With so many cows, more workers would have to be hired. Milkers, and preferably good ones.

"I was here as a student, so I had to return to Brantgum, of course. That was April 1989. And there the adventure settled down a bit. I met Simone! We fell hard for each other. Dad and I continued farming together in partnership.

"I began to think about New Zealand again. And what happened? I became more and more homesick for New Zealand; I wanted to return to that beautiful rough country where everything was possible, where there were mountains, lakes, and huge herds of cows. True, it would get too rough there sometimes. They would shoot their old faithful dog without blinking an eye, and that bothered me sometimes in the native Kiwis. But I simply became homesick for my old dreams. I saw the green slopes, the rise and fall of the waves — just say it: I wanted to emigrate. To New Zealand, the most beautiful country in the whole world.

"After a few weeks, I wasn't the only one anymore who dreamed of a new beginning on the other side of the world — Simone dreamed with me. As a girl of ten, she had spent a couple of years in Laos with her parents, who were engaged in development projects. We weren't even thinking about the possibility of homesickness then. Paradise lay on the Bay of Islands.

"And then the good-byes. That was in March 1993. I still don't like to talk about that. A friend of mine drove Simone and me to Schiphol. In Fryslân they wanted to bid us farewell together as one family. In the front room of the farmhouse on the Ids Wiersmastrjitte in Brantgum. And a lot of emotions came to the surface there. On the part of everyone. Tears.

"I bought a farm at the head of the North Island. Much hard work. A lot of money was involved in my adventure, so we couldn't afford mistakes. But the price of agricultural land goes up and down more here than in Europe, and there were setbacks. I never considered giving up, and that was a good thing for in the meantime Dad had sold the farm in Brantgum, including cattle and milk quota and everything else. After all, he didn't have to figure on a successor anymore. Instead, he bought a very nice place by Holwert with a hundred acres, with no milk quota, but good for 150 sheep or so, which gave him something to do. The cards had been shuffled.

"The setbacks in Okaihau weren't the worst part. We had a beautiful house worth more than $350,000, and I could always sell that if necessary. But Simone, she became so homesick. By the early winter months of 1997–98 it couldn't go on like that anymore. I felt so beleaguered, I would sometimes spend an hour on the phone with Grandpa Marten; first still in Dronryp, later in Nijlân-State, a Rest Home in Ljouwert. Expensive calls. He asked me tough questions; sometimes his voice shook.

"Simone boarded the plane with little Jacob. And in December I followed her. To be sure, issues had to be settled, but that could be done in Fryslân as well as in New Zealand. Simone didn't want to go back to New Zealand, she said. What was going to happen now? In Fryslân they were thinking: is he going to keep farming in New Zealand without Simone?

"We were in dire straits. It was hard to come home this way to Dad and Mom in Holwert. They really took it hard. No, this was not at all what we had planned for. Big decisions had been made which couldn't be reversed, and now it was up to me. What was I going to do! I dreaded most the visit with Grandpa in Nijlân-State.

Marten Dykstra Sr. in Nijlân-State says in his eighty-eighth year: "This is what I told the boy on the telephone: 'I want you to come here with your wife and the little boy. That would please me!'

"'We're coming right away, Grandpa,' he said. I was looking forward to seeing them come in the door. I wanted to tell them that I too had been homesick once, even though it lasted only a few minutes. That was when I had just moved from the Hearewei in Ryp to Nijlân-State. It was on a rainy Friday, and I felt so lonely. That was really bad.'"

"And I," said Marten Jr. at age twenty-nine about the meeting, "I really wanted to see Grandpa again, but I dreaded the confrontation like the plague."

Grandpa Marten: "When they got here, I said to Marten: 'Now I want you to sit over there, right across from me, and Simone with the little boy over there. And then I'm going to ask you *one* question.'"

Marten Jr.: "I came through the door and was shocked to see a shrunken little man, sunk deep in his chair. But his beautiful old face, those eyes, the spirit were the same as always."

Simone: "He didn't look, as I had expected, right through us; his eyes were mild. Then he asked us: 'Do you love each other?'

"'Yes,' we said, 'we love each other.'

"'Then for the most part you've already succeeded in life,' he said."

Less than a half-year later. It turned out that Marten didn't feel at home in Fryslân. He flew back to the land of his dream and desires: New Zealand. Simone stayed behind with little Jacob in Makkum. It's all over: the two young lovers have separated. Separated by more than twelve thousand miles.

Simone tries to make a go of it with a job in a catering establishment. As long as the grandparents baby-sit now and then, it's working out well.

Marten tries hard way up in the North Island to become and remain an independent farmer. It's not an easy road, and setbacks make it even more difficult. Recently, unidentified persons burned his house down, close to the milking parlor.

It's like a dream with a cruel ending. Marten's parents in Holwert try to make their peace with it. And that's also true of Grandpa Marten J. Dykstra Sr. in Nijlân-State, who now is tired every day.

"That's how in my old age I've discovered that love does not conquer all," the old man observes with disappointment. "There are other strong drives and powers too: adventure, restlessness, mysterious desires, the new age, the new world."

The Layers of Life

Melis van der Sluis from Hamilton, New Zealand.

"It was noisy where we lived on Steamboat Wharf in Boalsert. The rattling of beer crates that had to be loaded and unloaded was all around us. We also handled soda crates; we called those carbonated drinks 'bullet beer,' the drink for minors. There was a lot of racket going on all right, but it wasn't exactly a flourishing business. 'Once the war is over,' Dad judged, 'it's going to get better, then the volume will go up.'

"The janitor of the Great Church in Boalsert had a way with words; he said: 'Don't give up, van der Sluis, they're talking about a baby boom after the war. And mark my words: real Boalserters never give up drinking. If it ain't from wealth, it'll be from poverty.'

"Liberation came, and with it celebration. But the people already got drunk on tap water, so to speak. When all the celebrations were over, there came a time of new laws and sobriety. The economy got off to a very, very slow start. It was hard to get anything at first. And when things were finally beginning to look up a little toward the end of the forties, news came that the breweries wanted to reorganize the distribution system. Maybe they wanted to get rid of small businesses. On top of that was a severe housing shortage. It was almost impossible for young couples to get a house.

"Mother was adventurous and enterprising. Jeltsje Reidinga, a skipper's daughter from Terherne, came from a tribe of nine kids; if there was nothing to challenge her, she'd go looking for something. Dad, Abe van der Sluis from Langwar, was a more cautious type. Not that he couldn't take care of himself, to be sure. But that difference in temperament wasn't a problem between them, instead it seemed to make them a better match.

"I was going to high school and was not yet aware that I took after my mother. It was a spring day. I had finished my homework and was playing soccer on Friesland's top team. That evening the weather was exceptionally mild, and it stayed light a long time. At the Bargefinne I saw the daughter of van den Oever. She looked my way, and all of a sudden I didn't know what was happening to me. Just like that I fell hopelessly in love. Apparently it was love at first sight for both of us, for not much later the two of us were walking around the bulwark together, holding hands. We walked around the old city once; I don't believe we even kissed. But those feelings, that new experience of wonder, I don't think I'll ever forget it. The next day the priest stopped by. He said: 'Van der Sluis! I have a serious problem. The long and the short of it is this: I, and not only I, have serious objections that one of your boys goes around with a daughter of Van den Oever. You can understand why that's not possible.'

'I understand it completely, Father,' said Dad, 'we are not Catholic.' That evening he took me aside and said: 'I understand that you're chasing that young girl of Van den Oever, one of my Catholic customers. Find somebody else, my boy, because if I should lose my Catholic clientele, I might just as well hang it up.'

"What did they call that later? 'The pillarization of society.' In that kind of society, a lot of small shopkeepers and entrepreneurs tried to pick up the fragile thread of the thirties again. But after the war, returns and profit margins didn't amount to much. Besides, the households tended to be big. In our case, with five kids — three boys and two girls — we could just scrape by, but there were a lot of really large families in Boalsert. And what was the city like right after the war? The barges hauling ash still moved through the city, the dogcarts still rattled across the Apple Market, and no fewer than sixteen bakeries were competing against each other. The old, pre-war way of doing things resurfaced briefly after liberation but was at the point of being wiped off the map. The people of the forties couldn't have known that, of course, but I believe that the youth felt it coming. Especially the youth.

"And then there was Mom. More and more we heard the word 'emigration' coming from her mouth. New Zealand. Apparently money was being set aside for that. That mysterious country deep down in the Pacific Ocean, on the other side of the world; it was somewhere on another planet.

"But before making that big move, someone would have to go ahead of the family and explore the opportunities. Permission for emigration was granted only if a family had the guarantee of employment and a roof over their head. One evening — I wasn't twenty yet — I said: 'I'll go.'

"'What you've studied here is never wasted, not there either,' Mom said. I was going to teacher's college in Ljouwert, but I was ready to drop my studies.

"'If you're going, then I'm going with you,' said my sister Gretha. 'Otherwise who's going to cook for you there?' Gretha and I were two birds of a feather; we even liked to go dancing together. 'When we find work and a house there, Dad and Mom are going to follow us with Atze, Jan, and Sjoerdsje.'

"'Well, I declare,' said Mom, 'it sounds like it's really going to happen.'

"'Yep,' Dad said, 'I guess we better go ahead then.'

"December 1951, right before Christmas. I was twenty now, and Gretha had just celebrated her nineteenth birthday, when we boarded the bus with our suitcases at de Bargefinne. On to Rotterdam, where the *Sibajak* was waiting for us at the wharf of the Royal Rotterdam's Lloyd. I still remember that the Boalsert we left behind looked rather gray and colorless. But I don't believe that our farewell was sad or very emotional. Now and then a serious look would flit across Dad and Mom's face, but soon they'd be joking again. Witticisms. For weeks Gretha and I had been planning our trip, and predictably our enthusiasm had transferred to the whole family. Yes, all of them would follow us. The two of us hadn't really stopped to think of the giant step we were taking; it was more like we were just going on a fantastic school trip to the other side of the world.

"It wasn't until one evening when I was standing in the stern of the *Sibajak*, staring at the water churned by the boat's propellers, that it suddenly hit me. That water formed an endless white-foaming path that took us ever farther away from Steamboat Wharf. The steady hum of the ship's ten-thousand-horsepower engines kept us moving at a speed of more than fifteen miles per hour. Day in day out, week in week out. And always there was that wake. I must've been a pretty active little fellow in our small city, always in motion, involved in everything, with heart and soul. Because there on the rear of the ship, on that round rear end of the *Sibajak*, I felt the roots from the deepest layer of my being, the very core, tearing loose. Not that it hurt so much at that time, but in retrospect I became somewhat aware of the irrevocable break with something that one can call one's youth.

"The new, the unknown was beckoning. And Gretha and I, we really enjoyed ourselves. Gretha — now there was a strong, steady young woman! As soon as the orchestra on board struck its first note, we'd hit the dance floor, and then I thought to myself: we're dancing toward the unknown.

"Our journey to Wellington took five and a half weeks. When we disembarked with our suitcases, it was in the middle of the summer on the North Island. But where were we going to go? Between the two of us, all the money we had was about twenty New Zealand pounds.

"'We'll take the train to Auckland,' I told Gretha. We bought two one-way train tickets, which left a few pounds in our pockets. There was still a seat for us.

"'Maybe Auckland isn't even the best place to find a job with which to build a future,' Gretha observed, 'we should land in the right kind of city for us right away. What place would have the best future — I think a place a little bigger than Boalsert and smaller than Amsterdam. That kind of city has a future.'

"The train was already moving. I eyeballed our fellow passengers. New Zealanders, young and old. Gretha and I got up and in our best school-English asked six passengers a question. We selected people who looked pretty intelligent.

"Our question was: 'Which city on the North Island would you judge to be the most appropriate place for two young people who want to build a future; a city, in other words, with a lot of potential for growth and a future and work.'

"'Hamilton!' was the answer from four of the six.

"'We're going to get off in Hamilton,' I said to Gretha.

"It was a quiet Sunday morning when we sauntered into the city with our suitcases. We were dead tired, probably from all the tension, but we also felt kind of forsaken. The city looked tired too. I think that Gretha and I gave each other a little pep talk. And that's how we started roaming the streets.

"'I don't see a lot of factories,' Gretha said. 'I'm going to put an ad in the paper right away tomorrow, offering my services as a tailor's cutter.'

"We were walking in the shade of a high red wall, put our suitcases down, and wanted to rest a bit on a ridge. Gretha laid her ear against the wall.

"'I'm hearing something, the same kind of sound as at home,' she whispered. Then I wanted to listen too. Yes, there was a racket on the other side of the high red wall. It sounded like the racket of crates of bottles. We walked around the building. The windows were high up on the wall. 'Climb up on me,' I said to Gretha. When she stood on my shoulders and was able to look inside through a window, I heard her surprised exclamation: 'Bullet beer, Melis. It's a soda factory or something. But maybe it's beer.'

"When she got back down next to me, she had tears in her eyes.

"'What a break. Bullet beer!'

"She could have said: 'Melis my boy, now we're no further than we were at Steamboat Wharf.'

"Less than an hour later we had found the director of the factory. Plenty of work, we found out. We could start right away the next day, he said.

"'All right, sir, tomorrow, early in the morning!'

"Gretha immediately placed an ad in the paper: 'Cutter wants work.' One ad was enough. She too could get started right away.

"Work and save. Before long we had enough money for a house. I didn't want to get stuck in that soda factory for too long. At that time there were all kinds of opportunities in New Zealand, they were begging for people. They were even in need of students. That's why I was able to continue my teacher's training in Hamilton. A free education plus spending money, that looked to me like a fine investment. On weekends the two of us went dancing. To outsiders it must've looked like we were a couple, but if Gretha should meet a good-looking fellow and I'd spot a cute girl, then like a couple of youngsters making time we'd each go our own way for a while. But if on a night out I should hook up with a girl, and there wouldn't be anyone for Gretha, then we'd simply head home together. That was the agreement. And that's how we took care of each other during that time of running around on our own.

"Dad and Mom had seen two of their children leave for the other side of the world, and now the whole Boalsert family was going to follow them. But there was a snag. Dad had already turned fifty, and now they found out that he was no longer qualified. That must've caused a lot of anxiety there in Boalsert. I finally presented the problem to what was then the opposition leader in Wellington, and made it clear to him that the information given to the immigrants had been in error. They were given permission to come.

"'Did you have a good trip?' I can still see Dad and Mom coming off the ship in Wellington. 'Yep, it was a long trip, an endless trip,' Dad said. Mom said: 'We'd been sailing for about four weeks; one evening we were standing in the stern of the boat, we looked down on that long wake, and I said to Dad, 'What an endless ocean.'

"'Yep,' your dad said, 'there's no going back.'

"Mom and Sjoerdsje, who became Shirley here, immediately headed for the store. Words that had just been memorized were put into practice right away.

"Dad was critical at first of his new surroundings. 'I had heard that the potatoes here aren't nearly as starchy as at home, but I hadn't expected that they would be this bad.' And of course he couldn't get his chewing tobacco at first. What he did was buy a box of good-quality cigars, cut them in little pieces, and that's how he had his chew.

"He was happy in one way that he had work at the soda factory. After all, his family was together again and his kids were doing well. But at his age, with his roots deep in Frisian soil, he must've felt pretty wobbly every now and then. Eventually he found the balance between the old and the new, surrounded by his children and grandchildren, and with the help of his beautiful garden full of new kinds of flowers and fruit. 'I've tried to turn the soil here into my own.' That was also the soil in which he found

181

his final rest, completely at peace. We never heard him say, as so many others said, that he definitely wanted to be buried in Frisian soil, or that he wanted his ashes scattered over Friesland.

"My own thoughts are different. I don't want to get all emotional about the fact that I have my roots in two worlds. Some people feel that as being torn in two. I prefer to see it as a kind of privilege. Not everyone is able to say that he has roots on both sides of the world. Half of my ashes are going to be scattered over the volcanic soil of my new fatherland; the other half over Frisian soil. That's how I've arranged it.

"As a teacher I've tried to open the eyes of my students — New Zealanders, Maoris, immigrants from wherever — to the culture in which they were raised and in which they're now growing up. That's the culture that you carry with you, wherever you may go in the world. If you don't recognize that culture or if you deny it — some immigrants do that too — then you're fooling yourself. Then it's just like you're hiding the truth from yourself.

"Later on, wherever I exhibited as a ceramic artist, I always felt the breath of that particular culture all around me. But back in Friesland, when I had an exhibition in the Princess Garden of Ljouwert, I felt a moment of revelation. I felt all of a sudden surrounded by an age-old culture of which I myself had been a part. I've tried to give that feeling shape in my work also. Art objects that don't just portray the layers of the earth's crust, but also the stages, the time-layers of life. It's one eruption after another. If you're lucky, you become older and older, and take more and more risks. And the bottom layer is the first. And the oldest. You must not deny that first layer, because that's the layer that carried you first.

"Mom had become a widow; she was well along in years when once more she got a longing to go back to middle Friesland. By then I had already flown back and forth with her a few times. 'But now I'm too old,' she said.

"'Mom, you're never too old to talk with old Terhernsters about your early school years,' I said, and together we boarded a huge 747. When the airplane lifted from the runway, she said: 'You know, Melis, when Dad and I stood one evening in the rear of that large ship, there was no end in sight. But now it's as if I'm being shot home like a bullet.'

"I rented a room for Mom for three months in Akkrum. For three months she addressed 'the first layer of life,' about playing marbles and hoops — talking and dreaming about all the doings of Terherne some eighty years ago. After three months she said: 'Son, I'd like to go home now.' A couple of days later we were back in the land to which her own adventure had brought her.

"One day I said to my wife, Ruth, who's from Danish background: maybe we should take a trip with the children around the world on a passenger boat. And that's what we did. On the passenger ship *Canberra*. I took a great big box full of my own artwork along that I thought I might be able to sell on board. But the main purpose was to show our children the places of our roots. That's how they landed in Odense on Rosenornsvej and in Boalsert on Steamboat Wharf. But I couldn't help feeling a bit hurt when it clearly meant less to them than I had expected. They wanted to go to London. Yes, London! The old center of their Commonwealth.

"Ruth and I looked at each other. And then we understood.

"She said: 'They've grown roots in their own country, and that's how it should be.'"

The Widows of Abel Tasman

Evening Rest near Melbourne, Australia

Anny Cornelissen had her birthday a week ago; she's still glowing. It was a memorable day, and the joy of that day continues to linger. The day began with a small aubade. After that a drink, dinner, a group of friends, another drink, and even a bit of dancing "And just forget it that you're seventy-five already."

In the smoking section of Evening Rest, the retirement home southeast of Melbourne, Anny Cornelissen enjoys a cup of coffee, then lights a cigarette, and begins her story. Very abbreviated, because she doesn't want to go in detail or whine. Besides, she doesn't have much time for she's planning to make the rounds of the rooms. She finds it rewarding to visit old folk who feel lonely and need someone to talk to.

"Seventy-five years old, that's three quarters of a century. What comes on top of that is a bonus." Everyone in the smoking section agrees with the buxom, animated lady. The widow Anny Cornelissen's presence raises everybody's spirit, though her neighbor lady, Mrs. Snijder, isn't exactly a wallflower either. She's almost eighty, but still sails across the dance floor when the Dutch club, the Kangaroo, puts on a party.

Mrs. Snijder, freshly permed, slender, and pert: "This one, that's my husband. Willem. He's eighty-one, I'm eighteen, I mean that's how I feel. I wanted to emigrate from Ijmuiden in 1953 already, but Willem still had some loose ends to tie up. One Saturday evening he came back from Tholen — after that disastrous flood he worked there on the dragline — and he said suddenly: 'All right, let's go!'

"That Sunday night he of course left for Tholen again, where he was working on a farm. Not long after that I sent him the telegram: 'Come home, please!' A couple of places had opened up on the emigrants' boat, *Johan van Oldenbarnevelt*; and we were able to go."

Willem Snijder, the 81-year old son of an Ijmuiden fisherman who had turned his back on the sea, listens calmly and comments: "It was an evening toward the end of March. Spring was in the air. I came into the room and didn't even have time to shave. She had already sold the house, the furniture was crated, but we still had a bed to sleep on. Everything had been arranged. A day and a half later our relatives waved us good-bye from the pier.

"My wife is the engine that makes everything move, and I like that. Also because of her, it went well for us here. After three days I got a job at a British firm not far from Frankston. Again as crane operator. That's a specialty, by the way, did you know that? A real specialty."

She: "Willem is a reasonable man but a bit serious at times. Then he starts thinking about the good-byes on the pier in Ijmuiden. That family of his, those Snijders, they were such a tight-knit bunch, and that's why Willem in his dreams sees now and again his parents, brothers, and sisters waving their good-byes on that pier. Then he becomes melancholy, and I say: 'Watch out my boy, we don't want any trouble with homesickness in our old age. We've had enough of that already!'"

Snijder: "A priest here talked to us and said that the emigrant wife wants to go back to Holland during the first few years, and the man in the last years of his emigrant life. That's what the priest said when he had talked to the wife of Graat Verschaeren. Well, the widow Verschaeren can tell you about it; she had such a bad case of homesickness at first that it made her stutter.

"And now I feel that I'm getting it in my old age. I notice it every two weeks or so. . . . I'm not sure what it is. Gloom because of the way life is? Every once in a while it hits me."

His wife: "You shouldn't give in too quickly to getting older; you have to keep up your spirits. Let me be very honest about it: when he turns quiet and somber, I stroke him and then we end up making love together, and things are good again."

The smoking section, an open book. Anny Cornelissen listens, for she has known for a long time what life is all about. Twenty years ago she became a widow. "Both of my children live a day's flight away from me, but I can take care of myself fine. But there are a lot of old people here who had expected more from life. All kinds of things can happen to an emigrant, that's true, but ultimately you have to accept what life gives you. I liked it here from the start, just write that down.

"In Valkenswaard, my husband and I gave it everything we had for thirty years. We were already dreaming of taking it a little easier. And then he passed away, and I stood alone. It's as if everything around you suddenly falls away. I had a sister here in Australia. 'Come over here, Anny!' she wrote at the bottom of her sympathy card. She and her husband had a gas station here, and they had a beauty of a camping trailer near Mount Waverly where I could live in, they said. No, it wasn't an attempt to escape my misery, it was rather as if something lured me. Then my oldest son, just twenty-one, was transferred to Sydney in his job, and my daughter of sixteen wanted to go too. It was 1977, and I went. I just want to say this: a widow is mourned so long as her husband hasn't been buried. After that she's expected to take care of herself."

The widow Truda Josephina Verschaeren is almost ninety and prefers to stay in her room crowded with portraits and group pictures of her descendants. Her husband was almost forty-eight and she forty-three when they stepped off the boat with seven sons, a daughter, and ten dollars in their pocket. The oldest was almost twenty, the youngest nine months. They booked a November trip. For six weeks she was 'nigh unto death' from seasickness.

"My husband Graat and I stayed. Simply because the children after four, five years didn't want to go back. It was also the time that the first grandchildren came, and then there's no going back at all.

"But for Graat Verschaeren life remained difficult. He couldn't get used to another language and surroundings; his heart was and remained in Brabant. He was hard on himself and hard on others close to him. That's why I and the children had an especially hard time. He was a good man at heart, but in retrospect he was much too old to become an emigrant. His children cannot be blamed; some contributed their wages till they were past thirty. Just to get their father on his feet and provide him with a better life.

"Both of us as immigrant parents had had a hard youth. My parents had a small farm in De Peel [an area in Brabant with many small farmers who were trying to cultivate the peat soil for agriculture] with eight cows, ten sows, eighty chickens, and eleven children. There were seven girls, and one after the other was hired out to area farmers as full-time maid. I wasn't fourteen yet when I was already earning thirty guilders annually on an out-of-the-way place. True, it did include board and room. But you could be worse off than at home where we could keep our wooden shoes on in the kitchen and would all eat out of a communal pot of potatoes. Next to it was a large bowl of buttermilk porridge. Everybody had a spoon and dug in. Anybody who couldn't keep up would starve, of course.

"So, I was a lot worse off at that first farmer's place. At four o'clock in the morning we had to head out to the field to milk the cows. After that came the fieldwork: tying sheaves of grain or digging potatoes regardless of weather, and at four o'clock in the afternoon it was back to milking cows. In the summertime you worked as long as there was light, in the wintertime from dark to dark. Later I wondered sometimes why in the world homesickness wasn't finished off inside of me at that time. Because what in heaven's name did I get so homesick for later on?

"Graat was a hired man across from the place where I was. And then there was a carnival in Asten. Well, all the pent-up desires and frustrations of a year's slaving exploded there. There was a boy, and he asked if he could walk a ways with me. I would've preferred a factory boy or so, one in nice clean clothes, because it was obvious that this was a farmworker. But his face showed character. He came from a labor-class family of five. Gerardus Verschaeren.

"'Good news,' he began a week or so later when he stood with his bike by the hedge. 'I got a job in the brick factory of Schaesberg by Heerlen. It's not a dirty job.' Six weeks later he biked back from South-Limburg to Asten for the first time. He was so proud: he had bought a new carbide lamp for his old bike. I noticed white sweat rings in his new jacket. I began to have feelings for him, he had such a nice strong face, a good-looking guy. But then I discovered that he wasn't allowed in our house!

"'He's not a farmer!' exclaimed father, 'He's not coming in here.' Dad must've thought that he would never get ahead if all his daughters married from the labor class. Well, you know how it goes, in a situation like that you just don't let each other go. At last the priest was on our side too, and when one of my sisters made wedding plans, we decided to get married at the same time. After the church ceremony, we biked straight to South-Limburg where we were able to rent a room not far from the brick factory. And there it became clear to me what Graat had known for some time already: he wasn't meant for factory work. So it became peat digging in the Peel and then with a horse and wagon try to peddle the kindling turf in Beek and Donk, Eindhoven, Helmond. We were trying very hard to save enough to buy a small field, because with a small piece of land you're a bit of a farmer already. But we didn't get anywhere in the peat business.

"When my dad, Rinus van Heugten, passed away, a miracle followed, for despite all the poverty, it appeared that my parents had done quite a bit of saving. For each of their eight children there was a substantial amount of money. Now we dared to buy an old house in the Peel and rent a small piece of land. A good move, because war was not far off, and whoever had some land and pigs wouldn't notice much of the war. We sold and bartered cabbage, potatoes, and rye and didn't feel poor at all anymore.

"The Canadians and Americans came, and the fierce resistance of the Germans meant that nearly everything was shot right from under us. When liberation finally came, we could hardly make a living on that small piece of land anymore. In the meantime we were filling up the house with kids. Graat was the eternal optimist who expected to become a farmer. And why not? We had seven sons; when they in the near future would begin to pitch in, watch out. But we had no space or money and credit, and so we couldn't buy more land either. Right after the war there wasn't anything you could rent, as if already then the country was too crowded. And now it comes, listen closely: I had two sisters in Canada who were writing nice letters. In retrospect I wish that I had never received them, I mean those nice letters."

Truda Josephina Verschaeren speaks hesitantly about what happened next, at the end of 1946 and the beginning of 1947, with the Verschaerens and Van Heugtens in the Peel parish. Tension. Emigrate? That was certainly not a beloved subject in Roman Catholic circles. Why an exit from the rich culture of Catholic living, why get swept up with the force of numbers the way the Protestants were doing en masse. The episcopacy certainly didn't give its support. In the years between the world wars, Catholic publications openly warned against "the dominant illness known as emigration" and those warnings were still reverberating.

Still, in the case of Graat Verschaeren, the blood crept where it couldn't go. In the winter of 1951, he did go with Truda to the information meeting of the Catholic Emigration Council, established in 1947, an organization that originated from the Catholic Dutch Farmers-and-Gardeners Union when it was plagued by the scarcity of land.

Jos van Campen, retired information official of the Catholic Emigration Council in The Hague, remembers almost a half century later exactly how on that evening the mostly wooden-shoe crowd was enlightened about Australia. "We pointed out forthrightly to those men and women that they wouldn't be heading for an El Dorado; we minced no words about the phenomenon of homesickness. But they heard only what they wanted to hear. Homesickness? We'll handle that over there, they thought. It was as if at that time the masses got caught up in an irreversible movement. That's how it was. In 1948, one out of three Dutchmen between ages eighteen and forty considered emigrating. Just in 1952 alone, when the Verschaerens embarked with the ten of them, almost fifty thousand people left the country."

Truda Verschaeren: "They showed a nice film that night in Asten too. What a beautiful country that was, Australia. The parish priest, who was there to represent the North-Brabant Christian Farmers Union, had the emigrant prayer on paper. There was a couple that night who were going to leave in two days. With that prayer we too later on crossed the oceans:

"'Lord, Thou sowest us like the golden wheat that shall wax and bear fruit. Our future is in Thy hand as a kernel, and as Thou hast spread us among the nations with a gesture of blessing, Thou also knowest how we shall yield a new harvest in far-away fields. May our labor supply the food for the world, and may our life's walk reveal the bread for their souls. And should the weeds contest our place in the sun, Thy harvest, Divine Reaper, shall not thereby be diminished. For it is Thou who givest us the germinal force. . . .'

"We arrived and neither of us could manage the English language. Seasickness had already made us really skinny, now the language difficulty reduced us to skin and bones. Graat left right away with the boys for the forest. Cutting wood. Earning money. I too got busy. Picking tomatoes. A couple of weeks later I stood on a rickety ladder picking apples and pears. For pay that was much too low, as I discovered later. That was because we couldn't understand anybody. We were helpless.

"A neighbor lady had written something for me in English on a piece of paper for shopping: 'White cabbage and flour for porridge.' That was all. I never went anywhere without that scrap of paper. And so all we ate those first months was white cabbage and porridge.

"Besides the language, there were other enemies: the rock-snake and those huge lizards. Our son Jack was bitten by a rock-snake, the boy almost died in the hospital. Later on we got a solid roof over our heads all right, but the first five years we went inside only for sleeping. I sometimes prayed in the orchard that God would send a terrible storm, so that I together with the whole family would blow back to Brabant.

"Graat didn't fare too well and became bitter. 'We'll never make it,' and 'We'll never see the Peel again.' If you keep saying that, it's going to come true. But we managed to get him started as a vegetable market gardener. In the meantime the boys could go in construction because there the pay had gotten better. They went into masonry. It was Ger and Sjaak who stayed home a long time and contributed their wages. If Dad could only make some progress now, but Dad remained pessimistic, and that doesn't help at all.

"Still, the worst was yet to come. First our son Huub died in an accident on his way to work. He left a wife and five little ones behind. For a whole week I couldn't speak a word. And what happened to son Piet, that was so terrible too. His wife couldn't take the homesickness anymore and went back to Holland. They already had a son, so there was nothing else to do but for Piet to go along. He had grown up here, and there he got a job working a shift for Douwe Egberts in De Jouwer. He must've felt desperately unhappy there. Things hadn't gone too well between Piet and his wife for some time. At a certain moment he couldn't do anything but to go back to Australia. And she of course wanted to keep their little boy. To say good-bye to his only child — Piet just couldn't do it, and so he put an end to his own life. So don't be surprised when I say that our emigration was a failure."

Outside it turns out to be warmer than deep inside Evening Rest Home. The lights are lit now in the resident section; outside, the first tree cricket shreds the silence into tatters, and in the far northwest the lights of Melbourne glow above the horizon.

Two-and-a half days later at nine o'clock. The morning light conjures a rainbow above the garden sprinklers of this large retirement complex. The rainbow as the archetypal symbol for all people, proclaiming the end of disaster and the beginning of peace. But here the rainbow disappears when someone from on high turns off the faucet.

It's December 28 and the heart of summer. In a moment, in the main section of Abel Tasman Village, there will be a treat of *oranjekoek* [a traditional Frisian cake baked for special occasions] that's really not genuine oranjekoek. But then it's not a big celebration either, just a little birthday party for Liesbeth Niemarkt who was born eighty-six years ago. In all those years it's happened so often that a faucet was turned off from on high.

Fathers did not attend delivery rooms in those days; father Age Niemarkt didn't either, but at the moment of birth was a dockhand in the Frisian town of Jirnsum pulling a fully loaded lumberboat through the maddeningly difficult winding channel that connected Grou to the watercourse by Jirnsum. On the way he passed hotel-restaurant Oudeschouw, where in better times he had served as innkeeper. But that turned out badly; he had lost everything in that venture.

Liesbeth was number eleven in a family of thirteen children. When she turned eighteen, she married Wiebe Boersma, third navigation engineer on oceangoing trade vessels. But Wiebe was never able to stick to anything for very long. That was already the case when as young man he sailed on the vessels of the Royal Parcel Shipping Company (RPSC).

Liesbeth Niemarkt has never forgotten what happened. "It was at the end of the twenties. There was a dance night in Grou in the ballroom of Hotel Oostergo. A handsome boy in uniform came in, and I couldn't keep my eyes off him. And would you believe that he came heading straight for me, took a bow, and asked me to dance? It was a polka." The beautiful Liesbeth of that time now recalls, slightly bent over and with eyes pinched shut tightly, the sweet-sour memories of long ago. "It was summertime, there must've been at least half a dozen pleasure boats in the harbor, and he wore a white sailor's cap. I already kind of knew that I was good-looking. I became totally enraptured."

And that's how she walked into the arms of the man who flitted from place to place and never felt at home anywhere. Most of the time he drifted across the Indian Ocean on the vessels of the RPSC. But that wasn't what mother Pierkje Niemarkt-Kramer objected to the most; that sailor wasn't Catholic! So this couldn't and wouldn't be allowed to go anywhere. But it did. She was nineteen, he twenty-five, and they decided to marry by proxy. They sent each other the rings, already had a proxy in place — he in Tandjong Priok, she in Jirnsum. But then he suddenly appeared at her door. And that's how Wiebe Boersma married Liesbeth Niemarkt in person. Not only that, he also became Catholic for her and for the sake of peace.

"The RPSC was still based in the Netherlands Indies, and Wiebe served on the regular shipping line between Java and Australia. When on water, he wanted nothing more than to go home; when home, he couldn't wait to go back to sea.

"Again for the sake of peace, he turned his back to the sea forever. After all, he had plenty of diplomas, knew something about nearly everything, was very good in all things electric, was able to get all kinds of jobs on land. But a boss made him restless. So he went in search of something better. Though it was depression time, he wanted to try to start his own business. We bought a bicycle business on Midstraat in De Jouwer, but it turned out that the seller had taken all the customers along with him. Wiebe did not turn out to be a good businessman and went broke.

"Try again in Ljouwert, but this time as a salesman in somebody else's bicycle business. That's how we squeezed through the depression and the war years. After liberation, Wiebe became restless again. From 1947 on, the word 'emigration' was constantly in the air; in 1952 there was no stopping him anymore. We emigrated against my will with our three small sons to Australia. It took us two years of hard work to earn back the non-subsidized cost of the flight.

"First Wiebe found a job as electrician by the railroad, after that we moved to Brookvale where he got a job with a bus company. In Brookvale I thought: at last some rest and routine, but then he suddenly wanted to go back to The Netherlands. In spite of my homesickness, I had some serious objections to that. The children had just found friends in school, and now did we have to drag them back against their will? But Wiebe's impulse was too strong to control. After some four years we were back in Ljouwert.

"After a year-and-a-half I began to feel all right again. It wasn't one of the three boys who stayed homesick for Australia, it was Wiebe again who couldn't take it anymore. So all of us back to Australia. Three more times we wandered back and forth. That pulled our family apart. All the foundations were taken right from under me and the children. Now one of the children here and we over there, and then again just the other way around.

"One day our son Isaäk swore to us that he would never, never move again. He built a beautiful home for himself and his wife, and we began to settle along with him. When the maypole was placed on the crossbeams (it is an old tradition to place a green branch on it when the frame of a new home is completed), he fell from the ladder and died a few days later in the hospital. The second son, Age, embraced a strange faith, moved two travel days away to the Northwest, and didn't communicate with us for a long time. The third son, Lyckele, partly because of all that moving back and forth, was left by his wife and kids."

Wiebe Boersma never quite lost his restlessness. He and Liesbeth Niemarkt had been married almost fifty-eight years when he became seriously ill.

Liesbeth: "Just before his death, he himself began to talk about it. 'Lies, at long last I'm going to find peace!' He didn't want to be buried according to the strict Catholic rules in hallowed ground in Australia, no, we better take him to a crematorium. After that his ashes should be shipped to Fryslân, where they could be scattered above the pastures and the Pikmar."

The home journey of Wiebe Boersma across the Seven Seas, even the one in which he had returned to dust, proved not to be his last one. For even after his death he remained a wanderer: the small package with his ashes took six months on a freighter, then in the process of unloading got lost for a while, resurfaced and was delivered to relatives in Snits, and later in Ljouwert. But the somewhat distant relatives didn't know what to do with these remains. Somehow the package with his ashes seemed to represent a bizarre spirit and kept the relatives from sleeping. No one wanted or dared to scatter anew what had been so thoroughly scattered already. At last it was delivered to the director of the municipal North Cemetery on the Schapendijkje in Ljouwert. The man who appeared in the door said: "I'll take care of it," which in effect means: "I'll see what I want to do with it."

Frisian Dream

Henny Westerdijk and Wietske Westerdijk-Popma,
Gosford, New South Wales, Australia

It's less than an hour flying from Batemans Bay to Wollongong in the old airplane that used to fly the mail for the Australian Postal Service. We have a hard side-wind. Now and then the plane doesn't seem to have any gumption left, and then the metal body trembles like a newborn lamb. "It's blowin' hard enough to suit me," the pilot comments in his high-pitched voice. "One time it was so bad, I decided to put the crate down on Highway 42. Of course you have to land with the nose facing the storm. That was near Goodiwindi. When I touched it down on the asphalt, it came to a quick halt. And you know what happened then? Then the wind blew me with the whole business backwards off the road."

How often haven't I placed my lot in the hands of a total stranger at the wheel? Just the same, I don't like the way this trip is going. It's foolishness to fly along the coastline in this weather. It's not only the sea but also the sky that appears in turmoil here. But what am I complaining about; I'm the one who asked the pilot this morning to take this route, for I wanted to see (in the worst way) Botany Bay from the air.

Below me the Pacific Ocean licks the continent, an ocean with foam on its mouth. I see a frayed and endless shoreline that twists itself into a thousand bends and disappears into the mist. Steep inclines, narrow beaches, bays with interior lakes. And then suddenly there's the gushing of the Heathcote waterfall. We descend and make a turn to give me a better view of the scenery.

"I've seen enough, Sammy, let's try to get to the other side of Sydney."

His name is Samuel McKinsey, and that's the only thing I know about the man. Like most of the Aussies, he's at home with you in no time. "It's going to be all right," he calls out in a shrill voice, "I'll put 'er down on the ground perfect for you pretty soon. Perfect!"

At that moment I indeed spot, off to the side below me, what I wanted to see so badly: Botany Bay. I had had the image of this bay in mind ever since reading *The Fatal Shore*, the engrossing epic about Australia. In it, Robert Hughes, the Australian who immigrated to America, describes how two centuries ago Captain James Cook explored and tried to map these shores. What Cook and his crew encountered here at that time was still a totally mysterious continent. Never before had a white person set foot on this shore. It was the same shore, with the same land behind it, which a few years later would be made into a prison for thousands of misbehaving Anglo-Saxons. They were folk who had been spared the gallows but needed to be "cleared out of the way" for good.

Were they really all criminals? In any case, it concerned an oppressed people. Out of sheer poverty, someone had stolen the neighbor's shirt from the wash line. Or someone was caught grabbing a lamb from a farmer with a hundred sheep because his kids were dying from hunger and misery. That horrific misdeed came at a good time, because at the end of the eighteenth and beginning of the nineteenth century, England could use some cheap labor in its new colony at the other side of the world.

Hughes writes that these people in this remote spot would forever after be surrounded by the sea and sky: "the whole transparent labyrinth of the South Pacific would become a wall fourteen thousand miles thick."

Botany Bay slides away below us. The bay is larger than I had expected. "When the first ship with its cargo of criminals sailed into Botany Bay," Samuel McKinsey informs me, "a bunch of aboriginals happened to be there fishing. After their nomadic existence that had been in place for thousands of years, they were suddenly being disturbed. And how! A strange monster was pushing into the bay!" Sam tells me the story as if he had been there himself: "Some of those savages ran in fright into the forest, others stayed, ready to throw their spears, and still others bothered to look up only briefly and then just kept fishing. That's how it goes." Sam has all his information from hearsay; it turns out that he, like most Australians, has not yet read *The Fatal Shore* or other history books about their own country. And who, after all, wants to be confronted in such penetrating fashion with the fact that a large percentage of the population descended from riffraff?

I view the fatal shore below me and recall the scene: 80 percent of the people who survived the terrible voyage of nearly 13,000 miles were chased off the ship. I see them, heavy chains around their ankles, stumble up the beach. I hear the whip fall on bare backs. A bit farther on they were put to work by the military and early colonists. That's how it went.

Eight generations of descendants of all those criminals, supplemented by many more free colonists from many different countries, made Australia into the land that I see gliding past below me: the urban structures of Sydney, surrounded by an endless sea of houses; an open city with a square mile area half the size of Fryslân. Of the country's approximate population of 16 million, some 10 million Australians live in the five large cities.

"Here too we're losing more people from our huge rural area that's already so sparsely populated," Samuel said this morning. He's flown for the postal service and the veterinary service in all corners of the country and knows how it's gone and still goes: In the village, the agricultural cooperates have to merge, the silos stand empty, and the small creamery therefore has no future. From the domino effect, the agricultural loan bank might as well merge or close too. In three years time, 25 percent of the households in rural villages have left. And that's left the grocery store and the post office in trouble. Fewer customers, less business. Throughout the world, the small town is destroyed by the statistics. The most painful hit comes when the school closes. "Only then does the community begin to bleed to death," I heard Samuel claim. Fifteen hundred feet above the "fatal shore," he again asserts that this rural phenomenon is a global matter; it just goes a bit more slowly and deliberately in one area than in another. "Yeah, we're living in a global village." The whole world has become one and the same village; where did I hear that before?

The cafeteria on the corner finally closes too, because McDonald's took the spot of the closed agricultural lending bank. That's how it goes also in Kawerau in New Zealand, in Smithon on the island of Tasmania, in

Rafaela in Argentina, in Rocky Mountain House in Canada, in Warns in Fryslân. When another schoolchild was killed there by a car this past year, a sign was posted by the road with the words: "Watch for children."

A half hour later, Samuel McKinsey sets the machine down in the red-brown dust of the landing strip of a large sheep farmer near Gosford. I will be picked up soon by Folkert Lammerts Popma from Ljouwert, who happens to be in the area, visiting his sister Wietske and brother-in-law, Henny Westerdijk. They retired around here. To reach Folkert, I had to dial his mobile phone the night before, the same number that I dial in It Hearrenfean when I want to call him in Ljouwert. It worked beautifully: he answered someplace in Australia while sitting in the garden drinking coffee. Global village.

Less than fifteen minutes after our landing, a car turns onto the landing strip. When the dust clears, Folkert stands before me. He takes me across hills that are as dry as cork. Farther on, the landscape turns much greener. We keep on riding, past forests and through open fields. "Look, there it is, there on those slopes." In the distance the heights of Mangrove become visible. "Sometimes in a cold July month, several inches of snow will fall." A little while later we can see from the top of a hill the hazy blue of the Pacific Ocean.

We turn onto the yard of a large bungalow. Apparently, company comes to visit here every afternoon. Steady guests: a swarm of at least seventy small, brightly colored parrots. These birds visit Hindrik and Wietske Westerdijk to tell them a story. It is the story of dead-silent forests with giant eucalyptus trees, gigantic trunks that apparently reveal their secrets only to these beautiful green-orange birds with red bibs and a large beak.

We're in luck: when we arrive, the parrots have just finished telling their tale and in a wild cloud are flying back to the forest. In the garden I smell the coffee. And for this occasion there are also sweet cakes from Sint Jansgea. The offshore wind that rustles through the trees has turned into dry blasts of air, heated above the deserts of Queensland. A little farther on, the gum trees are budding. In a few weeks, around Christmas, they will show off what is perhaps the most beautiful red known in the Southern Hemisphere. Still farther, the deep-blue jacarandas are preening. The showy trees could no longer contain themselves and are in full bloom. Only after they lose their flowers in a few weeks will the leaves emerge on the jacaranda. Australian logic: the springtime calls for color, the summer screams for shade.

Henny and Wietske, getting on in years. Her eyes mirror the deep-blue of the jacaranda. The skin on his muscular workman's hands has been ravaged by the Australian sun. First the conversation features an English word mixed in now and then, later they sink deeper into their first language.

"We emigrated twice," says Henny, "first to Tasmania, and later from there to here on the continent. The fact is that we didn't make it easy on ourselves."

"We have it good now, at least we are content," says Wietske.

He grabs his walking cane, gets up with some difficulty, wants to fetch the old photo albums. "Yes, he's worn out both hips," she says, "he's had hip surgery four times already. It must've bothered him terribly in his work. But when work is your passion, then it seems to act something like anesthesia. He's almost seventy-five, but he can't resist building yet another new yacht. I'd like to fly back and forth to Fryslân more often, but Henny can't take it emotionally anymore. It's as if he doesn't dare to yield himself anymore to the land he loves. Not so long ago I happened to remind him, how, the last time we were in Fryslân, we rode with our daughter Jentsje from Ljouwert to De Lemmer. The sun was shining so beautifully that day, the landscape so pretty, and we saw a whole fleet of sailboats on the Jelte waters. Well, I discovered that to talk about that, to remember that moment, was too hard on him: he couldn't take it anymore. He started crying. So we better not talk too much about those things pretty soon."

"Those first two years on Tasmania," she continues a little later, "my oh my, that was so tough, so lonely. Henny lost himself in his work, but I wanted so badly to visit with my mom for a while. I shed a lot of tears in that time."

"We survived that," he says. "It's true, I found fulfillment in my work. And you gradually got more and more support here. It's strange, but lately I have times myself when I have trouble with longing. For example, when we get together as a bunch of Frisians and we talk about the past, and they get the notion of singing from the Frisian Songbook, then I have to get out of there, then I lose control."

Their story begins in Ljouwert in the twenties and thirties. He's a boy from the Hollanderwyk in Huzum. At home it's no banquet; the motto of railway machinist Hindrik Westerdijk Sr. and his wife is: The world is rough, to succeed you have to be tough. "We weren't as close a family as yours, Wietske."

She's a daughter of actor Lammert Popma from Ljouwert, the best of the evening entertainers, the director of many a regional play, the artist who dealt in textiles on the side at first, and later had his own textile business on Ruterwei. "We had a busy, or let's call it a dynamic household," she says. "Dad and Mom, my sister, Sita, and the four big boys were all pretty sharp. It always turned into playacting. Who knows, maybe we acted out our lives, because we really didn't have it that good either."

There was a lot of racket sometimes, but the Popma family was close. "It was a home full of personality and warmth," Henny adds, "I enjoyed being there." And that had its consequences, as it turned out: he fell in love with the daughter of the play director, and they married in December 1950.

At first there was no indication that Henny Westerdijk and Wietske Popma would end up emigrating. A half-century later it's still hard to explain why it indeed went that far. "Maybe it had something to do with the war, with the razzias, with being jailed, with the Canadians and Americans, those heroes from the new world where everything was possible. After the liberation, we too were expecting more possibilities, but that became a big disappointment. We had nothing except our dreams. And that's why we flew away. When at first we had such a tough go of it in Tasmania, when you, Wietske, were so homesick, we stuck it out. We didn't want to come back as failures."

"We were going to talk about back home," she says. "Father Lammert was a striking personality, through and through a man of the theater. When there would be an auction at Klopma's on the Langemerk street, Dad would function as both the auctioneer and entertainer. His sale items were always drenched in dramatics, and Dad would now and then make a comedy in three acts out of it. Pure 'performance.' And then Mom. Mom came from a skipper's family of nine children. Grandpa Jentsje Vlietstra, who was a resident of Frjentsjer, couldn't stay in one place as a skipper. So all of his nine children were born in nine different cities, villages, and hamlets. The marriage certificate booklet of Grandpa and Grandma Vlietstra is the unique document of an ambulatory existence (in the Netherlands, the names and birthplaces of the children are also recorded in this marriage record).

Father Lammert on stage. "Toward the end of the wartime, he was wanted by the Germans. One day the *moffen* came crashing into our store on the Ruterstreet. Dad had just sat down in a chair in the back of the store for a minute. The show-offs came prancing in their high boots toward him. It was too late to try to escape. So Dad played the absolute idiot there in his chair: the long gray hair in his eyes, his mouth sagging and agape, saliva drooling down his chin. And he had a ferocious expression in his eyes. When the Germans encountered him in that condition, he made some gurgling sounds and stretched out his hands, pretending that he would love to be hauled out of there. Dad tried to get up, but he couldn't manage to get out of his chair. The Germans decided that they could do without a wretch like that and left Dad behind, looking like an imbecile. When the soldiers slammed the tinkling shop door shut behind them, Dad fished his false teeth from his pocket, pushed them back into his mouth, and said to Mom: 'I believe that I got a fine review!'

"In spite of all those impressive performances and adventures, I think it really was Mom who was mostly in charge at home. It was Mom who kept the family together. Whoever wanted and was interested in an education, would get an education. Even in the bad thirties. She was a stately and beautiful woman, but also one who wasn't above keeping everything neat and clean, and doing the sewing and the knitting and the darning herself. Though a middle class woman, she would usually wear an apron; only when visitors came, would that thing disappear in a hurry."

"And then the war came," Henny takes up the story. "I was in hiding at Wietske's place on the Ruterstreet. The war got pretty tense in the winter of 1944–45; Wietske's sister, Sita, was a courier for the resistance. Folke was just a boy of around fourteen, but the other three boys were at a dangerous age. Jan, the oldest, was secretary for Baron van Harinxma thoe Slooten, the judge in Ljouwert who was saddled by the Germans with the responsibility for overseeing civilian evacuation, should the need arise, but who was no friend to the enemy occupation forces.

"In the evening of the 12th of February, Mrs. Harinxma called the Ruterstreet. 'Jan has to disappear as quickly as possible.' At that moment, a group of Belgian SS men had already arrested van Harinxma. It became clear later that they had shot the baron in the back right by the Blokhús Square. Brother-in-law Jentsje at that moment was hiding in his little houseboat in Earnewâld, his brother Fré had his hiding place in the tollhouse, and fortunately Sita was out of the way as well. My mother-in-law had hardly hung up the telephone, when sixteen *moffen* plunged into the room; we had nowhere to go. I still found time apparently to crawl behind a curtain, and soon heard how the raiders a couple steps away smashed everything to smithereens. They carried on like beasts. I tried to make myself as small as possible. Suddenly I felt the barrel of a revolver pushing against my chest. I tore the curtain aside, and looked the German straight in the eye. 'Here I am,' I said. They took Jan along and manhandled him badly. He landed via the Burmania House by the *Sicherheitsdienst* (Security Service) in the Scholtens Home in Grins and ended up on the List of the Dead. Father-in-law Lammert, Sita, and I landed in the *Huis van Bewaring* (Retention House), with future transportation to the concentration camp of Neuengamme. We tried to stay in touch with each other through rapping signals.

"One evening I heard the beating of prisoners in other cells. It sounded like the brutes were doing their work with a hose and ice-cold water. Then the moment came that I too had to take off my clothes . . . , no, let me stop here, it wasn't good at all. And then it was the time for us to be shipped out. I was loaded with others into a requisitioned truck from the Hoekstra firm. At first it was pitch-black in the cargo hold. As we rode out of the city, I felt every bump and counted every turn. That's how I knew roughly where we were. Like: now we are on the Suder Square, here we cross the tracks — farewell Hollander Road — and here we are on the Skrâns across from the Gerard Terborch Street.

"I figured that we were entering Goutum then. At that moment I found a crack in the truck I could look through. I couldn't believe what I then saw in a flash: the two brothers Siderius were standing by the side of the road. Men from the underground resistance. They were swinging a Sten gun (a World War II–era machine gun). The truck slowed down. I couldn't contain myself anymore and smashed the window between the cargo hold and the cab of the vehicle, and screamed 'Stop now! We're being liberated!' The truck stopped, and I noticed how someone outside was already fussing with the flap in the back. 'The Canadians are coming!' I heard, 'it is the liberation!' I hadn't seen daylight in ages, but the cargo flap fell down and it blinded me; I wanted to jump down on the road, but I couldn't manage, it was as if I didn't have any feelings in my legs anymore. I was empty, completely empty, but at the same time I felt deeply, deeply happy. I was free. Ladysmocks were blooming on the shoulder of the Werpsterhoeke Street, and it was as if another kind of light shone on this new day."

"That was April 1945," Wietske continues. "A good six years later we left the Skrâns together in the bus to Schiphol. Yes, we took the big step. Why? We did it, that's all I can say about it now. Dad was standing along the street, halfway to the Werpsterhoeke, his head held high. Jentsje stood beside him, waving a young green branch. We said our first good-byes on Ruterstreet. Like I said, it was more a theater performance than a dramatic parting from each other. Mom and Sita came along to Schiphol. When the time came, her voice shook. That sound, sometimes I hear that still; Mom said: 'You must take good care of each other.' Soon thereafter the airplane's engines began to roar. It was a Super Constellation with a double tail, the Surabaya."

"At that time a sky monster," interrupts Henny.

"Two-hundred ninety miles an hour — I wrote everything down — four days and three nights in the air with quite a few landings in between. Fifty-eight passengers and nine crew members in two rows of double seats. The stewardesses gave us plugs for our ears and American chewing gum. That was to keep us from going deaf. Yes, it was on Sunday, June 3, 1951; I watched fields loaded with flowers slide away underneath me."

"Why did we go! Let me tell you why." Henny is silent for a long moment. And then: "We had been liberated, all right, but . . . , that's when I went to Abe Hainja in It Hearrenfean. A job in auto body work. There was no glass in the windows of the train to It Hearrenfean, I just about got blown out from the draft. Eight cents an hour, that's what I started at. When I turned twenty a couple of months later, Hainja said: 'You're learning fast, I'll give you a couple of cents more an hour.' That made me feel proud because I wasn't doing it for the money, I just wanted to become a skilled tradesman as soon as possible so that I could start on my own. After three months I got a job with Anema in Ljouwert. That was on the Roodborst Street. Now I began to earn more of a decent wage. After that I started with a friend of mine for myself on the Dryltserkade in Snits. Take out dents. Working eleven hours a day. I'm certain of this: I delivered first-rate work, but I was afraid to charge enough."

"He's a master at his job," interrupts Wietske.

"If I had been a good businessman," he says, "I would've been filthy rich here long ago. We rode to Schiphol. And a little while later we were flying. We had to pay five thousand guilders for the trip. Frosted airplane windows at an altitude of twenty thousand feet, little flames leaking from the engines and licking the wings. In Karachi the whole machine had to be sprayed to disinfect it. And to keep us from boredom, we played games led by the first stewardess: guessing the cumulative age of the crew members, etc. We landed in a nice hotel room in Bangkok, where we slept under a mosquito net, and where we also saw naked children wandering on the street; I thought to myself, we've never had it *this* bad. We rattled and shook in that crate across our Netherlands Indies, right over Borneo, where we crossed the equator. The plane landed and took off three times, and we all got a card with the signature of the director of KLM, Albert Plasman."

"Later, around evening we saw the coast of Australia," Wietske continues. "When we got closer, the contours faded, it was getting dark, the airplane began to shake, and they told us that we were heading into bad weather. It became a struggle against nausea. Those hours were terrible. When the weather finally cleared up, we stood on shaky legs in the airport of Sydney. That same day still, the train left for the reception camp Bonegilla. We had a room of eight by ten feet. There were two single beds. They told us that we would stay here for a week. The first morning we heard men talking German. *'Die Männer aufwachen!'* ('Wake those men up!') Henny rushed out the door to find out what those idiots wanted from us. They said that they were in charge and that it was necessary to have 'law and order' in the camp. They were, as we found out later, Croatians who had been on the wrong side during the war and were placed in charge here. Let me tell you, we had a bad week in Bonegilla."

Henny: "Fortunately, the next week an ancient DC3 from the Australian army flew us to Melbourne. After that we didn't have to wait long for the flight to Burnie on Tasmania. It was like being liberated for the second time. But on Tasmania there was really no decent housing for immigrants. Dilapidated wooden shacks. The next day we had a roof over our heads and sat on wooden crates looking at each other. The luggage was to come later by boat. I went to explore the immediate area. What I saw was beautiful nature, but I got the impression that they were way behind the times here on Tasmania. Pre-war conditions. The local gas station operator was still pumping gas with a crank."

Wietske: "The Tasmanians kept very much to themselves. There was really only one couple that paid some attention to us and were interested in having something to do with us: Max and Dora Ford. So at first I learned a lot from Dora: something of the language, the customs, baking your own bread. Fortunately I soon got work in a design-and-paper factory."

Henny: "After nearly a year I considered going back. In fact, there was a period of time when I was working hard just to earn the cost of the return trip. Further on, in Pinguin, was a Christian Reformed Church. 'Just say so, Wietske,' I said one Saturday night, 'if you need somebody to talk to and want to go to that church, you just let me know.' She said, 'I want to stay free, I want to become Aussie.'"

"After the first two years, it was getting better," she still remembers.

"Wietske has the ability to attract people to herself. Eventually she had a circle of good friends, people of high standing. I'm more reserved, but I'm happy when Wietske is happy. And for the rest I just lose myself in my work."

"It doesn't happen by itself," she says. "It was a matter of sticking with it, of perseverance. After a while I thought to myself: I wasn't in Quick [a famous Dutch gymnastics team] for nothing in Huzum, so in my spare time I began an exercise class for the personnel of the paper factory. And I was enrolled in a language course for women. We tried to put off having children as long as possible. After two years we had more friends and the longing to go back became more bearable. After four years, when I was thirty-one, we got a baby boy. Henry. Such a handful can be a good remedy, but after a few months I suddenly got a terribly strong urge to show the little fellow to Mom and Dad. And I could sense from Mom's letters that they would love that too. My bond with Mom became stronger and stronger. So sure enough, we were in trouble again, I wanted to go home, could hardly sleep sometimes, but we didn't have enough money in hand yet. I can't describe it.

"One morning, I was nursing the little boy, the telephone rang. My youngest brother, Folkert. He's always needed only a few words to know what I was trying to say; Folkert sensed the lay of the land immediately, was doing very well himself financially, and quickly arranged for me to come by boat. With the little boy, with Henry. It was a beautiful voyage on an Italian passenger boat, but there were some problems attached too: the Italian boat officers who invited me in the evenings for a gala dinner had a hard time later leaving me alone. I was in a tough spot; apparently they saw me as a young widow. In Genoa I took a train to Amsterdam."

Henny: "Wietske has always been a very attractive woman."

She: "There's no better remedy for homesickness than a trip home while your husband stays behind. For then it begins to work the other way. Already after three days I was so homesick for Henny, even for Burnie on Tasmania. Knowing that I *could* go home already made it more bearable. Still, a year later I had a tough time of it again. But what a mother I had: though she was old now, she got on a boat in Rotterdam and sailed to Melbourne. All by herself. On the *Rotterdam*. Without knowing a word of English. An old mother who had never really gone anywhere — for six weeks all by herself on an ocean liner. Dad couldn't undertake a trip like that anymore, not even with Mom along, but she did it. To make her daughter happy. When I picked her up from the boat in Melbourne and asked if she had had a good trip, she said: 'It was worth it to me!'"

"On Tasmania I got my own body-shop business," he resumes after a pause. And it didn't go so bad, but there was a change when the Ford dealers started their own bodywork. That was in the beginning of the seventies. In this part of the world they don't get together so easily on minimum charges and so, it usually quickly turns into cutthroat competition. It didn't take long when there was no living in it anymore. I tried to sell the business, but I couldn't get rid of it. So then I rented it out, which meant I could start building yachts in the evening hours without going into the hole too much. But of course I did have to go to the bank for some money. After a while it became obvious that my new renter couldn't raise the rent. That meant that I could get out from under the mess only if we sold our beautiful home on the sea; the house for which I, myself, had baked the bricks one by one into the night; the house from which we could view the ocean and the harbor. That was terrible. It was a time of recession; the sale price of the house turned into a disappointment too. But I saw a future in yacht building and wanted to start over somewhere else. Not on Tasmania, but on the continent of Australia. That's why we moved to New South Wales, here in Terrigal. Emigrated again.

"Here I built the *Marijke*, named after our daughter, a seagoing round-framed yacht; designed by Van der Stadt; you have to go far to do better than that. I wanted to show the Aussies and Kiwis that they aren't the only ones who can build fast seagoing racers. When the boat was finished, I signed up for the Melbourne-Tasmania race. I was at the helm myself. And I won the cup. That was of course good advertising."

"Just say it," she interrupts, "you were Sportsman of the Year, Henny! You don't have to hide that. What's more, racing on the ocean is a little different from sailing three laps up and down the Snits and Terkappel lakes."

"However, I got the commission to build a Frans Maas [a famous Dutch yacht designer] design from the contractor, Peter Rijsdijk. Rijsdijk didn't pinch his pennies. Man, how that yacht ran! Peter and I tacked the new boat in a stormy north wind to Sydney. We encountered a rough and vicious sea, but I wasn't worried for a second. When a boat is tight and well-made, it's like a bottle with the cork safely in place. When Rijsdijk's boat won prizes, the telephone calls started coming from the USA and Canada. Here in Australia I got all the work I wanted. Seventeen seagoing yachts I built and delivered myself. They sail all over the world, and their skippers have all become good friends of ours. That's worth more to me than a bagful of dollars.

"In the meantime we didn't have it so lean anymore, because we did end up with some money after all from the sale of the body-shop business and the house on Tasmania. Everything turned out all right after all."

"Yes," she says, "we don't really have to go back anymore. The children and grandchildren are here. After Henry, we got Robbert, and then Marijke. They live in Perth; that's three days and nights by train."

Henny Westerdijk gets up and, without the cane, has to grab hold of the garden bench for a second. "Come along," he says then, "I want to show you something yet." We trudge around the house and land in the spacious backyard. In the valley below us, the Australian dusk sneaks closer, the sharp wind has gone to rest. Henny Westerdijk walks ahead of me, around the barn. For a moment I can't believe my eyes. Am I staring here at the height of surrealism? I see, rising high before me in the dry landscape, a large Lemster barge [a specially designed barge that looks like the typical Frisian barge but, to make it more seaworthy, whose forepart is built bigger and higher in relation to the hind-part, thereby raising the rounded head above the waves].

"You're seeing right," he says, "I gave it the old Lemster sheer [a unique upward curve of the longitudinal lines of the ship's hull as viewed from the side]. But the head is made a bit higher. And I outfitted it with a lead-heavy keel of about forty inches. A barge on the large waters like the Indian Ocean is better off without a leeboard. I made everything twice as strong."

A bit timidly I climb up the steep ladder behind him. When he's reached the top, I notice how he's stumbling rather unsteadily into the self-draining open wheelhouse. I follow him. He unlocks the heavy steel doors to the deckhouse, lowers himself down a narrow stairs into it, searches for a match, and lights a candle. The warmth of a brown skipper's deckhouse wafts toward me. I want to see everything: the chart table for the navigator, the two berths, the galley, the engine, his impressive craftsmanship.

"I don't have any pure gin in the cupboards yet," he says, while pouring us a blended whiskey.

I don't ask how the boat is ever going to get out of here, how it's ever going to taste the salt of the ocean.

"It's as good as finished," he says, except for the name." When we stumble down the ladder later on, he says: *"Friso,* what do you think of the name *Friso."*

"That's a nice name," I hear myself say.

While we walk up the yard, he turns around one more time. In the dark I see between the gum trees the contours of a silent Lemster barge. Now I see the *Frisian Dream* as its name. The boat has a nearly impossible voyage ahead.

The Statue by Zadkine

Okke Jansma from Highton, Australia

The glow of the afternoon sun outlines the villas of Highton-Victoria in a colorful mosaic, their pale-red and green rooftops shimmering in the summer heat.

Two oceans meet in the bay of Geelong, then slow down into sluggish waves, and at last cease their panting when they hit the beach. How long ago is it since the last "Anchors Aweigh!" resounded across the water? It must be a good century since the last schooner-rigged boat left the bay of Geelong. Maybe it was one of the wool-carrying boats, maybe it was the boat that had functioned as a prisoner transport on its outward passage. For it can't be all that long ago since the last loads of tens of thousands of petty and major criminals, troublemakers, whores, and other misfits from the sewers of old England and Ireland were dumped on the shores of Sydney, Melbourne, and Tasmania. Not far in the past, the sails of the barks and barkentines and clippers disappeared forever over the horizon, signifying the end to a bizarre episode. The backs of the colonists who followed were not beaten raw from the leather whip.

The shadows have not yet lengthened, and the shimmering heat seems to separate the colorful rooftops from the hills in the background. It's a warm afternoon in the city, a city much like all cities around the globe. Here too is the new affluence that erases all the old tracks, the tracks of the "originals," of the naked primitives, those pitch-black Aboriginal-nomads, the last of whom — a married couple — were driven from their cave in 1967 as if they were the last dangerous predators in the world. And gone too are the tracks of the horses and wagons with bales of wool from the dry outback; gone are the tracks of the little Australian gold diggers and all the other fortune seekers.

The day is ending in Geelong. A mild southerly wind is chasing the fog from the coastline; not far away an oil refinery comes into view. It's clearing up as the evening approaches; eighty kilometers to the northeast, the low sun turns its murky spotlight on a group of skyscrapers: the city of Melbourne. A Boeing 747 approaches, searches for its prescribed path as it climbs, and high above the old tracks begins its journey back to the old continents, at a new and fantastic speed.

We drive in the heavy jeep on a six-lane highway, then a four-lane, and then on two-lane roads to the home of Okke, the son of Wiemer and Bartsje from the small town of Sumar. His home is actually in Highton, one of the suburbs of the South-Australian Geelong. Not till several days later, on one late evening, he would confide that his ashes will be scattered. Not across the Geelong bay or the forests of gigantic trees, but across the land where he used to play and dream and first tried to find his way: ashes across the heath of Sumar and the Bleense where he struggled so hard to win the first prize in the skating race for schoolchildren; across the Hege Geasten, old hedgerows, ponds, and uneven paths. Across farms which today, so much later, he probably wouldn't even take note of, for the old countryside has been turned upside down and changed so much that one hardly recognizes it anymore. And of course a few flakes of his dusty remains are intended for the place where he was born: the *Mounepaad* (Mill-path) in Sumar.

Okke Jansma. He lives in an idyllic home with a beautiful garden at the end of Brassey Avenue. A gentle woman is waiting there for him, one who also has her roots in old Europe, in Portsmouth in the south of England. Janet, but he calls her Jantsje. "Regardless of how much you love each other as husband and wife," she will observe later, "each hangs on to his or her own emotions and roots. There are some things that one can scarcely understand about each other. That's the lot of the first generation emigrants from two different countries who marry each other. But that plight also brings you closer together."

She serves us tea in the garden and listens for the first time in a long while to the heavy music of his mother tongue. The shadows are now at their longest, the roses are closing. Then the night falls, and the stories begin. About her roots in Portsmouth and his in Sumar. They're stories that can't be mixed together, for the paths are too deep and run too far apart.

"A new millennium is before us, maybe just the right moment to take stock," he says. "Because the planet has shrunk so much and is still getting smaller and smaller."

His wife uses the English common to Portsmouth: "Whatever, as an immigrant Okke has done very well. When he came here, he began at once with the study of chemistry. He completed his studies in Melbourne, and that's quite an accomplishment. Some time later he was top man of the Shell laboratory in charge of a lot of people working under him — there's always a variety of nationalities here — and he survived both as a person and as a manager. He's getting older but is still vital enough to be busy with all sorts of things. He still travels for Shell now and then, reports on the effect of pesticides on crops, and generally is totally involved in life. I may be bragging him up a bit, to be sure, but he knows a lot more about Australia than the average Aussie; he knows a great deal about the history of this country, about current events, about the flora and fauna, about its literature. One would say then that as an immigrant of some forty years he's thoroughly integrated. But listen to this: he also knows a lot about Friesland, he's so attached to that little place, the people, and the language. And that makes the question of integration much more complex. He reads not only English and Australian poetry, but also Frisian. He didn't turn away from his old country as a kind of self-protection; he didn't want to cut the ties in order to give himself completely to making a new life. You see that kind of "double religion" is a stronger presence with the Frisians and Irish than with most other immigrant-nationalities. I know from experience: when the Irish and Frisians let their thoughts go back to their old country with its peculiar identity — when they start talking about it, their language turns lyrical. Maybe that is because their old languages are in jeopardy. Let me give you an example: the other day I was telling Okke about my grandpa. And afterward he started telling me about his grandpa. That's good, of course, to find out more about our grandpas and grandmas. But with Okke's story I began to see that old man come alive in front of me. When he finished, he was quiet for a while, and then he said: 'Jantsje, when I sit here and think back to the time when I stayed overnight with grandpa and grandma, I can taste the potatoes from Blije again.' Those are the kinds of emotions that I as an English woman can't generate anymore. I don't even know if Blije was a kind of soil or a village.

"Okke, tell that story about that café in Ireland, because it's about the same sort of Frisian and Irish peculiarities we've been talking about."

"I had to," he starts after a pause for recollection, "I had to go to Frankfurt and other places in Europe, and landed in Ireland. In a very unusual old pub. There they happened to be holding a Great Irish Storytelling evening. Storytelling for hearty prizes, the way they play shuffleboard in Friesland around *Sinterklaas* time (St. Nicholas Eve, celebrated on December 5) for *rolladen* and *oranjekoeken* (rolled meat and orange cake). Well, those Irish are great storytellers! Older men got going about the sheep-shearer strike, about their emigration and their return, about what their grandparents told them about the potato crisis. Stories from the moors, about the peat-land, about poverty and fortune, about ignorance and slyness, faith and superstition, love and hate. After a while it was my turn, and I told my story. Sumar. That won me the second prize. I told about my childhood years in that little village in Friesland; about the ice and skating racing in the wintertime; about going around as a boy with men like Lammert de Jong, Ids Boersma, and Durk Blom with the stink truck from Burgum to pick up cadavers from poor little farmers; about some of the little land managers who out of reverence for death, especially in the case of their best cow with a pedigree, would deck the cadaver out with a new horse blanket; about going out to play afterward with the smell of decay all over my clothes. I told the story about the conflict between father and son, about my boarding the ship at age twenty, about my good fortune and the catastrophe. And just as the Irish would occasionally play around with a Celtic word and then translate it, so I would occasionally throw in a Frisian word.

"When I finished my story, the people were quiet as a mouse at first; then an old woman said: 'Be so kind and tell us the most beautiful word from your old language.' And one word jumped into my mind just like that: *Leauwe* — faith. That is still my favorite Frisian word."

"Okke didn't put on a mask to keep his old identity hidden," Jantsje says. "That's both an advantage and disadvantage. Many immigrants crawl inside a shell, erect a wall around themselves, pretend to forget their first language, prefer not to talk about their birthplace. There are people here, not young anymore, who once stepped off the boat with their parents but no longer know in which province, let alone which city or town, they first saw the light of day. That means they're withholding something important from their children and grandchildren. It's true of a certain kind of person, the anonymous kind who lives as the 'invisible' immigrant.

"When you feel that you have roots on both sides of the planet, you have tensions now and then. Sometimes such people have the feeling that they were torn in two. Okke suffers from that occasionally too. When he gets in that state of mind, I just leave him alone as he 'unravels.' Sometimes he says: 'Just let me be, I need to shake the crumbs out of the tablecloth.' Then I want him to explain to me just what he means. Pretty soon I see him trudge to the garden shed where he carves beautiful forms from old blocks of Australian tree trunks."

He agrees. "Yes, that's when I sometimes talk to myself at my workbench or lathe. Sometimes I swear. At what? Let me tell you. At old Wiebe Paulusma, for example, at Wiebe and his little boat. Bleens ice-club once held a race for schoolchildren. We had a stiff wintry wind from the northeast, skating was petering out, I had beaten Chris Zwart already, and Chris's uncle was Eleven-City Race champion Karst Leemburg, so he radiated a bit of the magic of the ice-hero. But now I had to race against Okke, the son of Teade, my second cousin. Two of us boys, also products of a tradition of racing families, competing against each other. The first two races ended in a draw.

"So it was our turn again. But this was a tiebreaker: one of us had to win. I stood at the starting line. Through my tears from the cold wind, I saw all of a sudden the little boat of Wiebe Paulusma at the other end. Wiebe had once said to me: 'So, you're a grandson of Jabik Skunk!' That simpleton had the gall to call my grandpa by his nickname! In that last race I headed straight for Wiebe's little boat. I didn't see ice anymore, I didn't feel ice anymore. I screamed: I'm going to kick you in the balls with my ice-skates. And I won the prize. I won three brand-new guilder bills. I don't know if I felt it then the way I feel it now, here in my garden shed, the emptiness after the finish: there was no one to meet me, no one to congratulate me. Dad was always at work. I felt darn lonely there for a little while.

"So that's why I spend time in my shed, in my meditation chapel, to chisel and plane and polish away on my life. One day I heard through all the noise of planing the shrill voice of an old ice-racer and small-time skipper, Gels Brouwer. On that same skating rink of Bleens, Gels was loudly urging one of her grandchildren on to skate faster. The child did the best she could but didn't have a chance to win; and then Gels said to the defeated child: 'Now you're not my grandchild anymore.'

"The hard life of Sumar. It must've been the Monday before the children's races in 1947. I had skates that were bought at Hoekstra's in Wergea, really beautiful wooden skates, but they were as dull as a doorknob. O yeah, I knew all right that sharpening skates wasn't cheap: old Egbert Zijlstra charged one-and-a-half guilders and Bos two-and-a-half. I'd often watched them do it, eyes and ears wide open. I watched how Egbert tried to do his best, with his nose about to drip and the tip of his tongue between his lips. On a fine sandstone he sharpened the skates of men and women who were fast.

"Dad: 'You want somebody else to sharpen your skates? And that's going to cost me one-fifty? What?! Two-fifty? Are you nuts, I'm going to do it myself!' O goodness gracious, I noticed the fire in Dad's eyes, could already see the fire of his hard emery stone in the smithy of the chemical plant we called 'the stink factory,' where he had found his livelihood. Dad was going to sharpen my irons really flat; he wouldn't even grind the edge off the corners, because he had neither the patience nor the tools for that. And if I'd keep bugging him about it, I'd wind up getting my ears boxed. There was no way around it: Dad did indeed sharpen my skates and it was the worst kind of hit-and-miss job. That morning before school I tried them out and tried to skate off the edge, because I was going to participate in that race. I had to show Dad that I was the descendant of the great Okke van den Berg, the man they had written beautiful poems about in the newspapers. But it became obvious that I had to skate off so much edge that I raised a dust cloud of loose snow blowing around my pants.

"I've stood here in my shed, shouting 'why didn't my dad ever show an iota of interest in me!' I was about nine or ten when I got a small bench-vise from him on my birthday. What a surprise; I was crazy about that thing. I was constantly using it. But of course, there came a time when I didn't touch it for a while. Not much later I discovered that he had simply given it away, to a stranger. To me that was incomprehensible. I was furious and said to Mom, 'how's that possible, I made such beautiful stuff with that vise, it was my own, Dad gave it to me after all.'

"'Just calm down,' she said.

"But here, in this same Australian garden shed, I also saw Dad and Mom sit in apparent harmony at the table. It was in the evening in the fall, the lamp was burning on low, and my-oh-my, there was so little space in the house for studying. But now Dad had to study and learn the lines for his acting role. He had gotten a part in the comedy called *The Flirt* and this was going to be a big deal. Mom was plenty smart; she had helped him practice his lines so often that she knew the whole thing by heart. At last he had everything memorized too. I listened to the script and held my breath as he began to recite. Why was I at that moment so fascinated by Dad's declamation? Because I had just discovered that he was able to get close to the characters in *Flirt*, but in my opinion not to me.

"We didn't have much space in our house for studying, still I succeeded in getting into a kind of academic junior high school, known as the ULO. When I came home with my diploma, he didn't let on that he felt even a smidgen of pride or joy. It was rather the opposite: his face showed a trace of, 'What makes you think you're better than me!'

"After that to a university-prep school or HBS in Drachten. 'I'd like you to find your living in metal,' he said. It was as if Dad and I were endowed with totally different genes: he was an iron-man and I preferred wood. Iron to me was too hard and cold and inflexible. To me wood was alive, you could even read the age-rings in it.

"'I really love chemistry,' I decided one evening when I had come home with high marks in that subject. 'What crazy talk is that,' he shouted, 'just learn a skill and start working! There's plenty of work here for guys who're able and willing!'

"And then I heard that same night how that same man read the paper out loud for Mom. He presented the facts, so to speak, from the fullness of life in the world. Mom could read very well herself, but Dad's reading to her was like a final ritual of a well-spent day. He read the events of the day for her, now and then adding his own pithy commentary.

"When I reflect on that, it strikes me that there was a very solid loyalty between those two people. I also realized later that both of them were somewhat inclined toward humanism.

"What normal boy is in love with chemistry. 'Okke's going to go to HBS to become a piss specialist,' my neighborhood pals joked. But in HBS I got very high grades in that subject as well as in physics later on. I was really good in languages too. But then came a hitch: I messed up in math. I was probably out of sorts for some reason during that time, because in deportment and diligence I got a B and a C. When I came home with that report card, Dad ignored all the good marks but fell all over the lower ones. He gave me quite a tongue-lashing.

"A little while later I said to Mom: 'Mr. Lenstra wants me to have tutoring for a half year in math; he said when I get math under control, I'll breeze right through the rest.

"'Is that going to cost us anything,' she wanted to know. 'Yes, that's going to cost three hundred guilders for a half year.'

"'You better ask Dad,' she said. With lead in my shoes, I went to Dad. He had a fit.

"'Why for godsake didn't you try harder! Just remember fella, you have to make a choice: study your tail off or work with your hands.'

"I really messed up with math now, became discouraged, grew rebellious, was likely to flunk my fourth year, sold half of my schoolbooks, came home one afternoon, and announced with relief: 'I'm finished with school!'

"'Finished?' Dad paled; he was furious; the tiles seemed to come rattling off the roof. 'Finished? You quit HBS? Then get out!'

"I stood on the *Mounepaad*, mad, and sort of thrashed around like a wild man for a bit. Then I grabbed my bike from the shed and took off. I rode and rode, in the direction of the *Ofslútdyk*, and all of a sudden it struck me that I wanted to go to North-Holland, to Midden-Beemster, where Uncle Dirk was a cheese maker. I always got along well with Uncle Dirk and especially with Aunt Sjouk. I stubbornly stuck to my guns and stayed in Midden-Beemster for a good three months.

"Years later, here in the garden shed, I mentally made that trip across the *Ofslútdyk* again, and once more I felt that ambivalence of the love-hate relationship, that tension between detaching myself and the pressure of the strong loyalty to the dad who was becoming my antagonist. That trip across the *Ofslútdyk* had been for revenge and a search at the same time. I still remember: I had to wait by the lock at Den Oever for a couple of incoming fishing boats; I saw the water churning in the locks, and at that moment I felt, as if for the first time, the severing of the umbilical cord.

"Dad didn't know what to do with his emotions, his anger, his resentment. Being a craftsman was after all his social status, and status to him was everything and maybe nothing: smith in the stink factory. In the early years of the fifties he took home seventy-five guilders per week. For a household with four daughters and a son. He became irritable; everything he earned went to Mom, to his family — I have to grant him that. The struggle that men like Gerrit Roorda from Tynje could articulate — the simple Laborer vs. the Capitalist — hit home with Dad. But he would not and could not make that his dogma. He wanted to fight the injustice in the world in terms of the small world right around him. And in that small world he first of all met himself and, not to forget, that one son of his with possibilities beyond those he had himself. I wasn't able to understand that for a long time.

"One Sunday afternoon in 1953 he was about to listen to his favorite radio program. It was the music hour featuring the great English alto Kathleen Ferrier. What a liberating voice. Years later I reviewed that scene in my mind again, and I thought, Dad had his escape dreams too: his longings, his feeling for beauty, his need to let himself be transported toward the unreachable. He sat listening to 'Das Lied von der Erde' right after they announced that Kathleen Ferrier had died. Dad's heavenly voice, his alto, had died. Now, I had had many run-ins with the old man by that time. But here he heard Kathleen Ferrier sing Mahler and Händel one more time, and Dad sat at the table, crying.

"He had resigned himself to my dropping out of school, but when I announced that Shell in Amsterdam would train me as a chemical analyst, he exploded again. 'What kind of bullshit is that, what are you going to do all the way in Amsterdam, if you had wanted to you could have stayed in school. And otherwise you could've gotten a job here.'

"A serious clash followed, but I didn't succeed in making it to Amsterdam. There went my chemistry dream. And that in spite of the fact that I could've gotten paid for my studies in Amsterdam. Apparently I resigned myself, found work in the lab of the creamery in Ljouwert. I spent some time there; then I was old enough to join the service and opted for the Air Force. That gave birth to a new dream: to become a pilot for the KLM. I now made my plans without my dad's knowledge, but I couldn't avoid him: I came home with a contract for a six-year training hitch in the Air Force.

"Without a signature from the head of the family, I wouldn't get into the Air Force. He read the document and couldn't restrain himself after only one paragraph: 'I didn't raise you to have you get smashed to smithereens! I'm not going to sign this.'

"It was as if I had expected this reaction; I was edgy and said: 'Now I'm falling into the same manure pit as you: you had wanted to emigrate to Canada but Grandpa Okke was damned if he was going to sign, and that still sticks in your craw!' Those words apparently touched a raw nerve. 'You're not joining!' he thundered, pounding his fist on the table. I took the risk and argued some more. That did it; he screamed: 'Watch out, fella, I don't want to hear another word from you!'

"That's how things piled up. The day came when the bell also rang for me on the square in Ljouwert, the bell in the travel office of Lissone Lindeman. It was the first informational night on emigration to Australia. If 80 percent of the truth is a lie, then this was very possibly completely misleading. There was no mention of reception camps such as Bonegilla, which you couldn't avoid. The truth is that hundreds came to a bad end right off in Bonegilla. They gave no information about what must've been known then already, namely the high percentage of emigrants that since 1948 had come back from Australia. They didn't tell us that in this country there was hardly a house available for rent and that one had to work hard and long before being able to buy a home. Nothing was said about first living in such primitive accommodations as tents and chicken coops. What

Lissone Lindeman showed us were gorgeous pictures of children playing on golden-yellow beaches and limousines in front of beautiful villas.

"That's how they made money off people who were trying to escape their misery. Don't forget that in spite of considerable employment, some 17 percent were unemployed. The exodus from agriculture began, the first creameries were closing.

"Time went on, it became the middle of December, we hardly had any daylight anymore, and in the front room my two suitcases stood ready. One with clothes and one with books. Chemistry, physics, prose, poetry, Frisian, Dutch, English. The bus was on its way. Mom in her flowered apron stood by the graveled path, took a few steps, stopped in the open garden gate. Tears were burning inside my head, but I tried to act tough. A father who suddenly had less color in his cheeks than usual. Well yes, he would really like to go along to accompany me to Rotterdam. A mother with large questioning eyes, a kiss from her on the path. With the bus to Ljouwert, with the train to Rotterdam, getting off at what then was still the Maas station, and then to the Lloyd docks. A handshake from Dad, a large hand. Walking in wide, long lines with hundreds of others through a kind of shed. Then boarding. The *Sibajak*. Its nickname was *Sickojak*, because its voyages hadn't always turned out so well. Waving at a thousand faces below on the wharf. Where was that one face now under that one cap? All of a sudden it was as if everything fell away from me; I felt a sense of relief, but just for a moment. Then I was alone, with 1,700 other people on a ship built for 956 passengers.

"It must've been about five that afternoon; it was dark already, and I stared across an empty wharf. Still the *Sibajak* stayed in place; I thought: Let's sail! But it turned out that a crankshaft from one of the two Schelde-Sulzer engines had broken when the crew had tried to start it, and they had to go get a new one from the Schelde wharf in Vlissingen. We remained anchored at the dock for three long days and nights. That's how I got the chance to go ashore. I walked around Delfshaven and took a good look at the statue of Piet Hein. Then I walked all the way to the statue by Zadkine on the Square. What went through my mind then, there in front of that sculpture by Zadkine, I'll never forget. I was looking at the body of a figure from which a piece had been torn: *The Destroyed City*. Deeply touched, I trudged back to the Lloyd Wharf where the *Sibajak* was docked. But suddenly I didn't want to go back on board; I felt a terrible longing to go back home. It's true; I stood there wavering whether or not to take the train back to Ljouwert. But at the same time I knew that Dad and I would immediately be in each other's hair again.

"In bad weather and with now and then a flurry of wet snow, I set off to sea in the *Sickojak*. I must've been the only one on board who had read *All about Australia* by Dr. H. G. de Maar and J. D. Rempt. I still feel sorry for all those mothers, most of them from the great river areas in the southern of the country, with ten, twelve kids. And fathers who didn't have a clue as to what they had done to themselves and to their wives. And all those kids? Nobody asked them if they wanted to go or not. But there were also a ton of women on board who had pledged themselves by long distance and were now sailing toward their future husbands. But romance flourishes easily in the southern oceans. After all, there were a couple of hundred bachelors on board as well, men who smelled the possibility of more than one adventure. On my first big trip, I became a man, as they say.

"But what does it take to become a real man? Work and study. Chemistry. And then right away, of course, a job with a future.

"A catastrophe entered my life: my young Australian wife, Betty, died unexpectedly. She died within hours from a lung embolism. We had two dear little girls; I was at my wits' end. During that awful time I would sometimes stand on top of the cliffs by the southern coast and scream at the ocean. The fatal coast. And when I had done all the yelling I could, I'd limp back to land, completely spent. I still remember how I shuffled back to the car and made myself promise that I would never feel sorry for myself again, that there was only one thing to do: to take care of the two little girls.

"I couldn't do it without help. But how was I going to get steady and trustworthy help in the house, in a country where I had no parents, let alone uncles and aunts and cousins. I was finally rescued by assistants from the Mormons. Two older ladies took care of the children in the daytime. Not to convert them, but only to help them and me. That's how the girls enjoyed a good childhood and how the three of us remained a unit.

"In 1969 one of my sisters, Klas, came over. She had taken a crate of stuff from Dad along for me. It turned out that there were things in there that he hadn't made for me but for his dad and mom — my grandpa and grandma. Fire irons made in 1932, stove tongs, a small coal scoop. I heard Klas say: 'Dad at the time really worked hard on these, but I guess with the rod and the coal scoop he wasn't thinking about you not having a stove in the house.'

"The crate with stuff stood in the shed for a long time. But the day came when I looked at the things again, polished them, and gave each a place.

I've been back in Sumar at least thirteen times. The airplanes could fly as fast as they wanted to, but for a long time the oceans between me and the *Mounepaad* remained immense and deep. Sometimes I saw in my hope-filled dreams how Dad and I biked together in the direction of Eastermar. As friends. Maybe this time I could tell him something about Australia and about what inspired me, about how the sun there doesn't move through the south but north to the west, about the dead being buried on the cold south side of the cemetery, because that's where the cold winds come from over there.

"I had a couple of tiny, delicately made tools for precision woodwork in the suitcase, when I flew home. Made with my own hands in my 'meditation chapel,' in the garden shed, and I had really worked hard on them.

"'You didn't make those!' he snarled, almost mockingly. I had one of my girls, Rebecca, with me. She exclaimed: 'Daddy did it with his own bloody hands, Grandpa!' And the child was so angry and frustrated, that she began crying. Rebecca crossed the language barrier in one step, apparently felt the tension unmistakably, understood her grandpa perfectly. The old man suddenly couldn't handle the situation anymore and ran outside. The next day he was gentle.

"With each homecoming I noticed both parents looking older and more fragile. With each passing day, the hour that the Grim Reaper would also have his way on the *Mounepaad* came closer. It turned out that Mom was the first to die. I flew home, reread all the letters I had received from her. Only then did I notice the beautiful sentences she wrote: 'I stood outside this morning and the weather felt balmy.' 'Jel was buried last week, her needles are now retired' (Jel was a champion sock-knitter). 'It is near the end of the morning and of the Burgum open market, the first wooden shoes are coming this way again across the bridge.'

"And I read Dad's letters, letters that invariably were about his work. I found the box with my own writing sent to them, sentences from the fifties. It shocked me: they were mostly short, almost terse announcements. There was a beautiful New Year's card, but with only the words, in English, 'Your ever loving son Okke.' Now that really said everything, but when I wrote it I must've wanted to keep myself at a distance, because I used what to them was a foreign language. As time went on, I apparently exposed more and more of myself. The prose became more plain and sincere.

"It was the fall of 1997 when my faithful friend Johannes Huisman from Burgum sent a little package to Brassey Avenue. Too light for a book. It was a videotape. When I opened it, I had a hunch right away: this is nostalgia under high pressure, these are images of Sumar, Burgum, and surroundings. This is just the thing for a Saturday night, with a drink. But I suddenly got such a strong urge to see the film that I slipped it into the recorder and turned it on. With bated breath I walked, so to speak, behind the camera. We landed in the Burgum care center, known as Berchhiem. Dad, over ninety years old, appeared. What I saw was a tired, bent-over man. A pair of helpless eyes looked at me questioningly. It was as if he wanted to say something to me, but he couldn't. I saw only his eyes, eyes that had always been so clear. Now they were smoldering, slowly dying embers. I went to the telephone, ordered tickets, flew to Amsterdam, and drove immediately to Berchhiem.

"The same image. He was sitting in a chair and wanted to say something, but he couldn't quite manage it. His shoulder felt bony and fragile. After some silence, I started to talk about how good he had been at making a rabbit noose when he was younger. Back then I hadn't appreciated his poaching tales; maybe I could get him to talk about it now. He didn't react, but he said: 'Mom suffered a lot after you left!' His voice was barely audible.

"'Maybe in my heart I hadn't even wanted to leave.' And then: 'I wrote Mom faithfully.'

"'I drove you away,' he said.

"'I had a lot of anger then,' I heard myself say. 'Not a day went by that I didn't think about you,' he said. Then I could hardly understand him anymore.

"'You didn't like me very much; you were against my going for analyst training in Amsterdam. I never could understand why.'

"'That was because I loved you, and I didn't want you to go so far away.'

"I told him later in the afternoon that he didn't need to feel guilty. 'What's past is past,' I said. Not long after that, on Monday afternoon at 12:55, he died. After the funeral that week, I biked the old paths, picked up some new books of poetry, and had to get back to Schiphol. Halfway to Melbourne, I dug out the volume *Home-sounds* by Baukje Wytsma from my suitcase. The poem was not about my dad in the present, but about the dad from long ago:

> 'Dad, a man in rubber boots
> with eyes searching the distance.
> His workplace a closed world
> with alien codes.
>
> What shall I ask him?
> What shall I tell him?
>
> His eyes beyond me,
> his arms too wide,
> his singing too scared.
>
> Even if I should step into his boots
> I would come no closer.'"